Protest State

PROTEST STATE

The Rise of Everyday Contention in Latin America

Mason W. Moseley

OXFORD
UNIVERSITY PRESS

OXFORD
UNIVERSITY PRESS

Oxford University Press is a department of the University of Oxford. It furthers
the University's objective of excellence in research, scholarship, and education
by publishing worldwide. Oxford is a registered trade mark of Oxford University
Press in the UK and certain other countries.

Published in the United States of America by Oxford University Press
198 Madison Avenue, New York, NY 10016, United States of America.

Library of Congress Cataloging-in-Publication Data
Names: Moseley, Mason Wallace, author.
Title: Protest state : the rise of everyday contention in Latin America /
Mason W. Moseley.
Description: New York, NY : Oxford University Press, 2018. |
Includes bibliographical references and index.
Identifiers: LCCN 2017055371 (print) | LCCN 2018005573 (ebook) |
ISBN 9780190694012 (Updf) | ISBN 9780190694029 (Epub) |
ISBN 9780190694005 (hardback)
Subjects: LCSH: Protest movements—Latin America. | Social movements—
Latin America. | Political participation—Latin America. | Government
accountability—Latin America. | Democracy—Social aspects—Latin America. |
Latin America—Politics and government—21st century. | BISAC: SOCIAL
SCIENCE / Sociology / General. | POLITICAL SCIENCE / Political Freedom &
Security / Civil Rights.
Classification: LCC HN110.5.A8 (ebook) | LCC HN110.5.A8 M633 2018 (print) |
DDC 303.48/4098—dc23
LC record available at https://lccn.loc.gov/2017055371

9 8 7 6 5 4 3 2 1

Printed by Sheridan Books, Inc., United States of America

CONTENTS

FIGURES

TABLES

ACKNOWLEDGMENTS

If there is a task more daunting than writing a book, it is that of offering adequate thanks to the cast of thousands who helped pave the way. This book's origins can be traced to 2009, as I first began thinking about my dissertation as a second-year graduate student at Vanderbilt University. My dissertation research was supported by the National Science Foundation and grants from the Vanderbilt School of Arts and Sciences, the Graduate School, and the Center for Latin American Studies—all of which were crucial for its successful completion. During my time at Vanderbilt, I was nurtured by a brilliant group of scholars who did their best to turn a naïve twenty-two-year-old fresh out of undergrad into a real academic. I at some point either worked for or took seminars with John Geer, Josh Clinton, Cindy Kam, Bruce Oppenheimer, Zeynep Somer-Topcu, Giacomo Chiozza, Suzanne Globetti, Liz Zechmeister, Mitch Seligson, and Jon Hiskey, each of whom went above and beyond to help me become a better scholar. I owe a particular debt of gratitude to Josh and Cindy, who generously lent their methodological expertise to this book despite the fact that neither was on my dissertation committee.

As for my dissertation committee and team of mentors, I have been extremely lucky to be able to count on a talented group with diverse interests and opinions, all of whom were fiercely committed to my graduate career and have provided excellent feedback throughout that has greatly improved this manuscript. I served as Liz Zechmeister's research assistant during my first semester at Vanderbilt, at which point I am sure that she was convinced I was the most clueless graduate student she had ever encountered. Since that time, I redeemed myself enough to secure her services as a member of my dissertation committee and one of my most honest critics, and I am forever grateful for her willingness to read countless drafts and provide meaningful, thoughtful feedback regardless of how hectic her schedule is. Similar to Liz, Mitch Seligson has, despite being the busiest person I know, always gone the extra mile to support my career through countless letters of recommendation, edits of grant proposals and paper drafts, and attending and thoroughly critiquing virtually every talk I have ever given. Tulia Falleti, the resident Argentine and expert in qualitative methods, provided invaluable advice on this project since she agreed to serve on my committee in 2011, and I am happy to have been able to continue our collaboration during my year as a postdoc at the University of Pennsylvania. The commitment of all three to my career not only reflects their considerable quality as leading experts on Latin American politics, but their immense generosity and concern for their graduate students, for which I am eternally thankful.

For all of the hours Jon Hiskey dedicated to guiding my progress at Vanderbilt, he deserves (at the very least) his own paragraph. Since we bonded over our common love for Tar Heel basketball, cold beer, and live music, and then realized we also shared some research interests, Jon has been the most outstanding mentor and friend any aspiring academic could ask for. His feedback is always immediate and incisive, his grasp of intricate theoretical issues never ceases to amaze me, and his commitment to his students is extraordinary. His tutelage is reflected in some way, shape, or form on every page of this manuscript.

At Vanderbilt, I also benefited a great deal from my relationships with fellow graduate students. First off, the diverse community of LAPOP-affiliated scholars has been incredibly supportive as I have developed and refined my research agenda. To name a few (but not all), Alejandro Diaz-Dominguez, Fred Batista, Gui Russo, Daniel Zizumbo, Daniel Montalvo, Abby Cordova, Juan Carlos Donoso, Whitney Lopez, Arturo Maldonado, Mollie Cohen, Matt Layton, and Daniel Moreno have all provided feedback on this project and friendship along the way.

Aside from the legion of LAPOP-ers, Mariana Rodríguez, Camille Burge, and Jen Selin entered Vanderbilt with me in 2008 and have all proven to be great friends and colleagues as we progressed through the program together. Mariana in particular has been like a sister to me over the past six years, and I cannot thank her enough for her friendship and support. I also want to acknowledge John Hudak and Brian Faughnan, who preceded me in the program and were always willing to talk me off the ledge when I was overwhelmed by coursework or comprehensive exams preparations, most of the time over delicious drinks and food. They are all great friends for life.

In addition to the wonderful support I have had at Vanderbilt, I must also acknowledge the many kind souls who made my fieldwork in Argentina productive and enjoyable. Carlos Gervasoni met with me on numerous occasions to discuss my research and provided me with contacts for interviews in Buenos Aires, Mendoza, and San Luis, in addition to offering his methodological expertise in measuring subnational democracy. Germán Lodola was incredibly helpful in obtaining an institutional affiliation with *Universidad Torcuato Di Tella* and organizing a presentation of my research, in addition to providing feedback on my dissertation. I must also thank Lorena Moscovich, Mariela Szwarcberg, Matias Bianchi, Catalina Smulovitz, Maria Gabriela Abalos, and Maria Celia Cotarelo for lending their support in helping me carry out my fieldwork. I am also indebted to all of the generous Argentines who lent their time for interviews with a *gringo* stranger. They were, without exception, kind and helpful.

The personal relationships I formed in Argentina were also pivotal for helping me better understand Argentine politics and society, though I will only acknowledge three here. Jorge Mangonnet, my roommate, colleague, and best Argentine buddy, was incredibly supportive in connecting me to local academics and helping me develop my research ideas. I owe him a great deal for his assistance in developing this project, and look forward to working with him in the future. Mercedes Guazzelli provided the civilian perspective on Argentine politics, and was my cultural liaison during my entire year in Buenos Aires. Finally, Natalia Lucentini helped me organize my fieldwork in Mendoza, while also serving as a welcome friendly face during my time on the road. One of the joys of fieldwork is making lifelong friends, and I count myself as lucky on that front.

In addition to Tulia, I want to thank a few more people from my time as a postdoctoral fellow at the University of Pennsylvania. Dan Gillion and Ernesto Calvo were gracious enough to lend their expertise at a manuscript workshop we had at the end of my year at Penn, and many of their suggested revisions made their way into the final version of this book. In particular, I want to thank Ernesto for pressing me on the idea of the "protest state," where he (I think) inadvertently sparked the idea for the title of the book. Rogers Smith was also a wonderful mentor at Penn, and played a pivotal part in giving me the opportunity to bring this book project to fruition.

This book was nearly complete by the time I started as a faculty member at West Virginia University, but I want to thank two people in particular who helped push it over the finish line. Scott Crichlow has been a tremendous department chair to work with, and provided me with every opportunity I needed to successfully complete the book. Kyu Chul Shin has provided excellent research assistance, and helped with data collection and organizing the manuscript for submission. The entire department at WVU—y'all know who you are—has been incredibly supportive, and I count myself as lucky to be part of such a supportive academic community.

I also would like acknowledge two people without whom I probably never would have even made the decision to go into academia. Lars Schoultz was, for me as for so many other students at UNC, the person who got me excited about studying Latin American politics, enough to eventually consider a career in the field. Throughout his career, he has been an absolute treasure to the Carolina family. Ryan Carlin, who was my graduate student instructor when he was completing his PhD at UNC, has over the years become an invaluable mentor, co-author, and friend. Along with Jon Hiskey, he has been as instrumental as anyone in lighting my path in academia.

I would also like to thank a few people at Oxford University Press, without whom this book never would have become a reality. It was Anne Dellinger who first believed in this project's potential, and provided me with the opportunity to submit my manuscript to OUP. Since being handed the reins, Angela Chnapko has expertly shepherded this book to completion, and it has been a pleasure to work with her and her talented editorial assistant, Alexcee Bechthold. Finally, I extend my gratitude to Anitha Jasmine Stanley at Newgen for her hard work (and patience with me) in leading the production process. All of you who played a role in the journey from submission to publication were truly first rate.

I have been incredibly fortunate throughout my life to be surrounded by a community of family and friends who have provided steadfast love and support in all of my endeavors. My parents, Allen and Cindy, my brother Walker, and dear friends from my time in Boone (from the Deerfield Estates crew to the Godfather), Chapel Hill, Nashville, Buenos Aires, Philadelphia, and Morgantown—you have all had such a positive impact on my life, and any personal accomplishment of mine can be attributed in large part to all of you.

To my mom and dad, for their unwavering love and support.

CHAPTER 1

Introduction

The looting is not about hunger. They are stealing alcoholic beverages. This is a political matter.

    —Argentine Interior Minister Ramón Mestre, *December 2001 (Quoted in Krauss 2001)*

November 8, 2012 began as an uneventful day in Argentine politics. In a country well known for its economic and political instability over the years, there were no pivotal elections approaching or economic crises erupting. No controversial votes would be cast in the Chamber of Deputies or Senate, nor did anyone anticipate an important announcement by President Cristina Fernández de Kirchner. Put simply, November 8, 2012 seemed to be an unremarkable day in the history of Argentine democracy. It remained that way until Argentines got off work.

At 7 o'clock that evening, hundreds of thousands of seemingly average citizens armed with pots and pans, homemade signs, and catchy anti-government chants took to the streets of Buenos Aires and cities across the country to protest against the current administration. Within fifteen minutes, *9 de Julio*, the widest avenue in the world at fourteen lanes across, was inundated with protestors for block after block, and the famous *Plaza de Mayo*—the site of so many seminal moments in the nation's political history—was a pulsating sea of angry protestors. Indignant attendees voiced their dismay over President Kirchner's rumored desire to reform the constitution and run for a third term, high perceived levels of insecurity and government corruption, and troubling signs of increasing inflation amid alleged attempts by the government to manipulate official economic statistics.

According to newspaper reports, the event—dubbed "#8N" for its ubiquitous Twitter hash tag, which began to appear a few days earlier announcing the gathering—was one of the largest anti-government rallies since the country's return to democracy in 1983, and marked the climax of growing discontent with a president who had only one year earlier garnered a healthy fifty-four percent of the vote in the first round of the presidential election (Wiñazki 2012). By 9:00 p.m., the mass demonstration was over. While the protestors' motivations were diverse, the rally's organizing forces mysterious, and the exact number of protestors hotly debated—estimates for Buenos Aires alone ranged from 70,000 to 700,000 by the government and opposition, respectively (*La Nación* 2012)—one thing was clear: *lots* of Argentines had decided to take to the streets to effect change in their democracy, in an incredibly organized and succinct way.

While #8N was perhaps the most dramatic example, it was only one event in an avalanche of contentious episodes in Argentine politics during the final months of 2012. On September 13, another massive *cacerolazo* had erupted in the capital city, as thousands of *porteños* converged on the Plaza de Mayo to voice many of the same grievances regarding the current government's performance. Not even two weeks after #8N, on November 20, union leaders called for the first general strike of Kirchner's presidency, as truck drivers, public transit workers, and farmers alike stayed home from work and transformed the bustling city streets of Buenos Aires, Rosario, and Córdoba into ghost towns. On Monday, December 3, rival subway worker's unions clashed in a heated debate over salary demands at a stop for the D line—an outcome of the ongoing conflict regarding plans to transfer the subway system from the national government to the Buenos Aires city government in 2013—resulting in the closure of all subway lines and forcing the city's one million daily metro passengers to seek alternative modes of transportation. In Argentina, protest is simply a way of life.

UNDERSTANDING PROTEST IN EMERGING REGIMES

While Argentina is undoubtedly unique in its enthusiasm for street-based contention, a casual glance at any major newspaper would reveal a long list of countries where protest has also taken on a central role in everyday political life. In Turkey, since the 2013 Gezi Park uprising, opposition protests directed at President Recep Tayyip Erdogan have continued to swell, highlighted by an attempted coup in 2016 and continued unrest surrounding Erdogan's attempt to expand executive powers via referendum in 2017. In Southern Europe, the rise of the *Indignados* movement in 2011 signaled a massive rejection of austerity measures implemented by the European Union, and quickly spread from Madrid's *Puerta del Sol* to Zuccotti Park in Lower Manhattan with the advent of Occupy Wall Street. In Brazil, what began as relatively spontaneous demonstrations regarding the staging of an international soccer tournament in 2013 eventually precipitated the impeachment of Dilma Rousseff in 2016, and protests have not subsided under new president Michel Temer. Perhaps most famously, the sharp uptick in contentious activity in the Arab world beginning with the Tunisian Revolution in 2010 has been unprecedented in impact and scope, and, while perhaps failing to effect meaningful transitions toward democracy, it has undoubtedly awakened civil society and offered a potential harbinger of changes to come.

The events of the "Arab Spring" and other recent uprisings provided a wake-up call not just for the leaders of the rebellious citizenries who declared an abrupt end to their quiescence, but for an academic community challenged with explaining such a sudden, and massive, upsurge in contention across the world, even in the last regional bastion of overtly autocratic regimes. Indeed, explanations of recent protests have often centered around the global crisis of authoritarianism following the demise of the Soviet Union nearly thirty years ago, and the proliferation of democratic and pseudo-democratic regimes across the developing world (Huntington 1991, Levitsky and Way 2005). Whereas anti-government demonstrators in autocracies were often brutally repressed, this so-called Third Wave of democratization produced a slew of young regimes in which protest was made legal and tolerated, if to varying degrees. Empirical studies drawing on cross-national data from the World Values Survey have found that political liberalization and economic development make protests more likely, increasing the structural opportunities and resources at the disposal of potential collective actors (Dalton et al. 2009). In fact, many contemporary protest movements in the developing world have coincided with election cycles, as opposition parties seize the spotlight provided by high-profile elections to marshal citizen discontent with perceived violations of democratic norms (Beaulieu 2014). Other accounts of the recent surge in contention have centered on the use of social media and modern technology to mobilize activists—undoubtedly an important variable in understanding the alacrity with which modern collective actors can assemble (Tufecki and Wilson 2012). In sum, a growing body of empirical research has taken note of surging contention across the world, giving rise to a litany of potential explanations.

Perhaps in no part of the world has protest occupied a more central place in contemporary academic research than in Latin America. Since widespread democratization hit the region in the late 1970s and early 1980s, scholars have paid increasing attention to protests in the region, as they have sought to understand how Latin American citizens choose to engage the newly democratic regimes they inhabit. While numerous studies addressed the role that social movements played in precipitating regime change throughout the region (e.g., Collier and Mahoney 1997, Roberts 1997, Trejo 2014), it was not initially clear that protest would persist as a prominent repertoire of political participation once countries had transitioned to democratic regimes, and formal vehicles for representation like political parties had consolidated. Indeed, it appeared that in several cases, like Brazil and Chile, important social movements moderated their actions and sacrificed many of their more progressive ideals to help guarantee peaceful transitions from military rule (Hipsher 1996).

Further, the almost immediate enactment of neoliberal economic reforms in young democracies across Latin America portended for many scholars a decline in mobilization capacity and civic association, as many classic organizational structures for potential protestors like labor unions were de-fanged by market reforms (e.g., Roberts 1996, Murillo 2001, Kurtz 2004). Beyond simply making mobilization more arduous for contentious actors amid privatization, high levels of unemployment, and increased inequality, it was thought that neoliberal reforms had shifted so much economic responsibility from the public to private sphere that the state would no longer be viewed as the primary target for collective protest (Kurtz 2004).

Though there were clearly a number of good reasons to expect that contentious political participation would decline with the creation of formal mechanisms for representation and the adoption of neoliberal policies, anecdotal evidence in the 1990s seemed to undermine the demobilization thesis (Silva 2009). Beginning with the *Caracazo* in 1989, Venezuelan society erupted in numerous mass protests that eventually paved the way for the election of Hugo Chávez in 1998. Social movements organized by the recently unemployed in Argentina gained traction throughout the 1990s, ultimately culminating in the mass demonstrations in 2001 and 2002 that would cause the country to cycle through several presidents over the course of a few months. In Ecuador and Bolivia, protests in response to neoliberal policies also precipitated premature presidential transitions in the early 2000s.

Further empirical investigation revealed that while in certain cases, neoliberal reforms had reduced citizens' capacity to contest the state—especially with respect to the diminished role of organized labor (e.g., Murillo 2001, Levitsky 2003)—other new modes of collective action were thriving, including neighborhood associations, indigenous movements, and mass street demonstrations (e.g., Yashar 1998, Garay 2007, Arce and Bellinger 2007, Arce 2008). Scholars of the "repoliticization" school argued that while neoliberal reforms had fundamentally changed protest repertoires in Latin America, the fact that they were adopted under democratic regimes provided citizens additional opportunities to mobilize and protest against those policies (e.g., Arce and Bellinger 2007). Moreover, the increasing evidence that market reforms contributed to heightened unemployment, a spike in inequality, and increased poverty rates meant myriad grievances to fuel collective action. In sum, the belief that protest would decline with the consolidation of democracy and neoliberalism in Latin America appeared misplaced.

THE PUZZLE

While the debate regarding the impact of neoliberal economic policies on protests undoubtedly revealed a great deal about that moment in Latin American history and the possibility for collective action amid seemingly atomizing political and economic forces, the past decade has been marked by a return to center-left governments and the abandonment of many of the harshest policies adopted during the neoliberal era. Moreover, Latin America has experienced one of its most prosperous decades ever, as a commodity boom paved the way for sustained growth, reductions in inequality, and millions of citizens climbing their way out of poverty across the region (Ocampo 2008, Mangonnet and Murillo 2016).

Despite these impressive economic gains, rates of protest appear to have actually *increased* in the post-neoliberal era. Figure 1.1 plots reported protest events in eight of the largest Latin American countries (Argentina, Bolivia, Brazil, Chile, Colombia, Mexico, Peru, and Venezuela) over the past thirty years. After an initial surge in reported protest events in the period surrounding many countries' democratic transitions, rates of protest ebbed briefly before surging again in the late 1990s. Over the past ten years, the region has experienced rates of contentious collective action that *double* those observed in the transition period, even as many of these countries have also enjoyed some of the highest economic growth rates in their countries' histories.

Thus, while there is certainly considerable variation in Latin America in levels of enthusiasm for contentious politics, protest has frequently served as a vital form of political expression in countries across the region in recent years (e.g., Eckstein 2001, Boulding 2010, Bellinger and Arce 2011,

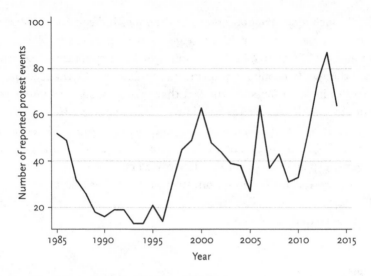

Figure 1.1 Latin American Protest in the Post-Transition Era
This graph tracks news reports on protests in eight Latin American countries (Argentina, Bolivia, Brazil, Chile, Colombia, Mexico, Peru, and Venezuela) over thirty years, as they appeared in several English-language newspapers: the *BBC World News Reports, The Guardian, The New York Times,* and *The Washington Post.*

Machado et al. 2011, Arce and Mangonnet 2013). From marching against low wages, high gas prices, or run-down schools, to clamoring for increased transparency in the face of corrupt political institutions; from demanding the truth about war crimes committed under dictatorships, to organizing roadblocks in the name of indigenous autonomy; it seems that myriad important issues and events in the last decade have been defined by instances of "politics in the streets."

In Bolivia, thousands of demonstrators called for and eventually achieved the deposal of sitting presidents in 2003 and 2005, and contentious participation has further crystallized as a common form of political voice in the country under the presidency of Evo Morales. The police riots in Ecuador in October 2010 offer yet another example of contentious politics having significant consequences for a Latin American regime, as hundreds of policemen, angered by a reduction in government-paid bonuses, threatened violence against the president, only to be restrained eventually by the military. The student protests for education reform in Chile had dire consequences for President Sebastian Piñera's approval ratings and offer evidence that even one of the region's more docile democracies historically is not immune to episodes of intense organized contention. Finally, street protests in Brazil that originally centered on the exorbitant costs of staging the 2014 World Cup amid decaying transportation infrastructure, public schools, and hospitals, and then transformed into calls for the eventual impeachment of President Dilma Rousseff during a far-reaching political corruption scandal, highlight a period of intense political instability in Latin America's largest and most influential country.

Evidence of heightened protest participation finds further support in recent survey data from the region. According to the findings from the 2008–2012 AmericasBarometer surveys, conducted by the Latin American Public Opinion Project (LAPOP) hosted by Vanderbilt University, nearly twenty percent of respondents (all voting age) reported participating in a protest during the year prior to the survey in Argentina, Bolivia, and Peru, while more than one in ten citizens had protested in Haiti, Guatemala, Colombia, and Paraguay (Figure 1.2). In all of these countries, rates of protest have rivaled those of "conventional" participation—for example, joining a political party or volunteering for a political campaign (LAPOP 2008–2012). From a regional perspective, it thus appears that rates of protest have been on the rise in Latin America since the mid-1990s, as contentious repertoires have consolidated in many regimes (Boulding 2014).

However, despite this region-wide trend toward higher rates of contention, not all Latin American democracies are as suffused with protests as the examples above suggest. While protest is a relatively common form of political voice in many Latin American regimes, it remains comparatively uncommon in countries like Costa Rica, El Salvador, and Panama (LAPOP 2008–2012; see Figure 1.2). In fact, in each of these countries fewer than 6 percent of respondents reported protesting in 2010. Indeed, it seems that for every Latin American country that is engulfed in intense cycles of protest, there is another where contentious tactics are seldom utilized, and citizen participation is primarily channeled through formal political institutions. Moreover, further variation in protest levels can be found *within* countries, as in the high-protest country of Bolivia, where demonstrations are almost a daily occurrence in El Alto but far less common only a dozen kilometers away in La Paz (Albó 2006, Lazar 2007). In short, while the rising tide of protest across Latin America plainly merits further investigation, the fact that this wave of contention has not reached certain countries, and even subnational contexts within otherwise contentious national regimes, is perhaps even more perplexing.

With this variation in mind, the following questions motivate this book: *Why has protest surfaced as a common form of political participation in certain Latin American contexts, but not others? Further, can we identify common factors at the national, subnational, and individual levels to help explain variation in protest across Latin American polities?*

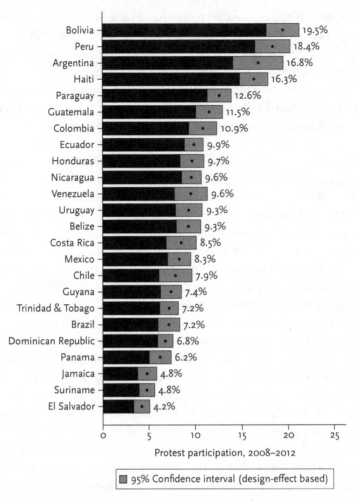

Country	Value
Bolivia	19.5%
Peru	18.4%
Argentina	16.8%
Haiti	16.3%
Paraguay	12.6%
Guatemala	11.5%
Colombia	10.9%
Ecuador	9.9%
Honduras	9.7%
Nicaragua	9.6%
Venezuela	9.6%
Uruguay	9.3%
Belize	9.3%
Costa Rica	8.5%
Mexico	8.3%
Chile	7.9%
Guyana	7.4%
Trinidad & Tobago	7.2%
Brazil	7.2%
Dominican Republic	6.8%
Panama	6.2%
Jamaica	4.8%
Suriname	4.8%
El Salvador	4.2%

Protest participation, 2008–2012

■ 95% Confidence interval (design-effect based)

Figure 1.2 Variation in Protest Participation across Latin America, 2008–2012
© AmericasBarometer by LAPOP

These numbers represent the percentage of individuals in each country that claimed to have participated in a protest march or demonstration during the previous year in 2008, 2010, and 2012. These surveys were nationally representative of voting age adults. See Appendix for question wording and descriptive statistics.

THE RISE OF THE PROTEST STATE

In this book, I argue that the variation we observe between emerging democracies in terms of contentious political participation can be explained by the interaction of two specific phenomena in recent history: (1) the persistence of weak political institutions and suboptimal democratic representation; and (2) the massive socioeconomic gains made in much of the developing world during the past decade, which in turn have produced some of the most politically engaged citizenries in the history of many emerging democracies. When these two factors combine—namely, low levels of institutional development and an increasingly active and knowledgeable democratic citizenry—social protest can "normalize" as a common strategy for effecting political change, utilized by a diverse cross-section of political actors seeking redress of sundry grievances. It is this dual process of political dysfunction and economic prosperity that produces what I call the "protest state."

In the protest state, contentious participation becomes the default mode of voice for citizens who are engaged in political life. Instead of relying on political parties and bodies of elected officials to represent their interests, active citizens in protest states take to the streets to make claims, regardless of the issue. Thus, rather than constituting unique situations in which severe grievances boil over into confrontational episodes of collective action, or where isolated minority groups advocate niche interests, protest in these regimes is a quotidian form of activism by politically engaged citizens that substitutes for what is perceived to be ineffectual participation via more official vehicles of representation. In turn, political elites often draw on street politics to pursue their goals, given its distinctive power in these regimes. Put simply, in protest states, faith in formal political institutions is low, while the capacity to organize among collective actors is high. It is this unique combination of political and social factors that I argue is on the rise in the developing world and has revolutionized the politics of emerging democracies.

To test my argument, I direct my gaze toward the fertile terrain of modern Latin American democracies. My emphasis on the importance of institutional weakness as a trigger for contentious participation falls in line with recent work on the Latin American context (e.g., Boulding 2014, Machado et al. 2011, Arce and Mangonnet 2012), while contradicting the notion propagated in research on advanced industrialized democracies that higher levels of democracy tend to produce amplified rates of protest—in other words, the argument that there is a positive, monotonic relationship between democratization and rates of protest participation (e.g., Dalton et al. 2009). In fact, I maintain it is precisely the *ineffectiveness* of formal democratic institutions in many Latin American contexts, which are often characterized by high levels of corruption, executive dominance, and weakly institutionalized party systems (Scartascini and Tommasi 2012), that reduces citizens' faith in formal vehicles for representation and pushes them to adopt more contentious, street-based tactics. Thus, while formal modes of participation often predominate in countries with strong political institutions like Chile, Costa Rica, and Uruguay, protests become increasingly vital in weakly institutionalized settings like Argentina, Bolivia, and Peru (Przeworski 2010, Machado et al. 2011).

However, this account departs from the existing literature on Latin America by underscoring the interaction between institutional factors and mass political engagement as the driving force behind swelling rates of contention. The vast literature on contentious politics makes clear that protests hardly ever materialize without the crucial organizational networks that facilitate mobilization (e.g., McCarthy and Zald 1973, Jenkins 1983, Meyer 2004). In recent years, Latin America has undergone a massive social transformation that has decreased the number of citizens living in poverty, increased access to secondary and tertiary education, and, I argue, mobilized a new generation of politically active citizens. Yet while certain Latin American regimes play host to an increasingly vigorous and diverse civil society, others lack the dense associational life that makes individuals cognizant of institutional deficiencies and capable of responding to those shortcomings through contentious popular mobilization. I argue that only where some minimal level of mass political engagement is present do the protest-producing effects of institutional quality emerge—in other words, the institutional arguments presented in the literature to this point are conditional on mass level factors related to community organization, which are increasingly present in twenty-first-century Latin America.

Another point of departure with the existing literature is my attention to the subnational level, and the ways in which many Latin American regimes might vary as much *intra*-nationally as they do across countries. I argue that the well-documented "unevenness" of democracy in Latin America (e.g., O'Donnell 1993, Fox 1994, Snyder 2001, Gibson 2005, Gibson and Suárez-Cao 2010, Giraudy 2013)—namely the juxtaposition of illiberal, personalistic subnational regimes and liberal multiparty contexts—has important consequences for variation in contentious politics across regimes found *within* countries. Similar to the national level, institutional flaws can produce heightened levels of protest activity—however, I maintain that subnational regimes can also become so closed off to citizen voices that they actually thwart most protest activity, except in extreme cases where individuals are forced to adopt more radical modes of contention to provoke a response from institutional actors. In sum, subnational democracy tends to exert a curvilinear influence on peaceful forms of protest, which diminish at the lowest and highest levels of democratic quality, while having a negative impact on violent protest, which surges in the *least* democratic contexts. Thus, political context influences distinct protest repertoires in different ways heretofore unexplored in the contentious politics literature.

The theoretical approach presented and tested in this book thus pushes the literature forward by bridging the often-separate literatures in political science on political institutions and behavior, to craft an innovative explanation of one of the most important sociopolitical trends in Latin America today: swelling rates of mass contention. Moreover, I extend my gaze beyond the country level to explore the very real behavioral consequences of uneven democracy—a phenomenon that has garnered more scholarly attention in recent years, but still remains vastly underexplored in the literature on post-transition Latin America. By marrying sub-disciplinary divisions and levels of analysis, I aim to provide one of the more complete explanations to date of contentious politics in emerging democracies.

A ROADMAP

In the second chapter, I review existing work from the contentious politics literature on Latin America and beyond, and particularly that which speaks to the basic question of "Why do people protest?" Then, I discuss the more specific challenges related to explaining varying levels of protest participation across contexts, particularly in Latin America. Following this discussion, I propose my own explanation of swelling rates of contention in Latin American democracies and variation in protest activity within the region— one that focuses on the link between representative political institutions and individual-level political behaviors. Here I introduce the idea of the protest state, which I argue explains one of the most important political phenomena in twentieth-century Latin America: the rise of mass protest. The chapter concludes with a discussion of the methodological approaches utilized in this book to test this theoretical perspective.

This book's third chapter will be its first empirical one, focusing on the cross-national determinants of protest participation in Latin American democracies. In this chapter I use multilevel modeling techniques to evaluate how country-level institutional characteristics interact with individual-level indicators of political engagement to explain protest behavior. By testing my own theory against contending paradigms from the contentious politics literature, this chapter offers one of the most thorough cross-national empirical studies of the determinants of contentious participation to date. Rather than finding support for dominant grievance-based explanations of protest or theoretical perspectives couched solely within the resource mobilization or political opportunities traditions, I find that an interactive relationship between institutional context and mass political engagement best explains why individuals across Latin America choose to protest. I conclude this chapter by comparing Argentina, a protest state, with the case of Chile, a country where protest has not yet normalized.

In Chapter 4, I explore another observable implication of the protest state theory: the hypothesis that political elites in protest states actively mobilize protest participation on their own behalf, given its relevance as a mode of political voice in those contexts. First, using the same cross-national dataset from Chapter 3, I test the hypothesis that whereas linkages to formal political organizations fuel traditional modes of participation in regimes with strong democratic institutions, they incite more contentious behaviors in protest states. Then, defining clientelistic activities as a range of "political services" that clients provide to their patrons in exchange for particularistic goods and favors (e.g., Stokes et al. 2013, Weitz-Shapiro 2014, Szwarcberg 2015), I argue that clientelism, like other types of organizational linkages, can foment contentious political participation in protest states. Machine parties invest goods and favors in protest activities to build contentious power in the streets and influence public opinion regarding key policy issues. The second hypothesis I test in this chapter is, therefore, the expectation that having been targeted for participation, buying will have a powerful positive effect on the likelihood that individuals take to the streets in protest states. To test my argument, I compare model results from a special battery of questions fielded in Argentina and Bolivia in 2010, both of which exemplify the key characteristics of the protest state.

Chapter 5 introduces the case study of Argentina, which I argue is key to understanding the protest state. Argentina's history is peppered with episodes of mass contention, but never more so than the post-transition period, particularly beginning in the late 1990s. In this initial chapter on Argentina, I trace the political and economic roots of mass protest participation from Carlos Menem's election in 1989 to the current Mauricio Macri government, supplying evidence that protest has indeed crystallized as an everyday form of political participation in this regime. I then present descriptive evidence from longitudinal survey data and protest events–count data to support this argument, demonstrating that not only has protest become more common over the past two decades, it has consolidated as a common form of participation for Argentine citizens across demographic groups.

In Chapter 6 I put forth a subnational adaptation of my theoretical framework for understanding protest participation, which leverages Argentina's federal administrative regime and striking subnational variation in terms of economic development, democratic quality, and rates of protest. Initially, I narrow my focus to the Argentine provinces of Mendoza, Buenos Aires, and San Luis, where I draw on dozens of interviews with citizen activists, movement organizers, and politicians to craft three detailed case studies. These interviews were conducted from March to June 2013 with support from a dissertation grant from the National Science Foundation (SES-1263807). In this particular chapter, I utilize the comparative method (Lijphart 1971) to examine how distinct institutional characteristics in each province have produced diverse trends in terms of protest participation. Through the interview process, I obtain a qualitative, nuanced perspective of protest in each province as I endeavor to gain first-hand knowledge of how citizens view the political regimes they inhabit, and how those views govern their behaviors.

In the seventh chapter, I proceed to rigorously analyze variation in protest activity across Argentine provinces. Using two sources of protest events data collected during my fieldwork in Buenos Aires, survey data from the AmericasBarometer, and the inventive method of measuring subnational democracy introduced by Gervasoni (2010), I examine how characteristics of subnational regimes related to electoral competition and executive dominance, and patterns of mass political engagement, produce different protest outcomes over the past twenty years. This chapter thus uses time series analytical tools, Poisson regression, and multilevel modeling to observe how changes in political institutions and citizen engagement might lead to shifts in protest activity over time. Departing from prior studies of protest in Latin America, I focus on the differential effects of subnational democracy on distinct protest repertoires. Ultimately, I find support for my national-level argument regarding the two key components of the protest state, as protest has consolidated in certain Argentine provinces but not others. However, I also uncover a curvilinear relationship between subnational democracy and *peaceful* protests, while I find a negative linear relationship between institutional quality and *aggressive* protests, which I argue lends further support for the larger theoretical contribution of this book.

This book ends with a chapter on the implications of its findings, along with avenues for future research. Few scholars have examined the consequences of varying levels of institutional quality and citizen engagement for mass political participation in Third Wave democracies, making the research findings of this book an integral addition to our understanding of important political phenomena in the region. By connecting a growing trend in mass political behavior to specific features of Latin American democratic institutions and civil society, this book sheds light on the ways in which political institutions shape how citizens engage the political systems they inhabit. Further, I argue the key finding that intermediate levels of democratic quality—that is, suboptimal institutions coupled with a highly mobilized citizenry—spur high levels of contentious activity at the national and subnational levels and calls for a recalibration of the received wisdom on the interconnection of political institutions and contentious politics.

In focusing on protest, this book also speaks to a topic that is highly relevant to regimes outside the region under consideration. Given recent political upheaval in the Middle East, riots across Southern Europe, elevated protest participation in hybrid regimes like Turkey and Russia, and the emergence of the Occupy Wall Street and Black Lives Matter movements in the United States, this project will speak to a more universal audience, contributing to a growing dialogue on a type of political participation that seems increasingly important in regimes of all types. The lessons drawn from Argentina and Latin America are certainly germane to other societies that are experiencing similar cycles of contentious politics, therefore making the findings from this book relevant to students of protest and political behavior across the world.

CHAPTER 2
The Rise of the Protest State

Theory and Hypotheses

Until recently, empirical research on variation in protest across polities has been limited, primarily due to problems related to data availability. However, theoretical work and single case studies on the roots of protest abound, offering rich source material for any budding project on the causes of protest participation. Moreover, a growing body of scholarship has sought to leverage newly available empirical data, primarily from region-wide survey projects, to shed further light on causes of protest in Latin America. In this chapter I put forth an approach to constructing a theory of protest across polities that acknowledges the challenges associated with answering such an important, yet multifaceted, question. This discussion includes background on the current theoretical and empirical landscape, beginning with classic approaches and incorporating the latest frontiers in scholarly work on contentious politics in Latin America.

The chapter begins with a brief treatment of the concept of "contentious politics," which lays the foundation for the rest of the literature review and the introduction of my theory. Following this discussion I put forth the overarching argument of this book, where I maintain that the rise of protest in many Latin American regimes can be explained by the interaction of two specific phenomena in recent history: (1) the significant socioeconomic gains made in the region during the past decade, which in turn have produced the most politically "engaged" citizenries—via social media, community organizations, and professional or educational networks—in Latin

American history; and (2) the persistence of flawed political institutions and waning legitimacy in the eyes of citizens. Thus, rather than emphasizing how worsening economic conditions and mounting grievances fuel protest, my theoretical approach attributes rising contention to the *improvement* of socioeconomic conditions amid low-quality political institutions.

When these two factors combine—namely, low levels of institutional quality and an increasingly active and knowledgeable democratic citizenry—social protest can "normalize" as a common tactic aimed at effecting political change, utilized by a diverse cross-section of political actors seeking redress of sundry grievances. It is these regimes, in which protest crystallizes as a repertoire of participation so common as to render it quotidian and conventional, that I call "protest states."

CONCEPT FORMATION: ON "CONTENTIOUS POLITICS"

Generally, protest has fallen under the conceptual umbrella of *contentious politics*, a term coined nearly forty years ago to describe "disruptive," or at least extra-institutional, political behaviors (Tilly 1978). Therefore, to answer any question related to protest, one must first arrive at a clear conceptualization of what behaviors "contentious politics" includes (which is easier said than done), and then decide where the phenomena of interest lie within that conceptual framework.

Since contentious politics emerged as a burgeoning new field of study in the 1960s, the term has been used to describe a vast array of "unconventional" forms of political behavior, such that the term itself has become somewhat vague. Indeed, "contentious politics" encompasses work on civil wars and ethnic conflict, social movements, mass demonstrations, terrorism, and revolution—in other words, a category of political phenomena seemingly alike in their unconventionality but dissimilar in virtually every other respect.

Due to this nebulousness, scholars have continued to pursue a more parsimonious conceptualization of contentious politics, mostly for purposes of cross-country comparison. For in-depth conceptual work on contentious politics there is no better source than Charles Tilly, whose pioneering work on protest, revolutions, and social movements primarily in European states has paced the literature for decades. Throughout his illustrious career, Tilly made contributions to virtually every subsection of the contentious politics literature, making him one of the most important social scientists of the last half-century and the unofficial guardian of the term *contentious politics*, along with his frequent co-authors Douglas McAdam and Sidney

Tarrow. In their 2001 piece on the state of the literature, the three scholars define contentious politics as follows:

> episodic, public, collective interaction among makers of claims and their objects when (a) at least one government is a claimant, an object of claims, or a party to the claims and (b) the claims would, if realized, affect the interests of at least one of the claimants. (2001, 438)

According to McAdam et al. (2009), contentious politics is characterized by three critical components: (1) interactions, (2) claims, and (3) governments. The term *interactions* describes the cluster of political actors who join together to make particular "claims"—in other words, "calls for action on the part of some object that would, if realized, affect that object's interests" (261). These claims are by definition either directed at actors within *governments*, the third crucial property of contentious politics, or have important consequences for governments as third parties. Oftentimes, according to McAdam et al. (2009), contentious politics entails citizens utilizing confrontational tactics directed at non-confrontational government entities, such as "routine public administration, organization of elections, military conscription, tax collection, appointment of officials, and disbursement of funds" (262). However, the form and intensity of contentious politics are strongly conditioned by characteristics of political regimes.

Given the diverse nature of "contentious politics," it would seem necessary to take a few steps down on the "ladder of abstraction" (Sartori 1970), as it relates to this particular book project. Thus, in an effort to produce and empirically test a "middle range" theory (LaPalombara 1968) that combines conceptual rigor with some degree of generalizability, this book focuses on a subset of contentious politics: *public protests and demonstrations by civilians targeted at government actors in democratic polities.* This particular conceptualization excludes civil war, intra-institutional contention, and democratization or revolution, all of which fall within the purview of contentious politics according to Tilly and his associates. The primary rationale for limiting the discussion to this particular type of contentious politics lies in this book's focus on developing democracies in general, and the region of Latin America specifically. In contemporary Latin America (outside of Cuba), democracy is the dominant type of political regime, rendering democratization unnecessary and attempts at revolution nearly obsolete. Moreover, none of the Latin American countries examined here are currently experiencing civil war or prolonged militarized conflict.[1] Thus, I confine my approach to studying political claims made via extra-institutional methods, aimed at actors within the regime in an effort to induce political change.

Despite having narrowed the scope of this study significantly, one might still argue that the category of "public protests and demonstrations" encompasses a plethora of performances characterized by significant differences in terms of the *degree* of contentiousness. In other words, signing a petition directed at a particular public official is qualitatively different from blocking a major highway, yet both of these acts would fall under the larger umbrella of tactics that are examined in this book. In Chapters 6 and 7, I provide a more detailed account of how we might delineate between confrontational and non-confrontational acts of protest, based on their legality and the extent to which they disrupt everyday life. It is in this chapter that I argue for a more nuanced understanding of the relationship between institutional context, political engagement, and protest, where more confrontational tactics thrive in less democratic settings, while non-confrontational protests surge in moderately open political contexts. However, for the most part, this book examines all kinds of public protests and demonstrations targeted at national and subnational political actors in democratic regimes, and treats these extra-institutional tactics as being part of the same class of contentious behaviors.

It should also be noted that while the empirical focus of this book lies in the emerging democracies of Latin America, the universe of comparable cases extends far beyond the confines of the Western Hemisphere. Since the early 1970s, an unprecedented number of countries across the world have undergone transitions to democracy (Huntington 1991). This "Third Wave" of democratization spanned from Latin America to Southern Europe to the former Soviet Union, and even included regimes in the Asia-Pacific and sub-Saharan Africa. While high-quality democracy has proved difficult to construct amid democratic "recessions" in a number of recently transitioned regimes (Diamond 2015), mounting evidence has pointed to an increase in protest activity in developing countries, and particularly those that play host to at least minimally competitive, periodic elections (e.g., Beaulieu 2014, Norris et al. 2005). Thus, while the data used for this book are drawn from one particular region, the emphasis on disruptive protests in emerging democracies is certainly one that travels.

RECENT STUDIES OF PROTEST IN LATIN AMERICA

Zeroing in on contemporary explanations of contentious politics in Latin America, the comparatively high levels of protest in certain countries in the region have not gone unnoticed by social scientists, who have spent a great deal of time studying particular episodes of mobilization in the post-transition era. In the mid-1990s, the scholarly consensus held that protest in Latin America would quiet down following the tumultuous transition period of the 1980s as political parties came to replace social movements as the most important vehicles for participation (e.g., Hipsher 1996, Eckstein 2001). However, numerous case studies of specific episodes of protest and a handful of cross-national analyses have found no such evidence of this predicted downturn. For example, we have studies of social movements organized by the economic victims of neoliberal policies in Argentina and Peru (e.g., Auyero 2005, Levitsky and Murillo 2005, Arce 2008, Silva 2009) and research on the rise of indigenous protest groups in Mexico, Central America, Ecuador, and Bolivia (e.g., Yashar 1999, Jung 2003, Lazar 2007, Becker 2011). In sum, students of political science, sociology, and anthropology alike have documented the persistence of mass protest in countries across Latin America, focusing on a diverse array of political actors and contexts.

However, as revealed by the pieces cited above, most of the research on protest in the region initially dealt with a particular subclass of social movements or episodes of mass mobilization, favoring specific explanations tied to a particular set of actors or grievances over general explanations of protest participation.[2] While this tendency raises certain problems of generalizability, it has also reinforced the notion that instances of protest mobilization can be traced to a unique situation or set of grievances. Thus, while many of these studies illuminate the causes of particular episodes of contention—for example, how movements organized or the processes by which claims translated into actions—the literature has lacked for a more general explanation of the rise of protest as form of political participation across Latin America.

For example, even comparative studies of neoliberalism and/or economic crisis as a cause of mass mobilization essentially home in on a specific type of policy-related complaint or injustice as the driving force behind movement formation, rather than making broader claims about the conditions that seem to give way to high levels of protest activity in certain countries but not others (e.g., Vilas 2006, Levitsky and Murillo 2005, Silva 2009). Indeed, despite the dual emphasis of several works on neoliberalism and democracy as predictors of protest demonstrations across Latin American democracies (e.g., Arce and Bellinger 2007), one is still left to wonder what happens when the grievances associated with neoliberal reforms subside, or whether there are more general factors that might explain the persistence of contentious politics in Latin America's post-neoliberal era.

Though lacking in extensive empirical tests, the insights from recent research on institutional "weakness" (Levitsky and Murillo 2005) in the region's young democracies seem highly germane to explaining protest in Latin America, a region populated by numerous flawed democratic regimes (Diamond 2002). While every country in the region aside from Cuba and now Venezuela is widely characterized as a democracy, and peaceful forms of political participation are generally tolerated and even encouraged, Latin American regimes differ substantially in how effectively their formal political institutions channel participation. In other words, these regimes are open enough that groups are capable of organizing and sustaining contentious action without fear of harsh retribution, but they often lack the institutional capacity to fully incorporate citizens into the policymaking process (e.g., O'Donnell 1993, Levitsky and Murillo 2005, Gibson 2005).

Work by Machado, Scartascini, and Tommasi (2011; see also Przeworski 2010) on institutions and street protests in Latin America offers the most relevant example of this approach being put into practice in an effort to explain cross-national variation in protest participation. In the authors' view, widespread protest is a symptom of low-quality institutions rather than specific grievances or the maneuverings of organizational actors. Utilizing Latin American public opinion data from 2008 and aggregate measures of institutional quality for a set of seventeen Latin American regimes, they demonstrate that there is a strong correlation between institutional deficiencies and rates of protest activity, and that the individual-level characteristics of protestors differ a great deal across contexts.

In some ways, the argument outlined below echoes this theoretical emphasis on political institutions, but with several key distinctions. Most significant is my inclusion of mass-level political engagement—or access to mobilizing structures—as a critical moderating factor, rather than relying solely on institutional quality to explain variation in rates of contentious activity across countries. Without an assessment of general patterns of political engagement among a citizenry, it becomes difficult to account for those contexts where institutions are weak, but protest activity is also very low—for example, El Salvador or Jamaica. Explanations focusing only on institutional weakness therefore fail to capture the crucial role that mass-level patterns of political engagement and civil society play in fueling rising rates of protest, even in regimes of varying levels of institutional quality. This book also examines trends in protest participation both over time and within nations, thereby providing a "baseline" for a given society and moving beyond a snapshot, cross-sectional approach. The subnational component of this book accounts for the possibility that patterns of protest participation vary greatly within countries, and thus provides a more nuanced understanding of how context influences citizens' political behaviors.

In sum, numerous studies have offered rich empirical accounts of the processes underlying certain episodes of contention in Latin America, or applied cutting-edge methodological techniques to examine the relationship between institutional strength and protest. However, I argue that a gap in the literature persists, in that extant research either fails to put forth a general explanation of protest participation across Latin American regimes or neglects the mass-level factors associated with surging rates of protest activity. Below, I attempt to build on the strengths of the existing literature, while remedying some of the problems associated with prominent explanations of protest in Latin America.

FILLING THE GAP: CONSTRUCTING A THEORY OF PROTEST IN LATIN AMERICA

The goal of this book is to understand why protest is so prevalent within certain democratic contexts but not others, and how second-level regime characteristics interact with individual-level factors to explain rising rates of protest participation across the developing world, and specifically in Latin American regimes. In this section I first address the more general challenge of explaining levels of protest across countries, given the myriad moving parts involved in such an enterprise. This discussion provides the foundation for my own theory of protest—one that focuses on the importance of political institutions and patterns of citizen engagement in shaping individual-level protest behaviors across and within Latin America's democratic regimes.

Explaining Levels of Protest Across Political Contexts

All studies that set out to explain protest participation ask, at a very basic level, "Why do some people choose to protest, while others do not?" In many ways, this book is no different. At its root, this study seeks to unravel why individual citizens engage their political systems in diverse ways across and within regimes. Put simply, this book endeavors to explain why certain modes (or to use Tilly's terminology, "repertoires") of political participation are so common within certain contexts, yet infrequently utilized within other political regimes.

There are innumerable aggregate-level economic and political factors that could influence protest behavior at the individual level. Indeed, whether they might be short-term economic crises, long-brewing transitions to democracy, or simply unresponsive politicians, the potential macro-level stimuli for the emergence of protest are impossibly vast. However, one might reasonably divide the contextual factors that influence individual-level protest behavior into four categories: (1) grievances, (2) representation, (3) repression, and (4) mobilizing structures. All of these four categories of variables have been discussed at length in the protest literature, and this section focuses on how each might affect individuals' choices to partake of contentious forms of participation or not—thus altering the decision-making calculus across countries and subnational units, and determining the extent to which protest takes hold in a given society. I present the four categories sequentially, to approximate the process by which grievances might translate into contentious behaviors.

1. Grievances: The Initial Stimuli

The first, and perhaps most obvious, factor that might influence protest participation is the overriding grievance or motivating claim spurring individuals to action. Almost any historical treatment of a particular instance of mass mobilization attributes that movement's existence at least in part to a particular claim. Intuitively, this perspective makes a great deal of sense. When contemplating what drives an individual citizen to attend a protest demonstration or join a social movement, it seems self-evident that in the absence of a motivating claim, that individual would not engage in contentious political behaviors. When aggregated to the country level, one might therefore expect that potential grievance-producing conditions should also foment high levels of protest participation, as citizens are confronted with more fodder for contentious claim making.

Prominent grievance-based explanations of protest date back to the 1960s and 1970s, when the "disaffected radicalism" thesis argued that protest was a response to relative deprivation and constituted a rejection of the key representative institutions of the political system (Gurr 1970). According to this line of thought, widespread political protest is a threat to the legitimacy of democracies, as citizens express discontent not with particular leaders or issues but with the political system itself (Norris, Walgrave, and Van Aeslt 2005). Gurr's *Why Men Rebel* (1970) offers the classic articulation of this perspective, as he argues that relative social and economic deprivation greatly increase the likelihood that mass protest, or even revolution, will occur as an expression of discontent. For Gurr, contentious forms of participation can emerge as viable options when citizens face "shifts" in grievances—for example, an uptick in dire economic circumstances, racial oppression, or widespread government corruption (also, see Gusfield 1968). Put simply, it is the grievance itself that serves as the primary catalyst in producing mass protest, as frustration and alienation create a gap between citizens' expectations and objective realities and thus incite violent anti-state participation, which can in turn destabilize political systems.

According to this view of contentious politics, protest substitutes for conventional participation (Muller 1979). That is, protestors generally come from destitute socioeconomic backgrounds and do not take part in the political process through conventional channels like voting, party membership, and civic associations. Other scholars have drawn the connection between macro-level economic conditions—for example, income and land inequality—and violent participation, asserting that protest can take root due to relative deprivation in unequal countries (Muller and Seligson 1987).

When considering what contextual factors influence individual behavior, scholars must consider how the claim itself emerged and how that claim might drive individuals to action. At the aggregate level, certain large-scale economic shocks have clearly had mobilizing effects on citizenries throughout history. For example, it would be impossible to explain the explosion of protest participation that occurred in Argentina during the 1999–2002 economic crisis, or in Spain and Greece during their ongoing economic recessions, without referencing the considerable influence those national crises had on individual citizens' quality of life. In the Latin American context, the abundant literature on the effects of neoliberal economic reforms on social movements and protests exemplifies the importance of grievances in fueling contentious participation (e.g., Vilas 2006, Arce and Bellinger 2007, Silva 2009).

The existence of a motivating grievance is undoubtedly an important part of the "Why do people protest?" equation. Put simply, in a context devoid of grievances, individual citizens would have no reason to question or object to the actions of government. Unfortunately, no such idyllic political regime exists in the real world. Citizens of every country inevitably have reasons to expect more from their regimes, and even if the objective direness of the grievance might differ substantially depending on the regime—for example, a comparison between recent anti-Assad protests in Syria and student protests for education reform in Chile—there are endless possibilities in terms of claims that might mobilize protest in different political contexts. Moreover, studies have shown over the years that in many cases the political regimes characterized by the most ostensibly protest-inducing conditions—such as severe state repression, extreme poverty, or high inequality—are rarely home to the highest levels of protest (Dalton et al. 2009).

In sum, grievances matter. But to adequately explain why rates of protest participation are high in some democratic regimes and low in others, one must go beyond grievances. Indeed, there are too many cases where "extreme" grievances are present and protest does *not* result, or where "minor" grievances produce massive mobilization, to base one's explanation entirely on these initial stimuli. While a motivating claim on the government might therefore be *necessary* for an individual to take to the streets, it is not *sufficient*.

2. Representation: What Options Exist for Redressing Grievances?

After identifying the grievance(s), the next step in tracing the impact of context on individual-level protest behaviors is evaluating the representational outlets available for the aggrieved to make claims on their government. In making this evaluation, questions abound. Is the regime a democracy, where representatives are expected to listen to constituents and voice concerns on their behalf? Or is it an authoritarian regime devoid of meaningful feedback mechanisms for political leaders? If the country is a democracy, what are the most commonly utilized avenues for the airing and potential reparation of grievances? Are institutional actors generally "responsive" (Eulau and Karps 1977), or is the process of rectifying claims inefficient and/or inconsequential?

The growing emphasis on non–grievance related determinants of protest (primarily in response to the critiques mentioned above) eventually expanded into a focus on how political regimes influence the opportunities available to prospective contentious actors. The "political opportunity structures" approach to the study of protest—namely the idea that a particular movement's potential for mobilizing support and acquiring influence depends in large part on political context (e.g., Eisinger 1973, Tilly 1978, Kitschelt 1986, Brockett 1991, Meyer 2004)—thus offers another approach to understanding how protest movements emerge and evolve, and how particular tactics take root in a given society.

Specifically, scholars operating within this theoretical paradigm seek to uncover the institutional mechanisms that allow previously unexpressed grievances to blossom. This might entail a focus on processes of democratization and political liberalization or, within existing democracies, on the role of political parties, labor unions, or important legal decisions in structuring potential protest activity (McAdam 1982, Kitschelt 1986). Others have sought to compare regimes characterized by different levels of democratic "openness," as several scholars have posited a curvilinear relationship between political openness and protest (e.g., Eisinger 1973, Tilly 1978, 2006). According to this logic, protest movements arise and flourish more frequently in moderately open regimes—where opposition is tolerated and widespread, but representative institutions are not fully facilitative of participation—than in regimes at either end of the openness spectrum (Tilly 1978).

Yet even in democracies, the potential vehicles for pursuing the redress of grievances differ greatly depending on the nature of the grievance and the characteristics of political institutions in the regime. For example, in certain cases citizens might seek out local municipal or provincial authorities to make their claims, while in other cases claims are directed at national actors, including legislatures, political parties, and even executives. Regular elections inevitably serve as a vehicle to voice grievances and seek a response from government in any democracy, subnational and national regimes alike, whether through formal electoral processes or contentious movements organized around Election Day (Schumpeter 1976, Beaulieu 2014).

In cases where institutions effectively channel citizens' claims and eventually respond to them, one might expect that formal political institutions render contentious behaviors less necessary given the relatively lower costs associated with formal political participation (Machado et al. 2011). However, in cases where those institutional channels do not exist, or they are ineffective in producing meaningful government action, it would seem that protest could emerge as a viable form of political expression. In other words, high-quality democratic institutions should serve to diminish the need for contentious action, while low-quality institutions might push individuals to explore other options for obtaining the government responsiveness they desire. Further, this book argues that democratic institutions that *promise* viable mechanisms for representation but fail to *deliver* on that promise will likely induce higher levels of contentious political participation than if there were no such representative institutions in the first place. This becomes a key component of the theory presented in this chapter.

3. Repression: Are the Risks of Punishment Associated with Protesting Too Great?

Another crucial factor to consider when evaluating how regime characteristics might condition mass-level behaviors is the degree of political repression found within that context. In certain regimes, public demonstrations that challenge authority are strictly forbidden, in some cases to the extent that protesting is a crime punishable by death or imprisonment. In other contexts, institutional actors such as political parties, labor unions, or individual politicians actively work to mobilize protest participation on behalf of their interests and those of their followers. The extent to which public claims on government are allowed or even encouraged is thus an important component of any explanation of levels of contentious activity across polities (Tilly 1978, Muller and Seligson 1987).

In contexts that exhibit high levels of political repression—think Soviet Russia or North Korea—protest participation is likely to be severely limited, even if grievances are plentiful and no institutional channels are available for voicing those grievances, due to state repression of any potential challenge to the regime. Indeed, only in regimes that are at least partially open can protest movements emerge and thrive, making some minimum level of democracy often necessary for high levels of contentious politics to be present (see Dalton et al. 2009). However, if repression is used temporarily in a semi-open regime, it is possible that it serves not to discourage protest but to shift the strategies of protestors, pushing them to adopt more violent protest technologies (Lichbach 1987, Moore 1998). In this case, repression would have a negative impact on the utilization of moderate protest technologies but might increase the incidence of more aggressive protest repertoires, as individuals are forced to adopt more violent modes of collective action to influence politics. I return to this idea in the argument presented later in this chapter.

4. Mobilizing Structures: What Organizational Framework Is Available to Structure Collective Claim Making?

Finally, the existence of mobilizing structures that can be utilized for fomenting widespread contention are crucial to the emergence of protest in a particular society. Even when high-protest conditions are otherwise in place—grievances are present, representative outlets are suboptimal, and political repression is low or sporadic—prospective contentious actors still require the organizational resources necessary to solve the collective action problem and mobilize groups of citizens behind a particular cause (Olson 1965). Without established organizational structures via labor unions, political parties, churches and religious groups, or community advocacy organizations, grievances might go unvoiced and potential movements thwarted.

Following the rise of the literature on relative deprivation, another significant subset of scholarly work began to gain traction in the 1960s and 1970s based not on shifting grievances and the gap between expectations and reality, but the socioeconomic and organizational factors that underpin the formation and sustainability of social movements. Scholars adhering to this particular approach were classified under the banner of "resource mobilization theory"—or the idea that the primary determinants of whether or not social movements emerge and are successful lie in a particular movement's access to organizational resources and mobilizing structures. For scholars adhering to this school of thought, grievances are viewed as a constant, while the driving mechanism behind movement formation is related to a change in how easy it is for "political entrepreneurs" to spread their message and mobilize support (e.g., Jenkins 1983, McAdam 1982, McCarthy and Zald 1973, 1977).

Scholars from the resource mobilization tradition have frequently demonstrated empirically that these organizational apparatuses are crucial to fomenting protest activity, and that individuals with connections to mobilizing structures are the most likely protestors (e.g., Schussman and Soule 2005). In particular, the resource mobilization school received a boon from studies on the U.S. Civil Rights Movement that occurred in the 1960s. While in many ways, African Americans in the United States encountered the same grievances they had faced during the decades preceding this time period, access to organizational resources changed drastically in the direct lead-up to the Civil Rights Movement. That is, increased urbanization, the growth of historically black universities, and an expanding black middle class led to the removal of traditional paternalistic social relations between (particularly Southern) whites and blacks, and paved the way for a thriving national movement (McAdam 1982, Jenkins 1983). In sum, according to Jenkins, "the formation of movements is linked to improvements in the status of aggrieved groups, not because of grievances . . . but because these changes reduce the costs of mobilization and improve the likelihood of success" (1983, 532).

Recent work in the contentious politics literature has stressed the extent to which a thriving civil society can fuel rates of protest participation. Cornell and Grimes (2015) find that a corrupt bureaucracy can stimulate disruptive protests, but only where civil society is strong. Boulding (2014) focuses on the role that NGOs play in mobilizing protests in contexts characterized by weak political institutions. In democratic and non-democratic contexts alike, there is evidence that labor unions and professional associations can provide the organizational platforms necessary for once-isolated actors to mobilize (Robertson 2007, Mangonnet and Murillo

2016). In short, organizational resources must factor into any cross-national account of protest participation.

Of the four factors listed above, representation and mobilizing structures emerge as the two most critical factors to explaining rates of protest participation across democratic contexts in Latin America, for several reasons. First, as mentioned above, grievances themselves are rarely useful predictors of protest participation in and of themselves, as often times the most dismal circumstances result in little contentious activity, while seemingly minor grievances can provoke large-scale protest mobilization. Second, levels of repression are very important in explaining the differences in rates of participation across democratic and authoritarian regimes, but in democratic countries repression is by definition low, at least comparatively. For example, while China's high levels of political repression serve to squelch protest activity domestically whereas Greece's relatively low levels of repression allow protest movements to flourish, these considerable differences are not as present in a region populated by at least minimally democratic countries like Latin America.[3] Repression likely accounts for why democracies boast higher rates of protest than non-democracies (see Dalton et al. 2009), but this distinction might obscure the more nuanced institutional differences within these two categories that matter for explaining divergent patterns of mobilization (e.g., Machado et al. 2011).

On the other hand, representative institutions and mobilizing structures vary greatly in Latin America, which lends considerable explanatory power to these two factors. My argument thus rests on the assumptions that while grievances and repression should be viewed as fairly constant when considering Latin American democracies, with occasional exceptions, variation in terms of institutions and mobilizing structures drive the vast differences we observe in terms of protest across the region.

THE PROTEST STATE

Why is protest a normal, almost routine form of political participation in certain Latin American democracies but not others? In light of surging protests in countries across the developing world, this book answers this question through a focus on recent trends in the quality of governance and socioeconomic development in Latin America. Specifically, I argue that increasingly engaged citizenries coupled with dysfunctional political institutions have fueled more contentious modes of participation in Latin America, as citizens' demands for government responsiveness have overwhelmed many regimes' institutional capacity to provide it. Where weak institutions and politically engaged citizenries collide, countries can morph into "protest states," where contentious participation becomes so common as to render it a conventional characteristic of everyday political life.

Following this line of thought, politically active individuals utilize protest as a means of exerting their influence more forcefully on the regime, given their lack of efficacy operating through conventional channels. When this style of demand making persists over time, protest eventually becomes an integral component of everyday politics. That is, citizens active in traditional modes of participation become the most likely protestors, and political elites attempt to mobilize contentious participation on behalf of their policy initiatives. Thus, contrary to the commonly held notions that protest movements are either largely led by the aggrieved segments of society most victimized by economic recession, corruption, or crime, or that protest is a healthy byproduct of liberal democracy and economic development (e.g., Dalton et al. 2009), I argue that in contemporary Latin American protest states, protest has become part of the repertoire of *conventional* participation utilized by politically active citizens and elites in systems devoid of effective representative institutions. This theory thus rests on two converging phenomena: poor institutional quality and expanded citizen engagement in politics. I address each factor in turn.

Broken Promises: How Poor Institutional Performance Fuels Protest

The specific mechanisms that determine how well regimes channel and respond to popular demands can be found in existing representative institutions and include the number and quality of political parties, the capacity of legislatures to form coalitions and enact policies, and levels of corruption present in formal institutions (e.g., Kitschelt 1986, Przeworski 2010). Political institutions in Latin American democratic systems vary greatly in terms of their ability to offer a high-quality representational outlet for their population and in their capacity to translate citizens' policy preferences into government output. For example, while political parties have been relatively disciplined and programmatic in countries like Chile and Costa Rica, party platforms vacillate from election to election in countries like Argentina, Ecuador, and Peru. Though Uruguay has in recent years demonstrated the ability to form working coalitions in Congress, gridlock has been the norm in Bolivia, with President Evo Morales and his party pitted in a constant struggle against opposition legislators.[4]

Table 2.1 INSTITUTIONAL SOURCES OF MASS PROTEST PARTICIPATION

Institutional Characteristic	Mechanism
Party Institutionalization	Where party institutionalization is low, with inconsistent platforms and little party discipline, contentious participation is more likely, as citizens lose faith in formal modes of representation.
Legislative Effectiveness	When Congress is mired in gridlock and functional legislative coalitions fail to surface, citizens (and thus elites) might seek extra-institutional solutions.
Political Corruption	When formal institutions and politicians are delegitimized by corruption scandals, cynicism about the viability of "traditional" participation translates into protest.
Executive Dominance	Where the president holds ultimate power over important policy decisions, the opposition will be galvanized to protest due to their lack of faith in formal representation. Defenders of the president will also be motivated to take to the streets.

Whereas Chileans largely report low levels of vote buying or corruption victimization, citizens of other Latin American regimes like the Dominican Republic, Mexico, and Paraguay report high levels of clientelism and graft. These examples highlight the extent to which regimes differ in their ability to absorb citizens' preferences and produce representative public policy, and it is this variation that I see as critical to understanding varying levels of protest in the region (Table 2.1).

One key issue related to institutional quality in Latin America is the extent to which democratic institutions in many countries fail to deliver on the *promise* of democratic representation for citizens. In previous decades, when the majority of regimes in the region were authoritarian, there was little expectation that political institutions would produce representative outcomes given the absence of institutional mechanisms for responsiveness. However, in post-transition Latin America, democracy has swept across the region and become the only legitimate regime type. The fact that an increasing body of literature has lamented recent setbacks in terms of the quality of democracy in the region (e.g., Weyland 2013) underscores the extent to which regimes are failing to deliver the democratic outcomes they guarantee.

In their 2007 article on democratic learning in African hybrid regimes, Mattes and Bratton introduce the idea of comparing the *demand* for democracy—the degree to which citizens prefer it to other systems of government and support democratic norms and processes—with perceptions of its *supply* in a particular regime context. Drawing on Huntington's (1968) work on institutionalization, they define the supply of democracy in a particular regime as "the extent that these [institutional] structures effectively and impartially fulfill their functions, whether to make laws, oversee the executive, prosecute criminals, or deliver public services" (192). Based on their analyses of public opinion regarding democracy, Mattes and Bratton conclude that the deepening of democracy depends both on the cognitive sophistication of citizens and the improvement of regime performance with respect to rule of law, electoral integrity, and other indicators of good governance.

In Latin America, there is overwhelming support for democracy and the practices it entails (LAPOP 2012). Compared to sub-Saharan Africa, Latin America has a longer history with democracy, and Latin American citizens have on average a stronger commitment to democratic norms and processes. However, the supply of democracy in Latin America has often left much to be desired. Hence, not only does poor institutional quality plague a number of Latin American regimes—it does so in national contexts where a high percentage of citizens have strong preferences for democracy and are capable of understanding where the institutions of their own countries fall short. In regimes characterized by widespread demand for democracy, but where the democratic promise of representation appears tenuous or nonexistent, engaged individuals are particularly likely to seek out alternative modes of voicing their demands.

Bringing the Citizens Back In: Engagement as a Source of Contention

The second key component of the protest state lies in swelling rates of citizen engagement in politics. This focus on political engagement as a moderating variable speaks to the literature on resource mobilization and protest (e.g., McCarthy and Zald 1977, Tilly 1978, Jenkins 1983), which argues that the formation and survival of protest movements depends in large part on the political resources available to contentious actors. While political (also referred to as "civic" or "citizen") engagement might seem like a synonym for participation itself, rather than part of a causal explanation of protest, it in fact refers to the extent to which citizens are knowledgeable about and interested in political issues, and how connected they are to the types of social and political networks that can serve to foment collective action.

The degree of political engagement in a given context is thus well measured by survey items used to gauge political interest and knowledge, membership in community groups, connectedness to formal political organizations via traditional or clientelistic modes of interaction, or even Internet usage to discuss or participate in politics. In contexts where institutions are high performing, we would expect that highly engaged citizens would participate in politics primarily through formal (or "conventional") vehicles, much like they do in established democracies like the Canada or Sweden. However, where representative institutions are weak, high levels of political engagement can give rise to contentious modes of participation, as formal institutions do not adequately channel participation (Table 2.2). Regardless, some minimal level of engagement is a prerequisite for widespread protest to occur in any context, as individuals require some kind of linkage to fellow collective actors in order to effectively mobilize contention.

In the twenty-first century, Latin American society has been transformed. High rates of economic growth fueled by a commodities boom (Mangonnet and Murillo 2016) coupled with an unprecedented expansion of the welfare state throughout much of the region (Garay 2016) have resulted in massive reductions in poverty, the extension of educational opportunities to previously underserved segments of society, and the development of a vibrant middle class. All of these advances have produced more politically engaged citizenries, equipped with the cognitive and organizational tools to take a more active role in political life. Indeed, widespread linkages to mobilizing structures and individual awareness of political issues are a prerequisite for large-scale mobilization in any society. Yet in many ways, the expansion of the Latin American welfare state was not just important in that it fueled increased access to organizational resources; it also was in many ways a validation of social mobilization as a strategy for effecting political change. As Candelaria Garay (2016) argues regarding the emergence of social policy expansion throughout the region,

Table 2.2 THE INTERACTION BETWEEN INSTITUTIONS
AND POLITICAL ENGAGEMENT

	Effective Institutions	Ineffective Institutions
High engagement	Low protest/High levels of formal participation (e.g., Uruguay, Costa Rica)	High protest/Low or ineffective formal participation—*"protest states"* (e.g., Argentina, Brazil, Bolivia)
Low engagement	Low protest/Elite-dominated politics (e.g., Panama)	Low protest/Machine-style participation through formal vehicles (e.g., El Salvador, Guatemala)

the incorporation of political "outsiders" in the welfare state was in part an effort to appease more isolated protest movements. This included indigenous groups (Yashar 2005) and associations organized by the recently unemployed (Garay 2007), and resulted in many social movements actually being absorbed into the formal organizations of political parties and labor associations (e.g., the FPV [Frente para la Victora] and CTA [Central de Trabajadores de la Argentina] in Argentina, respectively). All of these changes increased the mobilizing potential of Latin American mass publics and confirmed the potential power of protest.

Finally, not only are engaged individuals more likely to have the wherewithal and access to organizational linkages to mobilize protest; I also argue that this group of individuals is more likely to *be aware of* the shortcomings of formal avenues for representation in their regimes. Given their higher levels of interest in politics, knowledge regarding current issues and political actors, and savvy with respect to navigating an increasingly saturated news cycle regarding political issues, engaged individuals possess the political awareness (Zaller 1992) necessary both to identify problems within the current system *and* do something about it. This connection between access to information and contentious behavior has been demonstrated in work on the importance of blame attribution in motivating protest participation (Javeline 2003), and even appears heightened in studies of digital media (Van Laer 2010). Recent trends in citizen engagement are thus crucial in understanding the emergence of the protest state in Latin America.

Put simply, I argue that protest is more likely to become a normalized tool of political participation in democracies where engagement among citizens is high, and institutional performance is low. Where these conditions persist, contentious politics can be absorbed into a society's repertoire of collective action and utilized regardless of the specific characteristics of the grievance being expressed, and even under conditions where institutions might have actually improved.[5] It is this combination of factors that I argue has produced an emerging number of protest states in twenty-first century Latin America.

A Subnational Caveat

As mentioned above, national governments in most Latin American democracies lack the willingness or capacity to repress or otherwise thwart contentious actors who oppose them. In other words, while these regimes might still suffer from weak political institutions and the occasional trespass against democratic norms, no national regime in Latin America other than Cuba maintains explicit authority to repress or otherwise punish opposition protestors, nor do they have such complete control over economic and political life within their national boundaries as to credibly hinder all contentious activities.[6,7] However, this is not always the case in subnational regimes within Latin America, which I will eventually examine in Chapters 6 and 7 of this book. Numerous scholars have documented the extent to which many provincial and state governments in the region have managed to retain tight control over political and economic life within their territories, preserving pseudo-authoritarian institutions and precluding real political competition (e.g., O'Donnell 1993, Fox 1994, Gibson and Calvo 2001, Snyder 2001, Hiskey 2003, Gervasoni 2010, Gibson 2012, Giraudy 2013).

In these subnational regimes, I argue that the interaction between institutional and individual-level factors is slightly different from the national level. In more authoritarian provinces, which possess the most flawed democratic institutions by the standards enumerated above, we might actually observe *lower* rates of certain types of protest participation, given organizational obstacles to mobilization and the costs associated with contesting hegemonic local political bosses, who often wield a great deal of control over provincial economies and even law enforcement. However, where protests *do* manage to emerge in such closed regimes, we should find that they are more aggressive and even violent in nature than in more democratic subnational contexts. Overall, though, I expect and test for a similar dynamic in terms of the interaction between institutional quality and engagement at the subnational level.

OBSERVABLE IMPLICATIONS OF THE PROTEST STATE

Figure 2.1 illustrates the individual-level decision-making process that results from this multilevel theoretical framework. To simplify, I assume that grievances are relatively constant, in that they will motivate certain individuals to protest, while many other citizens with similar claims will abstain from contentious participation. The first question any individual with a grievance must ask herself is, "Are there effective formal mechanisms for seeking some response to this claim?" If the answer is yes, that person will generally abstain from contentious activities and participate through formal institutional vehicles, given their relatively lower costs and proven effectiveness. If the answer is no, that citizen must ask herself another question: "Are the organizational structures necessary for mobilization present and accessible?" If such organizational tools are absent, individuals will lack the capacity to mobilize even amid low-functioning institutions,

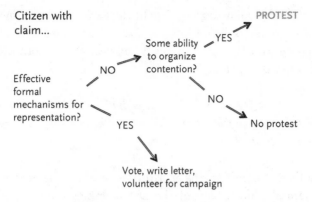

Figure 2.1 The Decision-Making Calculus of Latin American Protestors

resulting in either abstention from politics altogether or top-down clientelistic participation. However, in such societies where citizens lack faith in formal institutions but can draw on an extensive network of civil society organizations capable of efficiently mobilizing contention in response to a variety of claims, protest can thrive.

Below, I outline five hypotheses that emerge from this theoretical perspective and that I will test in the coming chapters:

> *Hypothesis One (H1): Where a high percentage of citizens in a particular society are engaged in political life, yet formal representative institutions fail to adequately channel citizens' demands, contentious action emerges as a vital form of political participation.*

Specifically, I expect that fragmented party systems, ineffective legislatures, and rampant corruption should correlate with higher levels of contentious mobilization at the national and subnational levels, as should high degrees of executive dominance or weak rule of law, as long as some minimal level of citizen engagement is present. This first hypothesis implies an interactive relationship between the strength of representative political institutions and the degree to which citizens are engaged in political life (see Table 2.2). In other words, where democratic political institutions are weak, yet the populace is not particularly informed about or engaged in political life—for example, there is low political interest and education, depressed turnout, and/or scarce participation in civic organizations—there is no reason to expect that protest movements will gain traction. Likewise, where institutions are high functioning and the population is politically active, aggressive modes of participation are not needed for citizens to feel efficacious. Rather, in regimes characterized by low-performing institutions *and* a high degree of political awareness and involvement among the citizenry, protest can normalize as a standard form of political voice—in other words, protest states. I return to this hypothesis in some way in Chapters 3, 4, 5, and 6.

> *Hypothesis Two (H2): Politically engaged individuals, who are interested in politics and active in their communities, are the citizens whose behavior is most affected by institutional context.*

Where formal policymaking institutions are seen as ineffective and inconsequential (due to any of the shortcomings enumerated above), and citizens thus cease to view them as legitimate, politically engaged individuals who are active in civil society are likely to adopt more radical tactics in pursuing their goals. My rationale for focusing on politically engaged individuals is twofold. First, engaged individuals are, *ceteris paribus*, the members of society most likely to have access to the organizational resources necessary to mobilize collective action. While many citizens might suffer from suboptimal political representation in weak democracies, only those who are plugged into their communities have the tools at their disposal to successfully mount contentious political action. The second reason I focus on the effects of political context on engaged individuals is that they constitute the portion of society most likely to have familiarity with the flaws of the democratic system they inhabit. By following politics, taking part in local organizations, and volunteering in their communities, these individuals are well *aware* of the representational deficits from which they suffer and are more likely to translate that additional information into action. I address this hypothesis in some way in each subsequent chapter.

> *Hypothesis Three (H3): While institutional deficiencies can trigger protest participation in certain cases, political regimes can also become so closed off that they render* most *contentious participation too costly.*

At a certain point, the limitation of opportunities for political expression becomes so complete that individuals can neither organize themselves nor hope that contentious actions on their part will have any influence on policymakers. That is, where the democratic promise of representation ceases to exist, so too does the motivation to take to the streets in demand of change. The argument that bad institutions generate protest is thus limited to democratic contexts, meaning a curvilinear relationship exists between political openness and the number of protests. This hypothesis becomes important at the subnational level in Latin America.

That said, while most forms of moderate street protests will virtually disappear in such closed off political contexts, it is also possible that authoritarian contexts do produce higher incidences of violent protests and confrontations between participants and law enforcement. In other words, while protests might be less likely in these regimes on average, when they *do* occur they tend to be more aggressive and confrontational than in more democratic contexts. I maintain that while at the national level, these types of closed regimes have become virtually obsolete in contemporary Latin America, with the exceptions of Cuba and now Venezuela, they continue to thrive at the subnational level in many federal democracies across the region. I test this two-pronged hypothesis in Chapters 6 and 7.

Hypothesis Four (H4): In protest states, political elites will mobilize protest on behalf of their goals, given its effectiveness as a vital, everyday form of political participation.

Where protest becomes a standard repertoire of participation utilized by a wide range of actors in everyday political life, given the relative ineffectiveness of formal political institutions, political organizations like parties and labor unions will seek to harness it in pursuit of their own ends. In this vein, Machado et al. argue in their 2011 paper that actors (i.e., unions, parties, etc.) who "have little or no chance of having their interests taken into account in the formal decision-making process" are more likely to use protest to influence policymakers than organizations operating in more high-functioning democratic contexts (11).[8] Thus, in societies where formal institutions are viewed as illegitimate, members of political organizations are forced outside of the realm of "traditional participation" to adopt more radical modes of behavior.

Furthermore, in protest states, clientelistic parties seek to invest material resources in protest activities to build contentious power in the streets and influence public opinion regarding policy issues, given its relevance as a key repertoire of political participation. Captured clients thus engage in protest activities that serve to support their political patron, so as to assure their rewarded condition and continued access to these goods. In sum, linkages to formal political organizations will be associated with distinct forms of participation, depending on the institutional context—whereas membership in a party or labor association is correlated with campaign voluntarism or voting in strong institutional contexts, it is associated with street-based activism in protest states characterized by low-quality institutions. I test this hypothesis in Chapter 4.

> *Hypothesis Five (H5): When institutions fail to improve in terms of transparency and responsiveness, protest can "crystallize" as a standard form of political participation akin to voting or volunteering for a political campaign, utilized by a diverse cross-section of citizens in response to various grievances.*

In protest states, where protest is firmly entrenched in the country's participatory culture and utilized as a primary representational vehicle, contentious behavior can become the norm among active democrats and even political elites. In other words, once citizens who are interested and active in politics regularly utilize protest to achieve their desired end, and politicians themselves mobilize protest on behalf of their policy initiatives, societies can settle on an equilibrium state where protest remains high regardless of the specific grievance or circumstance.

Another key implication of this hypothesis relates to the representativeness of protestors in protest states. In such contexts where institutions remain weak and ineffective, protest can become the go-to option for a wide cross-section of society, encompassing all varieties of citizens who are actively engaged in their communities. So while protestors might be made up of a less representative—and potentially more radical—subsection of the population in societies where protest has *not* normalized and is only utilized occasionally, demonstrators in protest states will tend to look similar in composition to participants in "conventional" activities and be no more radical in their political views than non-protestors. I will address this hypothesis in the following chapter and in the case study of Argentina.

TESTING THE THEORY: TRIANGULATING MEASURES, LEVELS OF ANALYSIS, AND METHODOLOGICAL APPROACHES

This is a comparative study, attempting to test a generalizable theory of protest across diverse political regimes to draw causal inferences regarding the role of political institutions and citizen engagement in moderating levels of contentious political participation. However, the empirical basis of this project is not a simple cross-national comparison. Rather, the primary methodological objective of this book is to triangulate methodological approaches and data sources in an effort to provide the soundest test possible of the theoretical framework outlined above. The principal strength of triangulating methodological approaches is that by corroborating the findings from an analysis of one set of units—or utilizing one measure of a particular concept—with findings from another data source, a scholar can become more confident that the theory he or she claims explains the relationship between X and Y is valid and borne out in empirical data (King et al. 1994). While a more specific description of methodological choices will be reserved for the coming chapters, this section will serve as a more general discussion of the methodological orientation of this book.

Triangulating Measures of Protest Participation

The key dependent variable in this book is protest—a notoriously difficult and controversial phenomenon to conceptualize and measure. As outlined above, according to the most commonly cited definition (Tilly and Tarrow 2006), protest is understood as the use of disruptive, extra-institutional techniques by actors who seek to make a particular claim, in which governments emerge as targets, initiators, or third parties of those claims. Naturally, this type of definition raises thorny questions about operationalization. Almost by definition, protests do not occur on a regular schedule, nor are they officially registered and documented.

From a practical standpoint, when it comes to measuring protest, scholars interested in conducting quantitative research on the topic are left with two realistic options: (1) event-counts data of protests, usually culled from newspaper articles; and (2) individual-level participation data based on surveys of everyday citizens. This book utilizes both types of data in an effort to triangulate measures and carry out a more thorough empirical evaluation of my theoretical approach and its implications, thus increasing the explanatory power of the theory. For the individual-level data, I look to the Latin American Public Opinion Project's (LAPOP) 2008, 2010, and 2012 AmericasBarometer surveys. Depending on the year, the AmericasBarometer covers up to twenty-six Latin American and Caribbean countries from Mexico to Argentina, and over 40,000 annual individual interviews. Each of these surveys included a battery of questions on protest behavior, aimed to gauge whether or not citizens protested and what types of tactics they tended to approve of or utilize themselves.

As for the protest events data, I turn to datasets compiled by two separate Argentine think tanks: the *Programa de Investigación sobre el Movimiento de la Sociedad Argentina* (PIMSA) and *Nueva Mayoría* (NM). Each of these Buenos Aires-based organizations has collected information on protest events since the early 1990s for all of the country's twenty-three provinces and its autonomous capital, and generously has granted me access to these data. Thus, these two sources offer coverage of nearly twenty years of contentious activity across twenty-four provincial units of analysis, making for a subnational protest dataset of unprecedented temporal and geographic breadth. By combining a cross-national analysis of protest participation using survey data with this subnational analysis of Argentine protest using two sources of event-counts data, this book will thus triangulate multiple measures of protest in conducting the quantitative portion of the analysis.

Combining Levels of Analysis

As mentioned in the previous section, this book will also combine analyses of protest participation across levels—notably, a cross-national analysis of survey data and a subnational analysis of event-counts data. Testing my theoretical approach across levels of analysis is important for several reasons. By conducting a cross-national analysis, I aim to put forth a more general test of my argument, built on concepts that can potentially travel to other national contexts outside of Latin America (Sartori 1970). Carrying out an in-depth subnational analysis of protest in Argentina provides increased specificity regarding one particular national case, while at the same time avoiding the "whole nation bias" that can sometimes emerge in purely cross-national studies (Rokkan 1970, Snyder 2001). It also sheds light on the importance of subnational political institutions in shaping individual-level political behaviors in Latin America, which is a growing concern of scholars in the region (Fox 1994, Hiskey and Bowler 2005, Falleti 2010, Hiskey and Moseley forthcoming).

Beyond simply serving as a subnational counterpart to the cross-national analysis, recent events in Argentina make it an intriguing puzzle for students of contentious politics. Even prior to the surge in contentious activity during the last quarter of 2012, the contemporary political climate there has been one of heated conflict, including widespread and often-times violent protest. Motivated by sundry grievances throughout the past decade, Argentines have taken to the streets regularly, banging pots and pans in the Plaza de Mayo, installing roadblocks throughout the country, and occupying factory and office buildings (Auyero 2006). In 2009 alone, there were over 5,000 roadblocks nationwide, frequently bringing everyday life to a screeching halt (Nueva Mayoría 2009). Nearly one-third of Argentines reported that they had taken part in a protest in 2008, placing Argentina second in the Americas in protest participation behind only Bolivia (LAPOP 2008).

The frequency and intensity of protests alone make Argentina a critical case in the study of protest behavior. One additional feature of Argentine democracy, though, makes it an ideal laboratory for examining the relationship between institutions and protest. Argentina is home to one of Latin America's most (in)famous federal systems, with vast differences in democratic quality found among the country's twenty-three provincial governments and autonomous capital (e.g., Chavez 2004, Spiller and Tommasi 2007, Gibson 2012). Given this variation in provincial-level political regimes and institutions, a subnational analysis of the role provincial political institutions play in shaping participatory repertoires offers a quasi-experimental setting that allows for tremendous analytical leverage in efforts to uncover the institutional determinants of protest—even more so than at the country level.

Bridging Quantitative and Qualitative Approaches

Finally, this book will also meld the rigorous quantitative techniques alluded to above with a crucial qualitative component. Each of these two major methodological approaches offers clear advantages in any effort to draw causal inferences, and used complementarily they provide a more well-rounded treatment of the political phenomena one seeks to explain. The quantitative approach allows for the examination of a larger number of cases and variables, permitting one to increase the amount of variance on the independent and dependent variables and control for alternative explanations (Lijphart 1971, King et al. 1994, Jackman 1985). This ability to systematically assess multiple causes and potential interaction effects—between individual-level engagement and second-level institutional characteristics in the case of this book—is crucial to scientific inference, and only attainable via quantitative analysis (Lieberson 1991). The large-N quantitative approach also offers a more effective means of avoiding selection bias—in this book, every major country in Latin America and the Caribbean minus Cuba will be included in the analysis, as well as every province in Argentina (Geddes 1990). Finally, the quantitative approach provides for probabilistic explanations while also offering quantified estimates of uncertainty via confidence intervals and error terms (Jackman 1985, Lieberson 1991).

The qualitative approach also has its own set of distinct advantages. Through small-N comparisons of units and individual case studies, the qualitative approach can generate valid "mid-level" concepts that are thoroughly crafted but can also "travel" (Almond 1988, Sartori 1970). Through the use of specific qualitative strategies like Mill's methods of difference and agreement (also referred to as the most-similar/different designs by Teune and Przeworski, 1970), qualitative scholars can closely compare two units in an effort to eliminate explanations or necessary and sufficient conditions (Savolainen 1994, Mahoney 2007). Qualitative approaches can also be more adept at avoiding problems regarding the quality of data, as researchers have a closer knowledge of the cases with which they are working and can better evade problems like the whole-nation bias (e.g., Linz and De Miguel 1966).

To better understand the Argentine case, I have carried out interviews with four groups of actors across the country: citizen activists, journalists, local academics, and politicians. These interviews took place in the provinces of Buenos Aires, Mendoza, and San Luis and the national capital, and provide the qualitative data for three in-depth case studies of protest behavior and a more nuanced understanding of the cross-provincial quantitative analyses. Perhaps most importantly, in a case study of Argentina based primarily on how macro-level provincial factors influence aggregate levels of protest participation, these interviews provide a crucial window into the individual-level motivations underpinning citizens' decisions to take to the streets or not, and the strategic choices of political elites.

Distinct institutional environments and wide variations in levels of contentious activity characterize the provinces of Buenos Aires, Mendoza, and San Luis. Mendoza is widely viewed as one of Argentina's most democratic provinces (Chavez 2004, Gervasoni 2010, Wibbels 2005) and is home to a competitive political environment and high-quality representative institutions. Conversely, the neighboring province of San Luis is one of the country's most notoriously authoritarian subnational political systems (Chavez 2004), with one family—the Rodríguez Saá—occupying the governorship since democratization in 1983 and controlling major local media outlets and the public sector (Gervasoni 2010). Buenos Aires, the largest province in the country according to population, lies somewhere in between its two western counterparts, with a relatively open and competitive political environment but low-quality institutions. Recently, it has played host to a number of important uprisings, including the standoff between agriculture and the Kirchner government in 2008 that produced nearly two thousand protests in Buenos Aires province alone (Cotarelo 2009). These provinces thus present an ideal opportunity to employ Mill's classic method of difference (1843), isolating key differences in terms of political institutions while holding constant basic structural, socioeconomic, and cultural characteristics in an effort to parse out the causal mechanisms driving variation in protest activity across subnational political systems.

CONCLUSION

In this chapter I have laid out a novel theoretical approach to understanding contentious political participation across and within Latin American regimes. This theory blends lessons from research on political institutions and behavior in emerging democracies with findings from the extensive study of the determinants of protest participation in the contentious politics literature, spawning a uniquely multifaceted theoretical framework to be tested at the country and subnational levels. This explanation of mounting rates of contentious political participation thus contributes to a growing literature on the institutional determinants of distinct patterns of political behavior, while also adding new wrinkles related to the centrality of citizen engagement as a necessary condition for mobilization, and the ways in which subnational political context can have diverse impacts on distinct protest repertoires.

In the following chapter I begin to test this theoretical framework at the country level in Latin America. The third chapter thus serves to both document the persistence (and potential corrosion) of low-quality political institutions in Latin America and then to provide evidence that political engagement has increased substantially in the region over the last decade. Then, I test the hypothesis that the two variables work in concert to explain the emergence of protest states, utilizing three waves of cross-national survey data and indicators of democratic quality from twenty-four Latin American and Caribbean regimes.

CHAPTER 3

Contentious Engagement

Evidence from Latin American Democracies

Despite widespread speculation that contentious protests would shift from being the norm to becoming the exception with the consolidation of democracy and passage of purportedly demobilizing neoliberal reforms, the past decade is peppered with examples of large-scale protest movements across Latin America, many of which have had important consequences for democratic politics in the region. Indeed, the recent salience of mass protest has been such that it would be understandable if a casual observer of Latin American politics assumed there was a band of disgruntled demonstrators banging pots and pans on every street corner from Mexico City to Rio de Janeiro. Yet for every Latin American country where protest has seemingly crystallized as a key feature of everyday political life, there appears another where contentious tactics are seldom utilized, and citizen participation is primarily channeled through formal political institutions.[1]

These highly disparate trends in protest activity across Latin American countries offer an important opportunity to better understand variation in terms of contentious politics in a region that much of the existing research treats as monolithic in terms of its institutional characteristics, trends in economic development, and protest behaviors. Why has protest participation exploded in certain countries while not in others in recent years? More specifically, how do individual and country-level characteristics interact to explain why some individuals protest, while others do not?

In this chapter, I begin to test my answer to these questions, which relies on the interaction between patterns of citizen engagement in politics and institutional context in Latin American democracies. As outlined in Chapter 2, I argue first that *ceteris paribus*, civically engaged citizens are more likely to protest than those individuals with lower levels of involvement in politics. Thus, one element to understanding protest across Latin America in recent years can be found in the region's socioeconomic and demographic trends that find higher percentages of educated, formally employed, and socially connected individuals than at any time in the region's history. In this chapter, I present compelling evidence that political engagement in the region is on the rise and plays a key role in explaining surging rates of protest in twenty-first-century Latin America.

However, citizen engagement remains only part of the story. For while these individuals will channel their energies through formal modes of political participation in political systems with strong, reasonably well-functioning formal political institutions, the same individuals are more likely to turn to protest when living in countries where political institutions fail to provide effective democratic representation. Here I present evidence to support the notion that Latin America is a region rife with flawed democracies, where high percentages of citizens lack faith in core political institutions and public services. This suboptimal representation via formal institutional vehicles thus constitutes the second of two key requirements underpinning the rise of the Latin American protest state.

In this chapter I test the argument that institutional failings in combination with rising rates of political engagement produce an environment ripe for contentious participation. In evaluating this interaction between institutional context and political engagement, which I argue has produced the protest state, Latin America offers an ideal collection of cases that vary across both of these critical dimensions. The primary contribution of the chapter, then, is to highlight the interaction between institutional context and patterns in citizen engagement with respect to individuals' proclivity to engage in contentious participation, representing a direct test of Hypotheses 1 and 2 enumerated in Chapter 2. In a series of cross-national analyses of survey data, I find that neither individual-level characteristics nor features of one's institutional setting alone fully explain protest behavior. Rather, only when viewed together do we have a more complete picture of why protest seems to have consolidated in certain cases but not in others. I conclude by comparing Argentina, a protest state, with Chile, a regime where protest has not yet consolidated as an everyday form of political participation. Whereas in Argentina, citizen engagement is associated with higher probabilities of partaking in protests, similar community activism in Chile correlates with formal participation but not protest.

From an economic standpoint, the twenty-first century has been good to most Latin American countries. Buoyed by new trade relationships with China and other East Asian countries, Latin America's largely commodity-based economies have grown at unprecedented rates in the new millennium (Mangonnet and Murillo 2016). From 2003 to 2007, Latin American countries experienced an average GDP growth rate of nearly six percent, marking the most successful five-year period of growth in the post-war era (Ocampo 2008; Figure 3.1). In 2010, while the advanced industrialized world was still mired in a severe economic crisis, Latin American economies expanded by about six percent (IMF 2012). More than just growth, Latin America has also made gains in terms of poverty reduction and education. The region's poverty rate dropped from forty-four percent in 2002 to thirty-three percent in 2008 (ECLAC 2013), while the number of Latin Americans with tertiary degrees rose from nine percent in 1990 to fourteen percent in 2009 (World Bank 2013).

Not only did Latin America experience an economic boom in the early 2000s—as Garay (2016) argues, a number of regimes across the region also carried out massive expansions of the welfare state, incorporating millions of former "outsiders" in the political process and offering unprecedented access to education, healthcare, and pensions. Garay convincingly argues that the social policy expansion that occurred in countries like Argentina, Brazil, Chile, and Mexico was the result of increased electoral competition and/or social mobilization from below, and produced a newly renovated commitment to previously ignored sectors of society, albeit through a

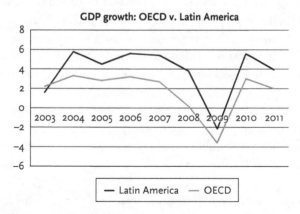

Figure 3.1 Recent Economic Growth in Latin America
The World Bank: http://data.worldbank.org/

diverse set of policies that ranged from restrictive (Chile and Mexico) to more inclusive (Argentina and Brazil). In tandem with the export boom, this newfound emphasis on social policy expansion had two important consequences for citizen engagement. First, it provided increased access to the types of material resources that serve as the foundation for community activism. Indeed, a consistent empirical finding from the literature on civic voluntarism is that activists are often disproportionately educated and enjoy stable economic situations (Verba et al. 1995). When millions of Latin Americans were fighting to make ends meet, they surely lacked the time and resources to devote to less tangible enterprises like attempting to effect political change. However, as the second component of Garay's theory maintains, the extension of the Latin American welfare state also offered a strong signal that policymakers could be influenced by mass behaviors, whether it be through the ballot box or in the streets. Governments' responses to citizen activism created a virtuous cycle, wherein activists observed the fruits of their labors and thus felt more efficacious participating in political life.

Indeed, in conjunction with these advances in terms of socioeconomic development, electoral democracy has finally consolidated as the only legitimate regime type in the region. Despite democratic "backslides" in countries like Bolivia, Ecuador, and Nicaragua (Weyland 2013), no country in Latin America has undergone a full-scale reverse transition to authoritarianism, with the possible exception of Venezuela. Within this context, there is evidence that Latin Americans have become more active democrats in recent years. According to cross-national surveys, Latin Americans overwhelmingly support democracy as the best form of government, and since 2004 have become increasingly interested in politics, active in elections, and participatory in their communities (LAPOP 2004–2012). The expansion of access to the Internet and social media has also had important consequences for politics in the region, with five Latin American countries ranking in the top ten in the world in terms of social network "engagement" (hours spent per month), and social media has increasingly been utilized for political purposes (*The Economist* 2013, Valenzuela et al. 2012). The end result of all of these trends is that Latin America has become a region where many (but not all) citizens are highly engaged in democratic politics and their communities via interpersonal and virtual activities, perhaps more than at any time in the region's history.

How might recent trends in economic development and increases in citizen engagement relate to protest? Beginning in the 1970s, scholars shifted their attention from grievance-based explanations of protest (e.g.,

Gusfield 1968, Gurr 1970) to the causal mechanisms that might explain why grievances translate into collective action in certain cases but not others.[2] As explained in Chapter 2, the "resource mobilization" approach offers an explanation based not on relative deprivation, but on the socio-economic factors that underpin the formation and sustainability of social movements. For scholars adhering to this particular theoretical construct, the primary determinants of whether or not social movements emerge and succeed lie in a particular movement's access to the organizational resources necessary for mobilization (McCarthy and Zald 1973, 1977).[3] Following from this line of thinking, prospective collective actors might actually find that their opportunities to organize expand as economic conditions *improve*, rather than resulting from periods of intense economic struggle. Recent empirical work from Latin America has corroborated this notion, as Mangonnet and Murillo (2016) find that the commodities boom actually provided incentives for rural labor associations to organize protests in Argentina, resulting in thousands of road blockades across the country during times of plenty. Likewise, Boulding (2014) and Cornell and Grimes (2015) find compelling evidence that civil society organizations play a critical intervening role in translating grievances directed at political institutions into protests.

In Latin America, studies have found that citizens who are more highly educated, interested and active in politics, and connected to civil society organizations are the most likely to engage in protest (e.g., Booth and Seligson 2009, Moreno and Moseley 2011, Figure 3.2). Thus, it would seem that at the individual level, the resource mobilization approach begins to explain why certain individuals are more likely to protest in Latin America than others, especially in an era when more citizens have access to organizational tools than ever before. Yet at the aggregate level, the resource mobilization approach predicts (and has found, in the case of Dalton et al. 2009) that rates of protest participation are highest in the most economically developed contexts, where more citizens possess the organizational resources to build movements and articulate their interests. This perspective is at odds with a case like Bolivia, for example, which ranks as Latin America's most contentious country while also being one of the region's most underdeveloped (LAPOP). Moreover, while countries like Peru, Argentina, and Ecuador grew rapidly in the early 2000s and played host to numerous mass demonstrations, other countries like Uruguay and Costa Rica also grew at impressive rates and failed to register high protest numbers. Thus, while resource mobilization and the expansion of political engagement clearly helps explain current trends in protest activity across Latin America at the individual level, on its own this perspective falls short

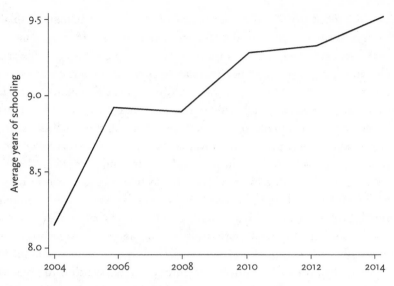

Figure 3.2 Increases in Educational Attainment in Latin America, 2004–2014
© AmericasBarometer by LAPOP

of a complete explanation of why individuals in certain countries in the region are so much more contentious than in others.

THE PERSISTENCE OF FLAWED INSTITUTIONS IN LATIN AMERICA

Latin America is a region populated by regimes of varying democratic quality (e.g., O'Donnell 1993, Diamond 2002, Levitsky and Way 2002, Gibson 2005, Spiller and Tommasi 2007, Levitsky and Murillo 2009, Levine and Molina 2011, Scartascini and Tommasi 2012).[4] While every country in the region aside from Cuba is widely characterized as a formal, electoral democracy (though some regimes, like Venezuela, probably require additional "adjectives" [Collier and Levitsky 1997]), Latin American regimes differ substantially in how effectively their formal political institutions channel participation and implement public policy. In this section I provide evidence for this assertion and explore the potential consequences of this variation in institutional quality for protest participation in the region.

Much of the recent literature on Latin American democratic political institutions has focused on institutional weakness in countries across the region, and how it might contribute to substandard representation and public policy outcomes. Two dimensions define institutional weakness, according to Levitsky and Murillo (2009): enforcement and stability. In many Latin American countries, the formal "rules of the game" (North 1990) often change rapidly or are not enforced. For example, presidents in countries like Argentina, Ecuador, and Venezuela (among others) have sought to change reelection laws so that they can remain in power, and despite explicit legal prohibitions against doing so, many presidents in the region have pursued "court-packing" strategies to attempt to establish political control over the judicial branch or have eliminated central bank autonomy (e.g., Helmke 2002, Boylan 2002). This degree of institutional uncertainty often has dire consequences for the quality of public policy, as it encourages shortsightedness among government officials, who in many cases are underqualified for the positions they hold (Spiller and Tommasi 2007). In addition, there is now evidence that the quality of Latin American political institutions is actually on the decline in many of the region's democracies, spurred by democratic "backslides" in countries like Bolivia, Nicaragua, and Venezuela, mirroring global trends in terms of political freedom (Puddington 2012, Weyland 2013, Freedom House 2015).

Shortcomings related to institutional weakness and poor governance are reflected in Latin Americans' attitudes. Despite widespread support for democracy as a system of government across the region, confidence in key regime institutions like political parties, legislatures, and law enforcement remains low in many Latin American countries—in other words, regimes suffer from low levels of legitimacy. In their 2009 book on the "legitimacy puzzle," Booth and Seligson argue that democracy has survived in Latin America in spite of low levels of faith in key regime institutions, in large part because the most dissatisfied citizens are able to voice their dissatisfaction through social protest. However, in cases like Honduras and perhaps now Brazil, these low levels of legitimacy have set the stage for government change through constitutionally questionable action on the part of local opposition movements. While disgruntled opposition leaders certainly protagonized these episodes of instability, as they sought power in the short term at the expense of long-standing democratic norms, public opinion undoubtedly provides a zone of acceptability (Stimson 1999) for political elites, and waning levels of support for the political system have spelled trouble for democratic regimes across the region.

In addition to low levels of legitimacy, even as Latin America has experienced unprecedented economic growth and reductions in poverty amid an export boom and widespread expansion of the welfare state, satisfaction with public services like education, healthcare, and transportation continues to be comparatively low (LAPOP 2012). High crime rates plague many countries in the region, and have increased exponentially in recent years across countries like Mexico, Venezuela, and much of Central America (Ceobanu et al. 2010, Bateson 2012). Thus, it would appear that a gap has emerged between Latin Americans' demand for democracy and its supply (Bratton, Mattes, and Gyimah-Boadi 2005), as diffuse support for democracy has consolidated while criticism of specific regime actors and dissatisfaction with government performance has persisted and in some cases increased (Booth and Seligson 2009, Mainwaring and Scully 2010).

Within the protest literature, numerous studies have discussed and in some cases tested the potential relationship between institutional quality and protest. Specifically, scholars utilizing the "political opportunities" approach have sought to expose the political mechanisms that allow previously unexpressed grievances to materialize as social movements and protests. This research has entailed a focus on processes of democratization and political liberalization, or, within existing democracies, on the role of political parties, labor unions, or important legal decisions in structuring potential protest activity (Huntington 1968, Tilly 1978, McAdam 1982, Kitschelt 1986, Brockett 1991). Others have compared rates of protest in contexts characterized by different levels of democratic "openness," as several scholars have posited and provided evidence for a curvilinear relationship between political openness and protest (e.g., Eisinger 1973, Tilly 1978, 2006, Muller and Seligson 1987). According to this logic, protest movements arise and flourish more frequently in moderately open regimes where public opposition is tolerated and widespread, but representative institutions are not fully facilitative of effective participation, than in regimes at either end of the openness spectrum (Eisinger 1973, Tilly 1978).

Empirical work on the impact of institutional quality on protest participation has produced mixed results. In their cross-national study utilizing data from the World Values Survey, Dalton et al. (2009) find that more democratic, high-functioning (i.e., "open") institutional contexts produce higher rates of protest participation than authoritarian regimes or weakly institutionalized democracies (see also Norris 2002).[5] However, in recent studies of Latin America, scholars have shifted toward examining how weak political institutions in democracies can push citizens toward adopting contentious tactics (e.g., Boulding 2010, 2014, Machado et al. 2011). A focus on more specific features of national-level political institutions by Machado et al. (2011) in their study of Latin American democracies reveals that institutional weakness actually increases the prevalence of protest participation within that regime. Boulding's research examines diversity in participation tactics utilized by non-governmental organizations (NGOs), finding that NGOs are more likely to encourage protest participation in weakly institutionalized contexts where voting and other types of formal partici- pation are viewed as less effective. Scholars have also found that electoral losses tend to foment more "protest potential" in new democracies than in established ones (Anderson and Mendes 2006), and that neoliberal reforms can spark contentious participation under democracy in Latin America (Silva 2009, Bellinger and Arce 2011). Finally, Cornell and Grimes (2015) find that more politicized bureaucracies provide incentives for disruptive protests, as political opponents seek to influence the political institutions that have frozen them out.

Despite the considerable contributions of these recent studies, a single-minded emphasis on institutional characteristics as the decisive determinant of contentious participation seems to ignore the critical role that swelling rates of citizen engagement have played in producing pro- test across Latin America in recent years. The list of national cases where institutions are low quality but protest movements fail to gain traction is long—in Latin America and the Caribbean, El Salvador, Guatemala, and Jamaica, to name a few—and includes virtually any authoritarian re- gime where representative institutions are non-existent or ineffective, but grassroots engagement is limited. Moreover, protests often materialize in countries with "good" institutions, as was the case recently in Chile in 2011 and in the United States during the Occupy Wall Street movement, due in part to the dense organizational networks that also exist in such democracies. For this reason, I argue that any cross-level explanation of protest must factor in individual-level political engagement, as these critical organizational linkages serve as a necessary condition for any po- tential institutional effect on contentious politics. Boulding (2014) and Cornell and Grimes (2015) begin to recognize the importance of this in- teraction between institutional characteristics and civil society, but stop short of fully elaborating how a wide range of organizational linkages and institutional features interact to make protest a "normal" strategy for active citizens of diverse backgrounds. This chapter seeks to advance that conversation.

In sum, this chapter presents strong evidence that in Latin America, re- cent economic progress has fueled swelling rates of political engagement, which has in turn produced a larger body of citizens who are in a position to partake of contentious politics if they so desire. Moreover, a wealth of evidence suggests that many Latin American democratic regimes remain deeply flawed—a reality that a growing percentage of Latin American citi- zens seems to understand. In the following section I put forth a strategy for measuring these two phenomena and for testing my argument regarding the rise of the protest state across Latin American countries.

DATA AND MEASUREMENT

The cross-national variation we observe in protest participation across countries calls for a focus on how political context interacts with mass-level dynamics to influence the rise of contentious political participation. In the face of trends related to citizen engagement and institutional quality in contemporary Latin America, I argue that a combination of high levels of political engagement among citizens and ineffective political institutions precipitates more radical modes of political participation, as regimes' ability to deliver on citizens' expectations fails to match the mobilization capacity of the citizenry. Thus, where individuals are engaged in civic life and interested in politics, but institutional quality is low—for example, characterized by unresponsive or inconsistent representational vehicles, fickle systems of checks and balances, and weak rule of law—protest emerges due to the inability of formal political institutions to adequately channel and respond to the voices of active democratic citizens.

To test the theoretical framework proposed above, I utilize data from the Latin American Public Opinion Project's (LAPOP) AmericasBarometer surveys from 2008, 2010, and 2012, which consist of representative national surveys of individuals from twenty-four countries in Latin America and the Caribbean. The key dependent variable comes from a question that asks respondents if they have participated in a street march or public demonstration during the previous twelve months.[6,7]

Figure 1.2 displays the percentage of respondents who participated in a protest from 2008–2012 in each Latin American country included in the AmericasBarometer biennial surveys. Clearly, significant variation exists in the region in terms of the extent to which protest has been adopted as a form of political participation. Bolivia had the highest rate of protest participation in Latin America at nineteen percent, followed closely by Argentina, Haiti, and Peru. Bolivia also experienced the most contentious single year rate of protest participation recorded by the AmericasBarometer surveys, at nearly thirty percent in 2008. These results immediately cast doubt on the notion that high levels of development produce high levels of protest (see Dalton et al. 2009), as Haiti and Bolivia are among the poorest nations in the Americas, while in such economically diverse countries as Jamaica, Panama, and El Salvador, protest appears to be extremely uncommon, with barely five percent of citizens registering participation.

The AmericasBarometer survey instrument offers an improvement on previous cross-national data on protest participation utilized in other studies for two primary reasons. First, the AmericasBarometer surveys from 2008–2012 always specify a time frame of the past twelve months when inquiring about protest participation—something that other cross-national projects like the World Values Surveys have not done. In all likelihood, questions that fail to establish a time frame for respondents are not measuring current levels of protest participation but are instead capturing an individual's lifetime account of protest activity. This would seem to favor higher rates of protest participation for older democracies where protesting has been permitted for many years, even if current levels are not particularly high. Further, while these data do not speak to present levels of protest, the predictors of protest—such as community activity, wealth, and even levels of education—do reflect current conditions. This temporal disconnect between the independent and dependent variables then casts doubt on the meaning of findings utilizing this measure of protest activity, such as those relying on World Values Survey data before 2005.[8]

Second, the AmericasBarometer survey offers multiple time points at which we can evaluate the determinants of protest participation for each country, which helps remedy any potential bias related to an outlier year for a particular country and increases the number of observations for second-level variables. For example, in the case of Chile, protest participation was relatively low in 2010 (and seemingly before, though we lack AmericasBarometer data to confirm) but skyrocketed to eleven percent in 2012, placing it in the top five in the region. A snapshot view using one round of surveys can thus capture an anomalous moment in a country's history, given the oftentimes sporadic nature of large-scale protest events. By taking into account results from three separate surveys, this study provides a more balanced view of a country's proclivity for protesting over time, less subject to exceptional years and episodes of mass contention.

At the individual level, the key independent variable for capturing community engagement is an index that gauges the frequency with which citizens participate in local civic organizations. Respondents were asked how often they attended meetings for a variety of different types of community organizations during the previous year, including community improvement associations, parent organizations, professional associations, religious groups, and political parties. The response options provided were "Never," "Once or Twice a Year," "Once or Twice a Month," and "Once a Week." The response levels were then coded from 0 ("Never") to 3 ("Once a Week"), and the five variables combined to form a single *Community Engagement Index*, which was then rescaled to 0–100. I argue that this index effectively measures the extent to which individuals are engaged in community activities and have access to the organizational structures that can serve to facilitate collective action.

At the individual level, I also include variables for interest in politics, years of education, and use of social media to share or receive political information—all of which approximate the resource mobilization approach to explaining protest participation by individuals. In addition, I draw from questions on support for key political institutions, satisfaction with public services, and external efficacy (the extent to which individuals feel politicians are responsive to them [Niemi et al. 1991]) to shed light on how perceptions of political institutions influence individuals' proclivity to protest. To test competing theories regarding the influence of specific grievances on protest participation, I utilize individual-level variables for presidential approval, evaluations of one's personal economic situation, evaluations of the national economic situation, and socioeconomic status. Interpersonal trust is also included, as many have argued in the past that trust in one's fellow citizens increases the probability of protesting (e.g., Inglehart 1990, Dalton et al. 2009).

For the second-level (i.e., country) variables gauging institutional quality, I turn to the World Bank's Worldwide Governance Indicators (WGI). The WGI offers measures on six dimensions of governance, three of which are relevant to this study: *Voice and Accountability*, *Government Effectiveness*, and *Rule of Law*. These measures represent the views of business, citizen, and elite survey respondents, and are based on "30 individual data sources produced by a variety of survey institutes, think tanks, non-governmental organizations, international organizations, and private sector firms" (WGI website). These indicators offer the best combination of coverage across countries and time, and are the product of rigorous measurement techniques for the countries included in the AmericasBarometer survey, though the indicators are certainly not without drawbacks (see Kaufmann et al. 2007). Descriptions of each dimension from the creators of the indicators can be found in the Appendix.

Each of these three dimensions captures an important component of institutional quality, and will be tested individually as a second-level predictor of protest participation.[9] The *Voice and Accountability* measure helps gauge the extent to which individuals can effectively participate in politics and obtain representation in government, while *Government Effectiveness* serves as a measure of regime transparency and capacity in the making and implementation of public policy. *Rule of Law* offers an indicator for how well regimes offer citizens equal protection under the law, a crucial characteristic of effective democratic governance. I combine the three variables in an index I call the *Institutional Quality Index*, which I use in the analyses below as an indicator of the institutional environment in which individual citizens operate.

In Figure 3.3, countries are listed in terms of average *Institutional Quality Index* score for the period 2008–2012. Chile leads the region in terms of institutional quality with a score of 1.2.[10] Venezuela and Haiti score lowest, unsurprisingly, while a large group of Latin American regimes hover around zero. These scores indicate that while democracy predominates in the region, the quality of political institutions and governance varies greatly, with the majority of regimes falling short of living up to modern standards of liberal democracy.

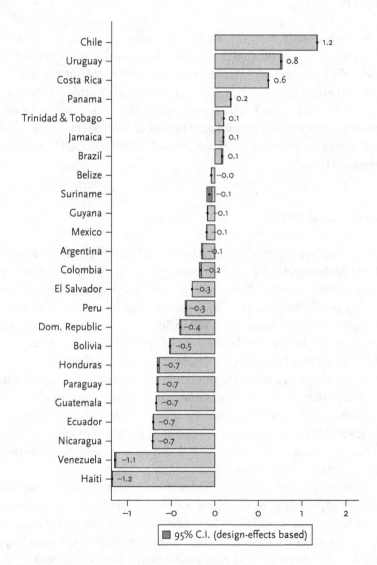

Figure 3.3 Mean Institutional Quality Scores, 2008–2012
© AmericasBarometer by LAPOP

As controls, I also include second-level measures of human development, inequality, and economic growth during the year of the survey. These variables will serve to test grievance-based explanations of contentious politics, in addition to providing assurance that the causal effects of variation in institutional quality on protest participation are not a function of an omitted variable linked to both institutional quality and protest levels.

ANALYSIS

The dependent variable in this analysis is protest participation, measured at the level of the individual. I therefore begin with two individual-level models of protest across Latin America that will highlight the socioeconomic and attitudinal characteristics associated with protest behavior. In the second set of models, I then incorporate the national-level variables discussed above in order to assess the impact of these second-level institutional factors on individual-level protest participation, in addition to cross-level interactions.

Individual-Level Models

Table 3.1 displays the results from the first set of individual-level models, each of which employs logistic regression given the dichotomous nature of the dependent variable.[11] In Model 1, we see that several variables emerge as strong predictors of protest participation, none more so than community engagement. An increase from 0 to 50 on the *Community Engagement Index* nearly triples one's probability of protesting, holding other covariates at their means (see Figure 3.4).[12] Moreover, a person at the highest value in terms of community activism is more than four times likelier to participate in a protest than someone who has no connection to any local organization, holding other variables constant at their means. In keeping with the resource mobilization approach to explaining protest participation, education and interest in politics also have strong positive effects on the probability of participating in a protest.

On the other hand, several variables seem to decrease Latin Americans' likelihood of participating in a street march or demonstration. Net of other factors, women are less likely to have participated in a protest, and age has a significant negative impact on protesting as well. Perhaps most importantly for the purposes of the argument presented in this book, system support has a significant negative effect on the probability of taking part in

Table 3.1 INDIVIDUAL-LEVEL MODELS OF PROTEST PARTICIPATION
IN LATIN AMERICA AND THE CARIBBEAN

VARIABLES	Protest Participation (1 = Protested) Model 1 Coeff. (s.e.)	Protest Participation (1 = Protested) Model 2 Coeff. (s.e.)
Female	−0.278***	−0.292***
	(0.025)	(0.049)
Age	−0.008***	−0.005***
	(0.0009)	(0.002)
Wealth (quintile)	−0.011	−0.078***
	(0.010)	(0.019)
Interest in Politics	0.011***	0.009***
	(0.0004)	(0.0008)
Education	0.325***	0.309***
	(0.021)	(0.039)
Community Participation	0.026***	0.0273***
	(0.0008)	(0.001)
Presidential Approval	−0.003***	−0.003**
	(0.0006)	(0.001)
Interpersonal Trust	−0.002***	−0.001
	(0.0004)	(0.0008)
Personal Economic Situation	−0.002***	−0.002*
	(0.0007)	(0.001)
National Economic Situation	0.0005	0.0007
	(0.0006)	(0.001)
Perception of Corruption	−1.89e−05	−0.002*
	(0.0005)	(0.0009)
System Support	−0.006***	−0.007***
	(0.0007)	(0.001)
Efficacy	0.0007	0.0005
	(0.0005)	(0.0008)
Satisfaction with Public Services	—	−0.006***
		(0.001)
Shared Political Information via Social Network	—	0.009***
		(0.0007)
Constant	−2.784***	−2.569***
	(0.090)	(0.168)
Observations	88,750	29,248

Standard errors in parentheses; *** p<0.01, ** p<0.05, * p<0.1; two-tailed tests

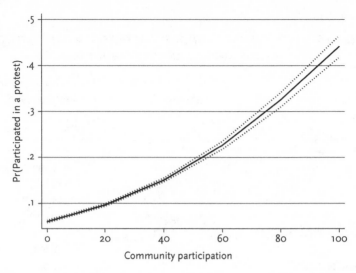

Figure 3.4 Predicted Probabilities Based on Changes in Levels of Community Engagement (90% Cis)

a protest march or demonstration, meaning that individuals who view key regime institutions more positively are less likely to protest, while those with more negative evaluations are more likely protestors. While this effect falls far short of the magnitude of the effect for community engagement, moving from the lowest quintile in terms of system support to the highest results in a twenty-five percent decrease in the probability of participating in a protest (from .12 to .09). In Model 2, we also observe a similar significant negative effect for public service evaluations—another key measure of individuals' perceptions of institutional performance.

In sum, based on these predictive models of protest participation in Latin America from 2008–2012, it appears that citizens who are actively engaged in their communities—they are interested in politics, participate in community organizations, and share political information via the Internet—and citizens who have negative views of key regime institutions and public services are the most likely protestors.[13] While these initial findings comport with the theoretical approach outlined above, the more important test of how institutional environment shapes participatory repertoires requires a multilevel approach, which follows in the next section.

Multilevel Models

In the second set of models, country-level variables were added to each model, and multilevel mixed effects logistic regression models were estimated to account for variation between countries during the three survey years under consideration. In other words, the second-level variables listed in each model describe "country years"—the national context in which individuals from each round of the AmericasBarometer responded to the survey questions. The results for eight models of protest participation are presented in Tables 3.2 and 3.3. In each model, second-level economic variables serve as controls, in addition to the individual-level variables that proved consequential in the regional analyses presented above. Variables for the WGI indicators of institutional quality were added one at a time in the four models in Table 3.2, and then interaction terms were inserted in the four models in Table 3.3.

First, it should be mentioned that second-level economic variables seem to play a minor role in explaining individual-level protest dynamics in Latin America during the time period under consideration. Neither inequality, human development, nor GDP growth during the year of the survey serve as significant predictors of protest participation, raising questions about the idea that macroeconomic forces are what drive cycles of protest. Although individuals' perceptions of their personal economic situation do continue to carry some weight, as do negative performance evaluations of the current president, wealth is not a strong predictor of participation. It thus appears that we can eliminate economic factors as the primary determinants of mass mobilization in Latin America with some degree of certainty. This does not mean that economic grievances fail to play any role in motivating instances of contentious behavior—rather, it indicates that many citizens experiencing economic hardship decide not to protest, while others in comfortable economic situations do choose to participate. At the same time, these results fail to reveal any positive relationship between economic development and protest participation, contrary to findings from accounts grounded in analyses of developed democracies.

The relationship between institutional context and protest participation is a thornier one to interpret. In each of the first four models, it appears that the institutional variables—while having the predicted negative sign—fail to attain statistical significance as predictors of protest involvement. This would seem to indicate that institutional environment itself does not have a significant impact on the probability that individuals within that context will protest, controlling for other individual and aggregate-level factors, which contradicts the findings of Machado et al. (2011).

However, the theory I put forth in this chapter is an interactive one, in which institutions interact with community engagement to affect individuals' likelihood of adopting contentious political behaviors. Model 7 in Table 3.3 includes an interaction between the *Institutional Quality Index*,

Table 3.2 MULTILEVEL MODELS OF PROTEST PARTICIPATION IN LATIN AMERICA AND THE CARIBBEAN

VARIABLES	Protest Participation (1 = Protested) Model 3 Coeff. (s.e.)	Protest Participation (1 = Protested) Model 4 Coeff. (s.e.)	Protest Participation (1 = Protested) Model 5 Coeff. (s.e.)	Protest Participation (1 = Protested) Model 6 Coeff. (s.e.)
	Individual-Level Variables			
Female	-0.272***	-0.272***	-0.272***	-0.272***
	(0.023)	(0.023)	(0.023)	(0.023)
Age	-0.008***	-0.008***	-0.008***	-0.008***
	(0.0008)	(0.0008)	(0.0008)	(0.0008)
Wealth (quintile)	0.005	0.005	0.005	0.005
	(0.009)	(0.009)	(0.009)	(0.009)
Interest in Politics	0.012***	0.012***	0.012***	0.012***
	(0.0004)	(0.0004)	(0.0004)	(0.0004)
Education	0.261***	0.261***	0.261***	0.261***
	(0.018)	(0.018)	(0.018)	(0.018)
Community Participation	0.026***	0.026***	0.026***	0.026***
	(0.0007)	(0.0007)	(0.0007)	(0.0007)
Presidential Approval	-0.003***	-0.003***	-0.003***	-0.003***
	(0.0005)	(0.0005)	(0.0005)	(0.0005)
Interpersonal Trust	-0.001***	-0.001***	-0.001***	-0.001***
	(0.0004)	(0.0004)	(0.0004)	(0.0004)
Personal Economic Situation	-0.002***	-0.002***	-0.002***	-0.002***
	(0.0006)	(0.0006)	(0.0006)	(0.0006)
System Support	-0.004***	-0.004***	-0.004***	-0.004***
	(0.0006)	(0.0006)	(0.0006)	(0.0006)

Second-Level Variables

	(1)	(2)	(3)	(4)
Gini Index (2009)	3.899	3.988	4.017	3.937
	(2.637)	(2.685)	(2.666)	(2.665)
HDI (2007)	2.909	1.106	1.386	1.731
	(2.365)	(2.111)	(2.090)	(2.206)
GDP Growth (annual)	0.005	0.010	0.011	0.011
	(0.039)	(0.040)	(0.040)	(0.039)
Government Effectiveness	-0.364			
	(0.268)			
Voice and Accountability		-0.032		
		(0.267)		
Rule of Law			-0.099	
			(0.211)	
Institutions Index				-0.177
				(0.263)
Constant	-7.255***	-5.804**	-6.100**	-6.313**
	(2.668)	(2.509)	(2.568)	(2.592)
Observations	92,567	92,567	92,567	92,567
Number of Country Years	67	67	67	67

Standard errors in parentheses; *** p<0.01, ** p<0.05, * p<0.1; two-tailed tests

Table 3.3 MULTILEVEL MODELS OF PROTEST PARTICIPATION IN LATIN AMERICA AND THE CARIBBEAN (WITH INTERACTIONS)

VARIABLES	Protest Participation (1 = Protested) Model 7 Coeff. (s.e.)	Protest Participation (1 = Protested) Model 8 Coeff. (s.e.)	Protest Participation (1 = Protested) Model 9 Coeff. (s.e.)	Protest Participation (1 = Protested) Model 10 Coeff. (s.e.)
Individual-Level Variables				
Female	-0.270***	-0.255***	-0.275***	-0.277***
	(0.023)	(0.023)	(0.023)	(-0.007)
Age	-0.008***	-0.006***	-0.007***	-0.007***
	(0.0008)	(0.0008)	(0.0008)	(0.0008)
Wealth (quintile)	0.005	0.003	0.006	0.005
	(0.009)	(0.009)	(0.009)	(0.009)
Interest in Politics	0.012***	0.013***	0.013***	0.012***
	(0.0004)	(0.0004)	(0.0004)	(0.0004)
Education	0.262***	0.265***	0.260***	0.331***
	(0.018)	(0.018)	(0.018)	(0.022)
Community Participation	0.025***	—	0.026***	0.026***
	(0.0008)		(0.0007)	(0.0007)
Presidential Approval	-0.003***	-0.003***	-0.003***	-.003***
	(0.0005)	(0.0005)	(0.0005)	(0.0005)
Interpersonal Trust	-0.001***	-0.0006	-0.001**	-0.001***
	(0.0004)	(0.0004)	(0.0004)	(0.0004)
Personal Economic Situation	-0.002***	-0.002***	-0.002***	-0.001***
	(0.0006)	(0.0006)	(0.0006)	(0.0006)

	(1)	(2)	(3)	(4)
System Support	-0.004***	-0.003***	-0.004***	-0.004***
	(0.0006)	(0.0006)	(0.0006)	(0.0006)
Community Dummy	—	0.737***	—	—
		(0.037)		
Second-Level Variables				
Gini Index (2009)	3.905	4.021	3.299	3.174
	(2.663)	(2.690)	(2.576)	(2.580)
HDI (2007)	1.822	1.079	2.000	2.063
	(2.204)	(2.227)	(2.128)	(2.132)
GDP growth (annual)	0.010	0.011	0.027	0.028
	(0.039)	(0.040)	(0.038)	(0.038)
Institutions Index	-0.107	0.020	-.484*	-0.822***
	(0.264)	(0.270)	(0.274)	(0.282)
Institutions Index * Community Participation	**-0.003***	—	—	—
	(0.001)			
Institutions Index * Community Dummy	—	**-0.313***	—	—
		(0.062)		
Institutions Index* Interest in Politics	—	—	**0.002**	—
			(0.0007)	
Institutions Index * Education	—	—	—	**0.194***
				(0.033)
Constant	-6.343**	-6.125**	-6.348***	-6.457***
	(2.590)	(2.617)	(2.453)	(2.457)
Observations	92,567	92,567	92,567	92,567
Number of Country Years	67	67	67	67

Standard errors in parentheses; *** p<0.01, ** p<0.05, * p<0.1; two-tailed tests

a country-level variable, and *Community Engagement*, an individual-level variable. The coefficient is negative, and obtains statistical significance at the p<.01 level. The fact that the effect for institutional quality is insignificant in this model indicates that it is not an important predictor of protest where community engagement equals zero. However, the significance of the interaction's coefficient reveals that this changes as the two interacted variables' values change (Kam and Franzese 2006).

Figure 3.5 displays predicted probabilities of participating in a protest depending on variation in institutional context and community engagement. By graphing changes in the predicted probabilities, we can clearly observe that the causal impact of institutional context changes drastically depending on levels of community engagement, and vice versa. Where community engagement equals zero—namely, citizens who have no ties to any of the five types of civic organizations referred to in the questions that make up the index—institutional quality has no effect on the probability of protesting. However, as engagement increases, the causal importance of institutional context begins to emerge. Where *Community Engagement* equals fifty, it seems that citizens in low-quality institutional settings become substantially more likely to protest, holding other individual and second-level variables at their means and modes. Where community involvement is high, the differences in probabilities are even starker—indeed, while a maximally engaged individual in a low-quality institutional

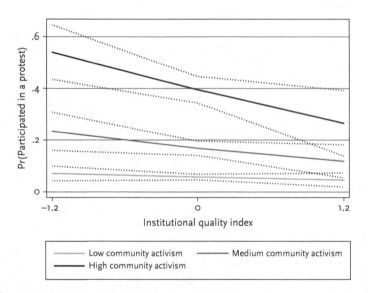

Figure 3.5 Predicted Probabilities: Interaction between Institutional Context and Community Engagement

environment (*Institutional Quality Index* = -1) possesses a .48 probability of participating in a protest, that same individual possesses only a .26 probability of participating in a high-quality institutional environment. Thus, active citizens are nearly twice as likely to have protested in low-quality institutional contexts compared to high-quality institutional contexts.

As a robustness check, Model 8 offers a similar interaction term with an alternative coding of the community engagement variable. In this case I coded *Community Engagement Dummy* = 1 for individuals who were at least minimally active in one community organization, and *Community Engagement Dummy* = 0 for those who possess no ties to local community groups.[14] Throughout Latin America, roughly twenty-two percent of respondents fall in the category of completely unengaged in their communities, while seventy-eight percent were coded as *Community Engagement Dummy* = 1.

Predicted probabilities for this interaction are presented in Figure 3.6. Again, it appears that the causal import of community engagement and institutional quality are highly dependent on one another. Engaged citizens in low-quality institutional environments are almost twice as likely to participate in a protest as their counterparts in high-quality institutional settings. Moreover, while engaged citizens are more than twice as likely as unengaged people to protest where institutions are poor, that difference is not nearly as glaring in strong institutional settings. Unengaged citizens are equally likely to participate in protests regardless of institutional context. Put simply, it appears that poor political institutions push the politically engaged toward adopting protest participation while having very little effect on the contentious behaviors of unengaged citizens.

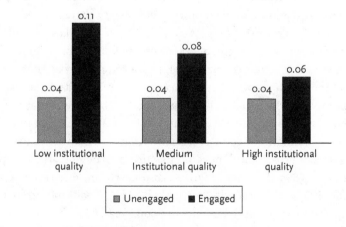

Figure 3.6 Predicted Probabilities: Unengaged vs. Engaged Citizens

Models 9 and 10 include interaction terms with institutional quality on one hand, and education (Figure A1) and interest (Figure A2) in politics, respectively, on the other. In each of these models the coefficient term for the interaction is significant. Both of these variables interact similarly with institutional quality, in that each becomes a stronger predictor of protest participation in weak institutional contexts, particularly in the case of interest in politics. For entirely uninterested citizens or uneducated citizens, institutions fail to exert much influence on the probability that individuals protest—however, as interest in politics and education increase, the causal importance of institutional quality begins to take off. The significant effects for interactions between institutions and civic engagement, education, and interest in politics corroborate Boulding's findings (2010, 2014) with regard to NGOs, but also indicate that NGO activity might simply serve as another example of a larger universe of organizational connections fueling protest participation in distinct political environments. In other words, it might not necessarily be the nature of NGOs specifically that motivates protest, but rather access to organizational resources more generally that produces protest participation in weak democracies.

COMPARING ARGENTINA AND CHILE

To further contextualize how political institutions and citizen engagement interact to produce the Latin American protest state, this section provides a more detailed account of two specific cases: Argentina and Chile. Argentina is a famously contentious country, which is the result of its unique combination of weak political institutions (Scartascini and Tommasi 2012) and a highly mobilized civil society characterized by dense organizational networks (e.g., Auyero 2007) and relatively advanced levels of development. As corroborated by the Institutional Quality Index presented above, Chile is known for possessing some of the strongest political institutions in Latin America, in contrast to its Southern Cone neighbor (Machado et al. 2011, Przeworski 2010). While student protests grabbed headlines in Chile throughout 2011 and 2012, it is not known as a particularly contentious country by Latin American standards, despite the importance of urban social movements during its democratization period in the late 1980s (Hipsher 1996). According to the AmericasBarometer data for 2010–2012, roughly six percent of Chileans reported having participated in a protest during the previous year, whereas Argentina registered nearly twice as many protestors (LAPOP 2008–2012).

In breaking down demographic trends in terms of protest participation in Argentina and Chile, several clear patterns emerge. In Chile, rates of protest participation are much higher among young people, the educated, and middle-class citizens, with the poorest quintile of Chileans registering the lowest rates of participation (Figure 3.7). Moreover, men appear significantly more likely than women to have participated in a protest during the previous year. On the other hand, in Argentina these differences become subtler, with few significant disparities in rates of participation across socioeconomic class, level of education, and gender. While young Argentines appear to be the most likely protestors, middle-aged citizens seem to utilize contentious tactics with much more frequency in Argentina than their counterparts in Chile (Figures 3.7 and 3.8). Thus, even at moments of heightened contentious activity, protest seems to be utilized by a narrower group of individuals in Chile than in Argentina, where it constitutes an important component of the participatory repertoire spanning a number of demographic groups.

As a point of illustration, I compare the effects of citizen engagement on protest participation and voting—the most common form of "conventional" participation in any democracy—in the two countries. Figure 3.9 shows the difference between Argentina and Chile in terms of the extent

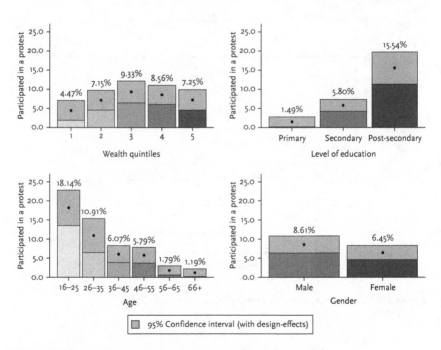

Figure 3.7 Protest Participation across Demographic Groups in Chile
© AmericasBarometer, LAPOP, 2008–2012

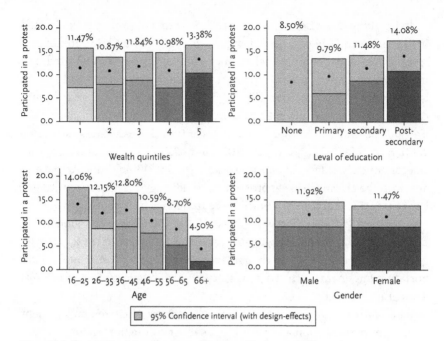

Figure 3.8 Protest Participation across Demographic Groups in Argentina
© AmericasBarometer, LAPOP, 2008–2012

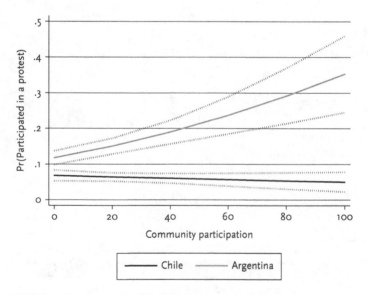

Figure 3.9 Citizen Engagement and Protest: Argentina vs. Chile

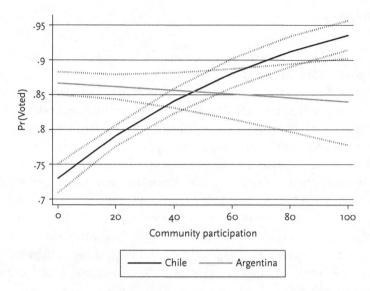

Figure 3.10 Citizen Engagement and Voting: Argentina vs. Chile

to which community engagement predicts protest participation. Holding other variables at their means in the base individual-level model presented earlier in this chapter, civic activity exerts a powerful positive effect on one's probability of protesting in Argentina, but not in Chile. Conversely, whereas higher levels of community engagement increase one's probability of voting in Chile, civic involvement actually has a slightly *negative* effect on voter turnout in Argentina (Figure 3.10). Thus, it appears that in a weak institutional context like Argentina, political engagement triggers contentious participation, whereas it motivates formal participation in the more high-quality democratic context of Chile. However, when individuals are not tied into these organizations or routinely exposed to the failings of the democratic system (*Community Engagement* = 0), institutions fail to exert much influence on contentious behaviors.[15]

Taken together, this evidence seems to indicate that (1) protest is utilized by a broader group of citizens in Argentina, of different ages, classes, and education levels, and (2) community involvement seems to have a much stronger impact on protest participation in Argentina than in Chile, where it is a stronger predictor of formal political participation via the ballot. Each of these trends indicate that while Argentina has become a protest state, where contention is a frequently utilized tool in the participatory repertoire of a wide swath of Argentine society, it has yet to take root in the same way in Chile—a country with far stronger formal institutions and vehicles for democratic representation.

CONCLUSION

This chapter has endeavored to understand how regional socioeconomic and political trends have produced variation in terms of protest in Latin American democracies. What the findings here suggest is an interactive relationship between social factors at the individual level and country-level institutional characteristics. Low-quality political institutions have an important positive effect on protest participation, but only among citizens who are at least minimally engaged in political life. In other words, low-quality institutions alone cannot determine whether or not an individual decides to attend a protest rally or demonstration—rather, the combination of high levels of individual-level political engagement and community involvement, and low-quality institutional environments where citizens feel underrepresented by formal democratic institutions, can greatly increase the probability that citizens resort to contentious tactics to make their voices heard.

Admittedly, this explanation of protest across countries is somewhat knotty. Rather than putting forth one variable or set of causal factors as the driving force behind contentious politics, I offer a more nuanced interactive theory that combines two seemingly contradictory phenomena—dysfunctional institutions and high levels of citizen engagement—to explain protest. Indeed, virtually any scholar of political behavior would argue that community engagement serves as a positive force in democracies, and that individuals across Latin America and other regions are only capable of participating in protests because of massive gains in political liberalization made during the last four decades, along with recent socioeconomic advances that have seemingly laid the foundation for an intensification of civic activism.

Both points are probably correct. However, the massive wave of democratization that has taken place since the 1970s in Latin America and other parts of the developing world has also produced a multitude of regimes where elections occur and basic civil liberties are observed, but where formal representative institutions fall short in terms of effectively channeling mass participation and public opinion. The results presented here suggest that when formal institutions fail to meet the needs of a highly engaged and determined populace, engaged citizens will adopt other means to make their voices heard. In short, mass-level democratic engagement has outpaced the consolidation of high-quality formal institutions in many Latin American regimes, creating a gap in terms of citizens' demands for democratic representation and its supply.

Moving beyond twenty-first-century Latin America, these findings might also help understand how gains in social development and civic engagement, coupled with low-quality formal political institutions, could lie at the root of mass protests in other regions and time periods. Indeed, an increase in citizen engagement and the use of social media to share political information clearly played an important role in Arab Spring countries, where citizens began to demand institutional reforms that made leaders more accountable to the citizenry. In Europe, individuals in countries like Greece and Spain—both of which possess myriad educated and engaged citizens—have not only been devastated by a severe economic recession, but frustrated by their inability to have their voices heard by policymakers amid European Union–prescribed austerity measures. Even in the United States, increased levels of contention organized by social movements like Black Lives Matter and a reinvigorated women's movement under the presidency of Donald Trump are seemingly led by active and informed citizens faced with exclusionary or nonresponsive political institutions. Thus, this chapter casts light on a broader set of phenomena, and informs scholars as they attempt to understand the causes and consequences of future episodes of protest participation across the world.

This chapter has demonstrated only that institutional context and citizen engagement appear to interact, to help understand which Latin Americans choose to protest and which ones abstain. However, I have said little about how organizations themselves seek to activate citizens to pursue their political goals—a defining characteristic of the protest state. In the next chapter I seek to explain how linkages to formal political organizations activate diverse patterns of political participation in distinct political milieus, tackling head-on the role that political elites play in creating and perpetuating the protest state.

CHAPTER 4

Protest from the Top Down

How Elites Marshal Contention in the Protest State

The theory and analysis presented to this point has established that contention has normalized in many Latin American democracies, as demonstrated by the models of protest participation presented in Chapter 3. In such protest states, I argue that individuals who are active in politics utilize protest as a more effective strategy for exerting their will on domestic political actors, and those political actors in turn mobilize contentious participation to help rally support for their cause. We observe the first part of this argument in different patterns of community activism across Latin American regimes, wherein individuals engaged in politics are more likely to adopt contentious modes of participation in weakly institutionalized contexts than in high-quality democratic regimes.

However, one principal observable implication of this theory remains unexplored: namely, the expectation that in protest states, where contentious repertoires have become so central to the day-to-day currents of political life, elites are more likely to actively mobilize protestors in pursuit of their political goals. How do linkages to political organizations influence patterns of political participation in protest states? In such contexts, do elites mobilize protests among their supporters to tilt the political playing field in their favor? This chapter puts forth the argument that political elites in protest states harness street-based participation to pursue their own ends, given its relevance as a form of political voice in those contexts. While formal political organizations are likely to mobilize protests in any minimally democratic context, their reliance on such contentious activities will be particularly heightened in protest states.

Drawing from a growing body of literature in Latin America and beyond, I unpack some of the ways in which elites seek to mobilize protests before connecting that research to my own theory of the protest state. First, I address a growing literature on the role that political elites play in mobilizing protests in democracies and non-democracies alike—a phenomenon that until recently has been largely understudied in the contentious politics literature. In particular, this literature focuses on two types of political organizations that play an active role in channeling interests and constructing contention: political parties and labor associations. Second, I shift my attention to discuss one particular method by which such organizations employ contentious repertoires to further their interests: clientelism. By defining clientelistic activities as a range of "political services" that clients provide to their patrons in exchange for excludable goods and favors (e.g., Calvo and Murillo 2013, Nichter 2008, Ujhelyi and Calvo 2010, Oliveros 2012, Szwarcberg 2012, 2013) and focusing on participation buying specifically, I argue that clientelism can coexist with and even foment contentious political participation. Specifically, captured clients engage in episodes of popular mobilization that serve to politically support their patron so as to maintain their rewarded condition and retain access to the allocation of goods.

Finally, I outline my theoretical expectations and empirical strategy for examining the extent to which political organizations mobilize contention in the protest state. In addition to the same cross-national dataset utilized in Chapter 3, this analysis also leverages a unique battery of individual-level survey questions from the cases of Argentina and Bolivia—two of the most contentious regimes in Latin America. This chapter thus contributes to an emerging body of research on elite-led contention through multilevel analyses of institutional characteristics and individual-level survey data, which reveal distinct patterns of elite/mass–level linkages in protest states. Whereas linkages to formal political organizations produce "conventional" participation in contexts of strong political institutions, such connections are associated with contentious modes of political voice in low-quality democracies.

POLITICAL ELITES AND THE PROTEST STATE

There is a long tradition in the contentious politics literature of emphasizing the role of movement leaders, or "political entrepreneurs," in fomenting collective action (McCarthy and Zald 1977). This line of argument can be traced to empirical research on the U.S. Civil Rights Movement, wherein U.S. academics underlined the importance of charismatic leaders like Martin Luther King Jr., who took grievances that had lain dormant for decades and channeled them into dynamic social movements. Much of this research dovetails with the resource mobilization framework, which emphasizes the structural factors that make collective action more likely, rather than motivating grievances, which are often present but fail to produce meaningful contention.

In most iterations of this theoretical approach, movement leaders are private citizens and activists who operate in civil society rather than within formal political institutions. Yet in recent years, inspired by events across primarily the developing world, scholars have sought to explain instances in which parties and other formal political organizations are protagonists in episodes of contention. Most notably, Emily Beaulieu's book (2014) on electoral protests examines contention organized by "individuals whose skills and objectives, first and foremost, are oriented toward competing in and winning elections" (7). She finds that where violations of norms regarding electoral fairness produce protests, and those protests attract the attention and support of the international community, electoral demonstrations can serve as a democratizing force in emerging regimes.

Empirically, Beaulieu's work on elite-led electoral protests spans democratic and non-democratic regimes alike, as she eschews classic dichotomous approaches to conceptualizing regime type; but other scholars have circumscribed their attention to subsamples of regimes with common institutional characteristics. Robertson (2007) explores how regional political elites mobilize labor strikes in hybrid regimes in particular, with evidence from Russia. In this case, Robertson argues that labor unions are not the representative organizations that they are in advanced industrialized democracies, but rather serve as instruments of control for political elites, who mobilize workers to serve as a bargaining chip in elite-level negotiations. On the other side of the coin, Trejo (2014) examines how autocratic rule affects the calculus of opposition parties, who in the absence of free and fair elections pursue a dual "socio-electoral" strategy that depends on the activation of sympathetic civil society groups. In Mexico, Trejo finds that protests crested at the outset of the regime's transition from one-party to multiparty rule, and then faded as opposition parties gained a real opportunity to contest democratic elections.

Likewise, there has been a proliferation of research emphasizing how political elites in democracies, in particular, tap into the potency of grassroots activism to pursue their goals. Auyero's (2007) rich ethnographic account of the 2001–2002 supermarket lootings that occurred across the neighborhoods of Buenos Aires offers one of the most compelling accounts of elite-led contention, in which he describes a dense organizational network within the "gray zone" of state power that conspires to wreak havoc on the incumbent government. In Argentina, the Peronists were able to tap into extensive grassroots clientelist networks built over decades to undermine the *Alianza*-led government after the Peronists lost the presidency in 1999, surreptitiously disseminating information to supporters about when and where to stage lootings and how to avoid arrest. Arce and Mangonnet (2013) corroborate Auyero's account of the organizing potential of the Peronists, as they find that in provinces with non-Peronist governors, roadblocks and other forms of aggressive protest are more common.

For Machado et al. (2011), repertoires of political participation are a direct response to the institutional context in which citizens operate. In regimes characterized by weak institutions, individuals are more likely to adopt "alternative political technologies" (Machado et al. 2011, Scartascini and Tommasi 2012), such as blocking roads or other aggressive protest activities, rather than engaging in more traditional modes of activism. While the authors are largely focused on the actions of individuals, they highlight that in weak institutional contexts, individuals who feel well represented by political parties will be more likely to have protested, whereas in regimes with strong institutions the opposite is true (Machado et al. 2011). Cornell and Grimes (2015) also examine the regime-level determinants of aggressive protests across Latin American democracies, but offer a different mechanism for why certain institutional arrangements fuel protests. They argue that it is not necessarily the quality of representation that drives contentious behavior, but rather political control of the bureaucracy that provides certain incentives to prospective contentious actors. Where individuals believe the government bureaucracy favors certain groups over others through patrimonial exchanges, they might also assume that only through aggressive direct action can they demonstrate their political relevance to the powers that be. This argument hinges on the notion that protest serves as a strategic tool that is yoked by elites in contexts characterized by corrupt bureaucracies.

Most empirical work in this vein focuses specifically on political parties—in essence the primary vehicles for representation in any democratic or pseudo-democratic regime and thus the chief conduit for elite-led mobilization. Even in protests that were ostensibly anti-establishment and spontaneous, like the Tea Party movement in the United States (Williamson et al. 2011) or the anti-government demonstrations that occurred in Brazil from 2013 until recently (Winters and Weitz-Shapiro 2017), a closer look often reveals the machinations of political parties in the shadows. In the famous 2013 Gezi Park protests in Turkey, opposition parties helped mobilize demonstrators, to which the ruling Justice and Development Party (AK) responded with pro-government rallies of their own (Traynor and Letsch 2013). Auyero (2007) and Machado et al.'s (2011) accounts of Argentine politics underscore the key mobilizational role of the Peronist party during times of political unrest. In short, there is abundant evidence that political parties activate protestors in democratic and non-democratic contexts to advance their agendas, which complicates classic narratives about the organic, mass-level roots of contentious collective action.

Not all accounts have revolved around parties as the primary representational vehicles for mobilization. Mangonnet and Murillo (2016) tackle the vexing question of why, during times of plenty, farmers adopt contentious modes of political participation. Zeroing in on the case of the export boom that occurred across Latin America in the 2000s, and specifically the soybean crop in Argentina, they find that where potential agricultural revenue is threatened by taxes, increases in rents can actually *fuel* contention, a finding that undercuts much of the research on grievances as a source of protest. However, the mobilizing impact of the export boom was most realized in districts with strong agricultural associations in place to foment collective action. According to Mangonnet and Murillo, "rural associations offer a forum for sharing grievances, establishing networks, and coordinating actions around leadership who aggregate demands, provide frames justifying protest, and bargain with government officials" (2016, 6). In sum, not only do parties serve as a mobilizing force in many emerging democracies—professional associations can also provide structure for collective action in regimes where protesting pays.

In protest states, political elites have particularly strong incentives to organize and deploy street-based activism in pursuit of their goals. One of the primary hypotheses enumerated in Chapter 2 is that in protest states, contention becomes so normal that it assumes a permanent place in the repertoire of institutional actors, complementing or even supplanting more "conventional" modes of political participation (Hypothesis Four). Similar to community engagement, formal political organizations can thus provide the necessary linkages for otherwise deactivated citizens to take to the streets. My chief expectation (H4.1) therefore is that individuals who have some connection to a formal political organization in weak institutional contexts will be more likely to protest, whereas that same individual will be a likelier conventional participant in stronger democratic regimes.

PROTESTORS FOR HIRE? CLIENTELISM AND PROTEST IN EMERGING DEMOCRACIES

Despite the conventional understanding of the relationship,[1] a growing body of work has posited a more complementary connection between political clientelism and social protest in Latin American societies. This literature posits that the two phenomena are, as Auyero, Lapegna, and Poma (2009, 1) underscore, "dynamic processes that often establish a recursive relationship." Drawing on the sociological contributions of resource mobilization theories that were popular in industrialized countries in the 1970s and 1980s, this line of research contends that clientelistic linkages between politicians and voters might lie at the root of contentious collective action.

As summarized in Chapter 2, the resource mobilization thesis asserts that organizational resources—such as money or physical facilities, information-sharing networks, media attention, alliances with political and economic elites, and so on—are necessary to translate isolated subjects into coordinated collective actors and, ultimately, mobilize people toward the fulfillment of a common goal (e.g., Jenkins 1983, McCarthy and Zald 1977). In a similar fashion, recent work has argued that clientelism, understood as the "distribution (or promise) of resources by political officeholders or political candidates in exchange for political support" (Auyero, Lapegna and Poma 2009, 3), can supply the key structures and the base of material resources for poor and low-income individuals to participate in different repertoires of contentious collective action (see also Auyero 2000, Collier and Handlin 2009).

Several scholars of this emerging school of thought have noted that, since the Third Wave of democratization in the region (Huntington 1991), resilient clientelistic networks have seemed to coexist with and even foster protest activities, abetting both sporadic and long-standing episodes of social unrest. In her study of peasant revolts in Colombia, for example, Escobar (1994) finds that clientelistic distribution was a useful incentive for the politicization of the peasantry and a viable mechanism for facilitating the eventual uprising of radical rural movements. Moreover, Penfold-Becerra (2007) argues that social welfare programs are selectively used by the Venezuelan national government to assure the allegiance and street mobilization of the nation's popular bases. In his analysis of Peru, Dunning (2014) also finds that party brokers direct private goods and services to help citizens to engage in unmediated direct action, or to recruit them to activities such as protests. As the author contends, clientelistic intermediation is "clearly an important element of direct action" (Dunning 2014, 18). To sum up, all of these studies shed light on the fact that clientelism can be "purposively activated to conduct politics by other collective (and sometimes violent) means" (Auyero, Lapegna, and Poma 2009, 12).

In protest states, clientelism can indeed coexist with, and even foment, social protest. Specifically, clientelistic networks often supply individuals with the organizational support necessary to mobilize. Where the aggrieved are privy to the mobilizational tools necessary to effectively organize, grievances can translate into action. Where those tools are absent, potential claims can go unexpressed. In more recent empirical studies, scholars have tested and confirmed the individual-level relationships that this theoretical tradition hypothesizes. Numerous articles—focusing particularly on the developed countries of Europe and the United States—have found that individual-level indicators like education, civic activism, and interest in politics have powerful positive effects on the probability that individuals take part in protests (Norris 2002, Norris et al. 2005, Dalton et al. 2009, Moreno and Moseley 2011). All of these individual-level characteristics serve as proxies for a person's connectedness to the vital organizational resources that allow citizens to consolidate and vocalize their collective claims.

Clientelistic relationships between patrons and clients can fulfill this mobilization role as well. In some cases, this might be as simple as a political patron offering cash or some other material item in exchange for their clients' attendance at a political rally they are organizing (Szwarcberg 2015). In other cases, clientelistic parties might offer public jobs to their political clients with the expectation that they turn out for party-sponsored events, including street marches and demonstrations, in the coming months and years (Oliveros 2014). In still other cases, retrieval of a cash stipend accessed in a local party office might link individual citizens to political apparatuses that also serve to mobilize rallies or episodes of other street-based activities. While these are three divergent examples, the common thread remains that clientelistic activities can supply the organizational push behind instances of collective action. Individuals with access to these mobilizing vehicles are thus more likely to partake of contentious activities than those who are not privy to clientelistic exchanges.

The key expectation I seek to test in this chapter with respect to clientelism and protest is the hypothesis (H4.2) that clientelism has a more powerful association with protest participation in protest states, where contentious behavior has been absorbed into the everyday participatory repertoire of citizens. In protest states, political elites seek to activate their followers in pursuit of their goals. One of the key strategies by which they do so is through the disbursement of excludable material goods in exchange for citizen participation. In conjunction with the first theoretical and empirical component of this chapter regarding the contentious consequences of linkages to formal political organizations in protest states, the chapter thus provides a thorough examination of the *who* and the *how* of elite-led protests in Latin America.

In this chapter, I adopt a two-pronged empirical approach that first seeks to demonstrate the extent to which political elites operate differently in protest states, drawing on individual-level data from across Latin America to test the argument that linkages to political organizations fuel protest in low-quality institutional contexts, and to support conventional participation in environments characterized by strong democratic institutions. The second part of my empirical approach endeavors to illuminate how one particular mobilizational strategy—clientelistic participation buying—fuels protest in some contexts but not others. To do so, I draw both on cross-national survey data from Latin America and a unique battery of survey questions asked only in Argentina and Bolivia in the 2010 AmericasBarometer survey.

Organizing Contention: Parties and Labor Associations in the Protest State

The first hypothesis (H4.1) I seek to test in this chapter is the expectation that linkages to formal political organizations tend to foment contentious participation in protest states, but not in Latin American regimes with strong political institutions. My empirical strategy for tackling this particular expectation is twofold. First, I utilize multilevel logistic regression models on cross-national data from the AmericasBarometer over multiple survey rounds to demonstrate that in contexts characterized by weak political institutions, linkages to political organizations produce heightened levels of protest activity, whereas in strong institutional settings such connections tend to be associated with amplified rates of formal participation. These data are the same utilized in Chapter 3, as are most of the individual-level control variables included in the two logistic models of participation. Each model also includes the same measure of institutional quality based on an index composed of World Bank Governance Indicators, with country-level controls for various economic factors including GDP growth, human development, and inequality.

At the individual level I focus on party membership in particular, given its relative universality as a linkage to a formal representative organization, and seek to demonstrate empirically that it has a distinct impact on the likelihood of participating in a protest versus volunteering for a campaign (a classic form of "conventional" participation) depending on the institutional context. In other words, whereas partisanship is associated with higher rates of protest participation in weak institutional contexts, it is correlated with higher rates of campaign voluntarism in high-quality institutional environments. This offers evidence that linkages to political elites fuel different types of political participation in the protest state versus democracies characterized by stronger political institutions.

The second component of this empirical strategy narrows the focus to four Latin American regimes: Argentina, Bolivia, Chile, and Uruguay. While Argentina and Bolivia represent classic protest states, Chile and Uruguay boast some of the strongest democratic political institutions in Latin America. In this analysis, I run country-specific models to determine the degree to which multiple types of linkages to two formal political organizations—political parties and professional associations—fuel different modes of participation across distinct institutional settings. These include partisanship, attendance of party meetings, contact with local officials, and participation in labor associations, each of which is operationalized as a dichotomous variable (see Appendix for original question wording). I find that whereas such linkages carry with them significant increases in the predicted probability of protesting in Argentina and Bolivia, the same cannot be said for Chile and Uruguay.

Assessing the Relationship between Participation Buying and Contention

To test my expectations regarding clientelism and contention in the protest state (H4.2), I begin by confirming that only in Argentina and Bolivia is receiving a participation-buying offer associated with protest, compared to Chile and Uruguay. I proceed to use a special battery of questions from the 2010 AmericasBarometer survey of Argentina and Bolivia, conducted by the Latin American Public Opinion Project (LAPOP). Argentina and Bolivia are ideal for testing the relationship between clientelism and protest for several reasons. There is a strong academic consensus (O'Donnell 1993) and empirical evidence (Brusco, Nazareno, and Stokes 2004, Calvo and Murillo 2004, Lazar 2004) that points to the widespread nature of clientelistic politics in both countries. Political clientelism is not completely new in Argentina and Bolivia, but its political, economic, social, and even cultural relevance has sharply increased since the 1990s, when market-oriented reforms deepened socioeconomic grievances (Van Cott 2000). Moreover, given that in Argentina political competition is programmatically weak, lacking an ideological cleavage, political parties are deeply reliant on the clientelistic allocation of public resources for electoral support

(Calvo and Murillo 2004). This has become even more pronounced since the nation's main political actor, the Peronist party, reconfigured its organization from a reliance on labor unions to clientelistic machines as a way to readapt its partisan structure to the changing trends of economic liberalization (Levitsky 2003). Since 2006, Bolivia has been ruled by the *Movimiento al Socialismo* bloc, a leftist party spearheaded by Evo Morales, the first indigenous president in the country's history, who has also relied heavily on clientelist networks (Anrias 2013).

In recent years, scholars have noted the extent to which protest has normalized in both countries, across socioeconomic class and demographic groups, as rates of participation have been among the highest in Latin America (Moreno and Moseley 2011, LAPOP 2012). As opposed to other South American countries like Chile, Colombia, or Uruguay, where episodes of social protest have been rare or exceptional, Argentina and Bolivia have witnessed an intense and at times violent resurgence of contentious activities all across their territory, making protest a "very salient and meaningful way to achieve certain political objectives and to express policy demands" (Machado, Scartascini, and Tommasi 2011, 7). Argentina and Bolivia are, therefore, appropriate cases to test the theory presented here that clientelistic exchange can indeed fuel protest participation in protest states, where elites attempt to mobilize contention on their behalf given its importance in everyday political life.

The 2010 survey of Argentina used a national probability sample design of voting-age adults, with a total N of 1,410 people taking part in face-to-face interviews in Spanish, carried out between January and April 2010. The sample consists of 74 primary sampling units (municipalities) and 61 final sampling units representing 21 of 24 provinces,[2] including the autonomous capital city of Buenos Aires. In the 2010 Bolivia national survey, LAPOP sought to oversample the population, resulting in a larger sample of 3,018 respondents that provides for equal representation from all nine Bolivian departments.[3]

Given the relevance of protest in each country, an extra battery of questions was utilized in the 2010 AmericasBarometer surveys of Argentina and Bolivia. These questions were designed to measure three primary protest tactics in each country: (1) street marches and public demonstrations, (2) roadblocks, and (3) labor strikes. As covered extensively to this point, the first group consists of typically non-violent modes of collective political action, often involving marches or campaign rallies in which political parties mobilize large groups of people to protest against or support the government in office or, alternatively, support an opposition party or candidate. Marches and demonstrations are particularly common in election years, when partisan actors seek to construct political power in the streets by convening neighborhood-level organizations and activists to support them (Szwarcberg 2015).[4] The 2010 questionnaire asked Argentines and Bolivians if they had participated in a march or demonstration in the last three years, and the data reveal that almost 20 percent had participated.

The next item on protests collects information on participation in street or road blockades (called *piquetes* or *cortes de ruta*), one of the most widely used and effective means of protesting in both Argentina and Bolivia (Arce and Mangonnet 2013, Assies 2003).[5] These events are somewhat similar to marches and demonstrations, but they make use of more aggressive, disruptive, and, on most occasions, anti-government techniques of mobilization. Although not necessarily violent, roadblocks spontaneously cause traffic interruptions, fomenting civic disorder and economic losses across populations (Bruhn 2008, Mangonnet and Murillo 2016). In their extreme version, they focus on disrupting commerce, laying siege to cities by cutting supplies and destabilizing the government in office (Silva 2009). While in Argentina and Bolivia they were originally confined to particular protest movements in periods of economic and political crisis—for example, the unemployed *piquetero* federations in Argentina in the late 1990s and early 2000s, and anti-government activists preceding the 2003 deposal of President Lozada in Bolivia—nowadays, roadblocks have expanded to different political actors, serving as a frequently utilized tactic. To measure this particular protest repertoire, the questionnaire asked if respondents had participated in a street, avenue, or road blockade during the last three years, showing that 10 percent of the respondents interviewed took part in these activities.

The final item on protest addresses individual participation in labor-based forms of protests, like strikes or work stoppages, providing a measure of one of the most traditional repertoires of contentious collective action in Latin American political history. As opposed to the former protest activities, strikes and work stoppages are a more formal, privileged tactic, not available to informal economic actors (Etchemendy and Collier 2007). Given their formality, it is thus unlikely that they are related to participation buying, as most of these individuals fall in economic brackets that make them less likely targets. To measure this item, the questionnaire asked if Argentines and Bolivians had participated in a strike or work stoppage in the last three years.

To measure the crucial independent variable, AmericasBarometer from 2010 provides information about participation buying, probably the most often studied clientelistic strategy in the extant literature on clientelism in

Latin America (e.g., Stokes 2005, Nichter 2008, Gonzalez-Ocantos et al. 2012, Carlin and Moseley 2015). The questionnaire asked Argentines and Bolivians if a candidate or someone from a political party offered a favor, food, or something else in exchange for his or her vote or broader political support in the last twelve months. The responses were originally coded on a 1–3 scale (1 for "never," 2 for "at least once," and 3 for "frequently"), but recoded as a dummy variable (0 = no, 1 = yes) to simply measure if respondents had been targeted or not for a participation-buying offer. When combining these categories, the 2010 AmericasBarometer data indicates that 17 percent of respondents in Argentina and 16 percent in Bolivia claimed to have been offered "something" by a candidate or a party in exchange for their political support, giving Argentina and Bolivia the second and fifth highest rates in the region respectively (only surpassed by Dominican Republic; Figure 4.1). Consistent with prior vote-buying surveys (e.g., Brusco, Nazareno, and Stokes 2004), the data also revealed that 49 percent of the vote-buying clients belonged to the lowest income ranges.

POLITICAL ORGANIZATIONS AND PROTEST IN LATIN AMERICA

For the first test of Hypothesis 4.1, I draw on the same cross-national data utilized in Chapter 3, including country-level variables for institutional quality along with various economic controls including GDP growth, human development, and inequality. Instead of focusing on the interaction between community engagement and institutional quality, in this chapter I am interested in how partisanship interacts with institutional quality to predict both contentious (Model 1 in Table 4.1) and conventional (Model 2) participation.

Table 4.1 reports estimates from two logistic regression models of political participation. In Model 1, the dependent variable is whether or not individuals participated in a protest during the previous twelve months. Because very similar models were already discussed in Chapter 3, I zero in on the coefficient of interest: *Party Member x Institutions Index*. The coefficient has a negative sign, and is significant at $p<.10$. Figure 4.2 graphs the predicted probabilities of protesting based on variation in both institutional quality and being a member of a political party. The results suggest a similar dynamic to that uncovered in Chapter 3 with respect to community engagement and institutional quality—whereas in high-quality institutional environments, party membership has no significant impact on whether or not an individual protested in the prior year, as institutions get

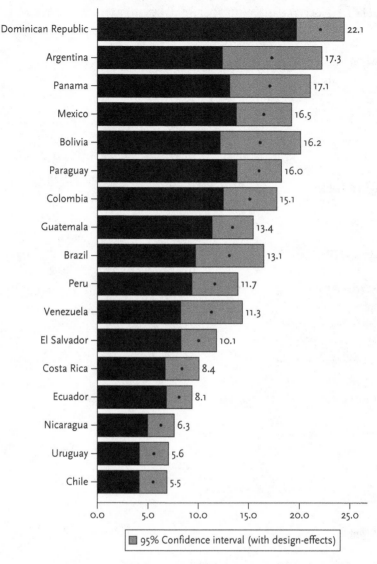

Dominican Republic — 22.1
Argentina — 17.3
Panama — 17.1
Mexico — 16.5
Bolivia — 16.2
Paraguay — 16.0
Colombia — 15.1
Guatemala — 13.4
Brazil — 13.1
Peru — 11.7
Venezuela — 11.3
El Salvador — 10.1
Costa Rica — 8.4
Ecuador — 8.1
Nicaragua — 6.3
Uruguay — 5.6
Chile — 5.5

0.0   5.0   10.0   15.0   20.0   25.0

■ 95% Confidence interval (with design-effects)

Figure 4.1 Clientelistic Participation Targeting in Latin America, 2010
© AmericasBarometer, LAPOP

weaker the causal import of party organization begins to shine through. In a setting characterized by weak political institutions—a −.5 on the institutional quality index is roughly equal to that found in Bolivia—party sympathizers are almost twice as likely to take part in a street march or demonstration as individuals with no party affiliation. This difference is similar at 0 on the institutions index, which corresponds to the scores of regimes like Argentina and Brazil.

Table 4.1 PARTISANSHIP AND POLITICAL PARTICIPATION IN LATIN AMERICA

VARIABLES	(1) Participated in Protest	(2) Volunteered for Campaign
Female	−0.189***	−0.138***
	(0.023)	(0.022)
Age	−0.008***	0.000
	(0.001)	(0.001)
Wealth (quintile)	0.009	−0.033***
	(0.009)	(0.008)
Interest in Politics	0.011***	0.016***
	(0.000)	(0.000)
Education (Years)	0.048***	0.038***
	(0.003)	(0.003)
Presidential Approval	−0.004***	−0.001**
	(0.001)	(0.000)
Interpersonal Trust	−0.001**	
	(0.000)	
Sociotropic Evaluation	−0.002***	
	(0.001)	
Pocketbook Evaluation	−0.001*	
	(0.001)	
System Support	0.114***	
	(0.025)	
Community Participation	0.796***	0.640***
	(0.024)	(0.023)
Gini (2009)	4.470*	0.396
	(2.559)	(1.115)
HDI (2007)	1.059	−2.615***
	(2.121)	(0.930)
GDP Growth	0.017	0.019
	(0.038)	(0.017)
Institutional Quality Index	−0.235	−0.123
	(0.256)	(0.112)
Party Member	0.454***	1.024***
	(0.032)	(0.028)
Party Member x Institutions Index	*−0.080**	*0.154****
	(0.048)	*(0.046)*
Constant	−6.249**	−1.979*
	(2.489)	(1.089)
Observations	91,198	103,590
Number of Country Years	67	68

Standard errors in parentheses
*** p<0.01, ** p<0.05, * p<0.1

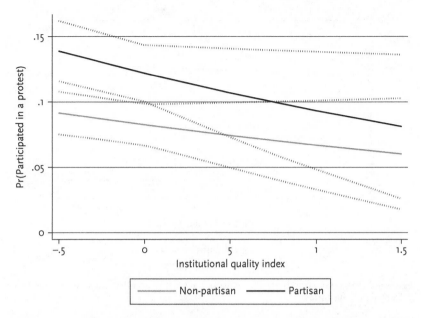

Figure 4.2 The Interaction between Institutional Quality and Partisanship as a Predictor of Protest Participation

On the other hand, the results presented from Model 2 in Table 4.1 tell a very different story. In this logistic regression model, the dependent variable is whether or not individuals reported volunteering for a political campaign during the past year. Volunteering for a political campaign represents a classic form of conventional political participation, common in advanced and emerging democratic regimes alike. My expectation is that volunteering for a campaign becomes more likely among partisans in strong institutional climates, where formal participation is viewed as relatively efficacious—in other words, the exact opposite of what we observe in terms of contentious political participation.

In direct contrast to the interaction between party membership and institutional quality in Model 1, the sign for *Party Member x Institutions Index* in Model 2 is positive, and significant at p<.01. Predicted probabilities are graphed in Figure 4.3, which demonstrate that the gap between party members and non–party members' odds of volunteering in a political campaign increase in the *most* democratic contexts. In other words, whereas party membership exerts a strong impact on protest participation in less democratic contexts, it is most powerfully associated with conventional participation in the strongest institutional environments. Party members are roughly three times more likely than non–party members to have volunteered for a political campaign at the highest value in terms

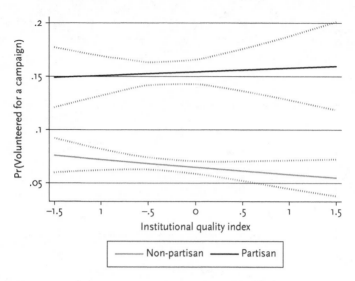

Figure 4.3 The Interaction between Institutional Quality and Partisanship as a Predictor of Campaign Voluntarism

of institutional quality, such as that of a country like Chile. While party members are more likely to partake of this behavior in less democratic contexts vis-à-vis those who have no party affiliation, the gap is not nearly as wide as in the most democratic contexts. In short, whereas linkages to political parties seem to fuel contentious participation in protest states, they are more strongly correlated with traditional participation in strong institutional contexts.

The second component of my empirical approach to examining how linkages to political organizations influence patterns of political participation in Latin America is to home in on four particular cases, similar to the comparison of Argentina and Chile in Chapter 3. I choose two classic protest states, Argentina and Bolivia, and two of the regimes with the strongest democratic political institutions in the region in Chile and Uruguay. I run a series of country-specific logistic regression models of protest, subbing in various measures of potential linkages to two types of political organizations: political parties and labor associations. My expectation is that connections to such organizations will have a much stronger stimulative impact on protest in Argentina and Bolivia, where protest is often weaponized by formal political organizations, than in Chile and Uruguay, wherein political elites more actively mobilize traditional political participation.

Table 4.2 presents changes in predicted probabilities derived from country-specific models of protest participation. Each column represents a distinct type of linkage to formal political organizations, and the change

Table 4.2 LINKAGES TO POLITICAL ORGANIZATIONS AND PROTEST IN ARGENTINA, BOLIVIA, CHILE, AND URUGUAY

Change in Predicted Probability of Protesting Based on Linkages to Political Organizations
(All variables dichotomous; holding other variables in models at means)

	Member of Political Party (1)	Attended Party Meetings (2)	Attended Professional Association Meetings (3)	Contacted Local Official (4)	Received Participation-Buying Offer (5)
Argentina	0.044***	0.176***	0.080***	0.116***	0.094***
Bolivia	0.056***	0.129***	0.079***	0.108***	0.020
Chile	0.030***	0.087***	0.027*	0.030**	−0.002
Uruguay	0.044***	0.094***	0.002	0.010	0.038

Standard errors in parentheses
*** p<0.01, ** p<0.05, * p<0.1

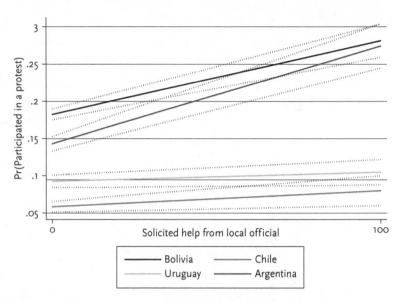

Figure 4.4 Protest Participation by Individuals Who Contacted a Local Official

in an individual's probability of protesting that results from having access to that linkage, compared to those who do not. All models include the same control variables from the models of protest participation presented to this point, which are held at their mean when calculating predicted probabilities. As observed in column 1, party membership does not seem to have a massive impact on protest participation in any of the four countries, though this impact is significant at p<.01. However, key distinctions emerge when considering attendance of party and professional association meetings, where the impact of such linkages is much stronger in the protest states of Argentina and Bolivia. In the case of labor associations in particular, linkages to such organizations are virtually unrelated to one's odds of participating in a protest in Chile and Uruguay—however, they have a strong and positive substantive impact on protest participation in Argentina and Bolivia. This would seem to echo the findings from Mangonnet and Murillo's (2016) study of labor association protests amid the commodities boom in Argentina. Likewise, whereas having had contact with a local official seems to be associated with amplified rates of contentious participation in Argentina and Bolivia, no real impact emerges in the two cases characterized by stronger political institutions. These differences are graphed in Figure 4.4., which highlights the differential impact of connections to political organizations on protest participation in distinct institutional environments.

CLIENTELISTIC VOTE TARGETING AND PROTEST IN ARGENTINA AND BOLIVIA

Using the measure of clientelistic participation targeting described above as the key independent variable, and the three unique measures of protest participation as dependent variables, in this section I test Hypothesis 4.2 regarding the relationship between political clientelism and contentious politics in two protest states, Argentina and Bolivia. Given the dichotomous nature of each of the dependent variables, the results presented below are from logistic regression models of participation in street marches and demonstrations, roadblocks, and strikes or work stoppages. Each of these models compares the relative impact of receiving a participation-buying offer on all three repertoires of protest participation. In addition, every model controls for standard socio-demographic variables like gender, wealth, age, and education, providing a thorough examination of the relationship between clientelism and protest and offering a challenging test for the argument that clientelism and protest are, in fact, interrelated phenomena in Argentina and Bolivia.

Before diving into the protest models from Argentina and Bolivia, column 5 in Table 4.2 lends some initial evidence that clientelism and protest indeed overlap in Argentina and, to a lesser extent, Bolivia. Having received a participation-buying offer increases the probability of protesting in Argentina by nearly .10. While it does seem that the relationship between receiving an offer and protesting in Bolivia is positive, it narrowly misses conventional standards of statistical significance (p<.18). Overall, given the lack of evidence of significant associations in Chile and Uruguay, these initial results provide some promising signals that clientelism and protest do indeed coexist in protest states to a greater degree than in regimes characterized by strong political institutions. However, using the three different measures of protest included in the special battery of questions in Argentina and Bolivia will ultimately provide a more rigorous empirical test.

Providing support for my hypothesis, having been targeted for a vote-buying offer has a significant positive effect on the probability that one participates in a street march in both Argentina and Bolivia, as evidenced by the results from Models 1 and 2 in Table 4.3. These results are significant at p<.05, and suggest that in each case, having received a participation-buying offer increases one's odds of protesting by about one-third. Notably, experience with participation buying also seems to be associated with higher rates of participation in roadblocks—a common repertoire of protest in both Argentina and Bolivia. While this translates into an increase in

Table 4.3 THE RELATIONSHIP BETWEEN PARTICIPATION BUYING AND PROTEST IN ARGENTINA AND BOLIVIA

VARIABLES	Street Marches		Roadblocks		Strikes	
	Argentina	Bolivia	Argentina	Bolivia	Argentina	Bolivia
	(1)	(2)	(3)	(4)	(5)	(6)
Female	-0.052	-0.267***	-0.099	-0.116	0.204	-0.357**
	(0.150)	(0.096)	(0.197)	(0.111)	(0.251)	(0.175)
Age	-0.166***	0.017	-0.197***	-0.002	-0.089	0.028
	(0.055)	(0.034)	(0.074)	(0.040)	(0.091)	(0.060)
Education (years)	-0.003	-0.024*	-0.038	-0.039***	-0.007	-0.019
	(0.020)	(0.013)	(0.027)	(0.015)	(0.034)	(0.023)
Interest in Politics	0.023***	0.013***	0.016***	0.011***	0.018***	0.010***
	(0.003)	(0.002)	(0.003)	(0.002)	(0.004)	(0.003)
Pocketbook Evaluation	-0.002	-0.007**	-0.007	-0.010***	-0.007	-0.008
	(0.004)	(0.003)	(0.005)	(0.004)	(0.007)	(0.006)
Sociotropic Evaluation	0.001	-0.012***	-0.009	-0.007**	0.001	-0.012**
	(0.004)	(0.003)	(0.005)	(0.004)	(0.007)	(0.005)
Urban	-0.758**	-0.456***	-0.794*	-0.265**	0.371	0.113
	(0.305)	(0.108)	(0.439)	(0.123)	(0.380)	(0.183)

	(1)	(2)	(3)	(4)	(5)	(6)
Wealth (quintile)	-0.058	0.059	-0.074	-0.014	0.132	0.053
	(0.060)	(0.036)	(0.079)	(0.042)	(0.101)	(0.065)
Presidential Approval	0.002	0.010***	0.012***	0.009***	0.004	0.011**
	(0.004)	(0.003)	(0.005)	(0.003)	(0.006)	(0.005)
System Support	0.176	0.000	0.225	0.047	-0.057	0.393**
	(0.166)	(0.100)	(0.222)	(0.115)	(0.274)	(0.177)
Received Participation-Buying Offer	*0.410**	*0.264**	*0.762***	*0.219*	*0.027*	*-0.164*
	(0.195)	*(0.116)*	*(0.232)*	*(0.133)*	*(0.335)*	*(0.221)*
Constant	-1.409**	-0.434	-1.339	-0.955**	-4.392***	-3.089***
	(0.637)	(0.410)	(0.848)	(0.474)	(1.029)	(0.737)
Observations	1,260	2,706	1,263	2,703	1,266	2,705

Standard errors in parentheses
*** p<0.01, ** p<0.05, * p<0.1

an individual's predicted probability of participating in a roadblock from .15 to .18 in Bolivia, having received an offer nearly *doubles* one's likelihood of blocking a road in Argentina, from .08 to .16. As predicted, participation buying is not related to work stoppages and strikes in either Argentina or Bolivia—a more sophisticated repertoire of protest reserved for the formally employed. Overall, it appears that political elites do indeed utilize clientelistic inducements to mobilize protest participation in countries where protest matters. In the following section, I briefly discuss the question of causality before digging into the implications of this analysis.

Addressing Causality

It is implied throughout this chapter that elites utilize mobilization strategies, including participation buying, to fuel protest participation. However, the opposite of this posited causal relationship seems plausible—that is, perhaps individuals are more likely to be targeted by political organizations because of their protest activities, rather than the other way around? More specifically, one might imagine a scenario where politicians attempt to appease protestors with clientelistic rewards or incorporation in a political organization, or where brokers take advantage of having close contact with protestors at demonstrations to distribute partisan propaganda or clientelistic goods. Indeed, in his seminal article on the topic, Auyero argues that clientelism and protest are actually intertwined in a recursive relationship, meaning that the causal arrow flows in both directions.

When dealing with cross-sectional data, there is no true panacea for concerns related to endogeneity. The strongest defense is always theoretical, and I contend that the causal story presented above—namely, that political organizations take the lead in mobilizing protest participation—is more compelling than the alternative explanation. However, there are statistical tools that enable us to further investigate the possibility of either a recursive relationship or one that actually flows in the opposite direction that I argue. I thus ran a series of two-stage least squares models and Hausman endogeneity tests to evaluate the extent to which causality flows in one direction from clientelism to protest in the second part of the analysis in this chapter, instrumenting for the various forms of protest participation. Given that this chapter focuses on one independent variable and three dependent variables across two countries, six models were run (see Appendix). I use ideology as the instrument, because empirically it is related to all three forms of protest—namely that people who identify with being on the left are more likely to protest—but is completely unrelated to receiving a vote-buying offer (see models in Appendix).

Sargan and Basmann tests confirmed that the instrument of ideology is "not weak" for each of the separate dependent variables (street demonstrations, roadblocks, and strikes). For every model, I was unable to reject the null hypothesis of exogeneity using Durbin and Wu-Hausman F-tests. Thus, this analysis finds that neither participating in a roadblock, strike, nor a street march or demonstration increases the probability of receiving a vote-buying offer, while uncovering strong evidence that the opposite is true.

THEORETICAL IMPLICATIONS

Moving forward, if political organizations do indeed promote protest participation in certain contexts, this raises a different set of questions about how we ought to characterize this relationship between elites and citizens. Specifically, should protest participation spurred by political elites actually be considered "contentious"? That is, if hierarchical relationships are exploited to mobilize participation in various repertoires of protest participation, should we view that participation as being any different from voting a certain way in exchange for material goods? Even taking into account the results presented above, it remains unclear if the relationships uncovered here constitute any sort of change from the traditional hierarchy that characterizes clientelistic practices, even if the actual participation that results is, on the face of it, more combative and polemic.

In my view, there are two distinct perspectives to contemplate in addressing these questions. The first is that the traditional view of clientelistic linkages remains accurate, as political patrons use their considerable resources to deploy clients through buying participation in "contentious" activities that are actually tightly controlled by elites. In other words, while at first glance activities like roadblocks and street marches might appear antagonistic and confrontational, in reality powerful political players deploy these tactics in societies where protest is common and strategically effective—that is, protest states. The relationship observed between clientelism and protest is thus not as striking an anomaly vis-à-vis the received wisdom—while clientelism *does* promote some kind of non-electoral political participation, this participation remains closely monitored and managed by the politically powerful. The same could be said for the positive association between linkages to formal political organizations and protest participation. Even if this is indeed the case, it does call for future scholarly work on elite–citizen linkages that takes into account other forms of political participation besides merely voting, as parties and other organizations might demand more than just electoral favors in exchange for clientelistic goods. While Szwarcberg (2012) and Oliveros (2012) have focused on other important "political services" besides voting that clients can provide, this analysis suggests that contentious behaviors like street protests and roadblocks offer two other potential participatory manifestations of clientelistic bargains between patrons and clients.

The second perspective is slightly more complicated, but also makes intuitive sense. While elites might initially mobilize protest participation that is in line with the goals of their parties or labor associations, the possibility exists that they eventually lose control over protestors once these networks have been established. If protest becomes a key component of a society's participatory repertoire, in part because parties or labor associations encourage the behavior in an effort to marshal support for their agenda, it seems that the practice could backfire when citizens take to the streets in the absence of those orders. The relationship between partisanship and protest, or being targeted for clientelistic exchanges and participating in demonstrations or roadblocks, might therefore be only part of the story, as the after-effects of the exchange could have unintended consequences for the parties who employ these tactics.

The survey data drawn upon for this chapter offer no direct test of these two competing perspectives, though a few possible trends surface at first glance. First, 90 percent of protestors in Argentina and 76 percent in Bolivia report receiving no pressure to participate in contentious behaviors. While this could imply that some respondents are not cognizant of or willing to admit top-down pressures to protest, it might also suggest that protest participation often takes on a more independent nature than political organizations would like. Or, perhaps individuals gladly participate in contentious activities at the request of political patrons as a sign of gratitude or because they genuinely believe in the party's program (Lawson and Greene 2014). Either way, it seems that most Argentines and Bolivians participate in contentious politics of their own volition, rather than passively marching in the streets at the behest of some domineering benefactor.

Second, in Argentina at least, there is no obvious relationship between political party affiliation or pro-government/opposition status and receiving a participation-buying offer, signifying that the ruling party (at the national level) does not exert hegemonic control over this type of clientelistic inducement. This is somewhat surprising given the perceived dominance of the Peronist party in this particular area, and its status as the ruling party at the time of the 2010 survey. Thus, even if the relationship between clientelistic goods distribution and contentious politics represents another form of purchased quiescence, it seems to be a strategy used by multiple parties on targets of various partisan affiliations, including opposition parties on the outside looking in. Moreover, the fact that only one-fourth of demonstrators were also targeted for a vote-buying offer, and that protestors are marked by high levels of partisan diversity, jointly signal that protesting in Argentina is still largely an independent source of popular mobilization utilized by a wide swath of the citizenry.

In sum, while certain individuals inevitably attend rallies, roadblocks, or strikes in response to an asymmetrical power dynamic with political elites, it seems likely that many others utilize those organizational structures to willfully partake of contentious participation on the behalf of causes they believe in. However, these individual-level motivations clearly require further research utilizing a more specialized methodological approach. In either case, one thing remains clear—this relationship between elite mobilization and protest only serves to entrench the protest state. If political elites are responding to a saturated protest environment, where street demonstrations and other forms of contention are highly useful tools to help pursue political goals, the deployment of protests in exchange for material rewards perpetuates the cycle. In this way, political elites, too, have contributed to the rise of the protest state in countries like Argentina and Bolivia.

CONCLUSION

In recent decades, there has been considerable theoretical debate on the role that elites play in mobilizing social movements and other forms of contentious politics. One of the key predictions of the theory of the protest state is that in such contexts, where institutional weakness and high levels of political engagement collide, elites will have incentives to mobilize contentious movements on behalf of their goals. This chapter has sought to articulate that perspective and test its observable implications. The first set of empirical analyses demonstrate that linkages to political organizations—specifically, political parties and labor associations—tend to provoke different behaviors in distinct institutional environments, producing contentious activism in protest states and traditional forms of participation in high-quality democracies. Thus, protest states persist not just through independent choices made by mass publics, but because political organizations realize the power of street protests and attempt to harness it for their own ends.

This chapter also seeks to shed light on how one particular strategy of elite-led mobilization—participation buying—could fuel contentious activity. In their seminal piece on the topic, Auyero et al. state, "further research should scrutinize the differential impact that variations in the form of clientelism have on the character of collective action" (Auyero, Lapegna, and Poma 2009, 3). This chapter has attempted to carry out that task in the Argentine and Bolivian contexts. In accordance with this approach, the empirical findings support the notion that in Argentina and Bolivia, rather than being opposed and antithetical political phenomena, clientelism can indeed coexist with, and even propel, social protest in assorted ways. In addition to demonstrating that these relationships exist, I have inspected how participation buying shapes the form of contentious collective action. On the whole, results show that Argentines and Bolivians who have been targeted for a participation-buying offer are much more inclined to participate in street marches and roadblocks as contentious strategies, but not in labor strikes. Thus, protest buying is both a symptom of the protest state and also a way in which it reproduces itself. For political elites in contexts characterized by low-quality institutions and high levels of political engagement, protest becomes a repertoire of participation worth mobilizing.

In the following chapter, I shift from examining the determinants of protest across countries to evaluate how protest has normalized in one particular regime over the past quarter century: Argentina. By examining this process in Argentina, I help support these cross-national findings by exploring an observable implication of my theoretical approach only hinted at in the past two empirical chapters.

CHAPTER 5

Tracing the Roots of the Protest State in Argentina

Argentina ranks as one of Latin America's most contentious regimes, according to data from the AmericasBarometer surveys from 2008 to 2012 (LAPOP). Anecdotal evidence would suggest that Argentina's contentiousness goes back further—indeed, the rise of the *piquetero* movement during the late 1990s and the role of public demonstrations in the country's dramatic economic and political crises in 2001–2002 have been well-chronicled by journalists and academics alike. But has Argentina always been a hotbed for contentious mass protests and social movements? How have contentious repertoires expanded and potentially "normalized" as a form of political voice since the country's transition to democracy, resulting in the country's status as one of Latin America's most preeminent protest states? Further, has this process occurred uniformly at the national level, or does subnational variation exist in terms of the prevalence and type of protest utilized by contentious actors?

To answer these questions, I shift focus from analyzing variation in levels of protest participation *across* countries at a particular point in time, to assessing the evolution of contentious politics *within* one regime over several decades. Thus, rather than utilizing cross-sectional survey data to assess the individual and country-level predictors of protest, this chapter endeavors to understand how protest evolves as a form of participation within a particular national context, and how this evolution may be a product of the same combination of rising levels of citizen engagement amid flawed institutions of democratic representation.

Specifically, in the chapters on Argentina, I seek to provide a richer treatment of each of the five hypotheses presented in Chapter 2. Namely, how do institutional characteristics and trends in terms of political engagement bear on patterns of protest participation in a particular political context? Might the behaviors of politically active citizens be altered where high-quality democratic representation via formal vehicles is lacking? Most importantly, I begin to analyze how over time, persistent institutional dysfunction and surging political engagement can result in protest normalizing as a form of political participation to the extent that it becomes a quotidian characteristic of political life—i.e., the makings of a protest state.

This chapter first outlines the previous twenty-five years of protest in Argentina, offering a summary of how a contentious "repertoire," to use Tilly's (1978) terminology, has advanced over the years within the country. I begin the discussion with Carlos Menem's first term (1989–1995), building toward the pivotal 2001–2002 protests that resulted in Argentina cycling through several presidents over the course of a month, and conclude with the recent mobilization surrounding the mysterious death of federal prosecutor Alberto Nisman, who was investigating President Cristina Fernández de Kirchner for an alleged cover-up related to the 1994 terrorist attack on a Jewish community center in Buenos Aires, and the growing *Ni Una Menos* movement against femicide and gender violence. I argue that since the early 1990s, the importance of protest to Argentine politics has steadily grown, and that a contentious repertoire of participation has consolidated to the point that it can now be considered "normal." I then turn to survey data from Argentina to demonstrate the degree to which protest has normalized in the country across demographic groups.

THE RISE OF THE PROTEST STATE IN ARGENTINA, 1989–2015

Perhaps as much as any Latin American country, Argentina has a rich history of popular mobilization. From the rise of the industrial working class in Buenos Aires in the 1930s and 1940s to the emergence of the *"madres"* of the Plaza de Mayo during the final days of Argentine authoritarianism and state-sponsored terrorism in the early 1980s, social movements have played an important role in Argentine politics for decades. But following the demise of the ruling military junta in 1983 amid widespread demonstrations (Collier and Mahoney 1997), the possibility existed that public debate would be channeled through newly created formal democratic institutions rather than the streets. Indeed, the initial decade of democracy in Argentina did little to dispel that notion. While the new regime certainly had its rocky moments, including President Raúl Alfonsín's premature resignation amid a spiking inflation rate in 1989, large-scale contentious protests would not reemerge in Argentina until the mid-1990s.

The Menem Years—Sowing the Seeds of Contention

In 1989, Carlos Menem, a Peronist (PJ) governor from the small north-western province of La Rioja, succeeded Alfonsín and embarked on an ambitious plan to reduce inflation and trim public excess by pegging the Argentine peso to the U.S. dollar, deregulating markets, and privatizing public services (Svampa and Pereyra 2003). This new economic model represented an abrupt departure from the previous import substitution in-dustrialization approach in Argentina, where a large percentage of workers were either public employees or members of powerful unions that served as intermediaries between the government and industry (Murillo 1997).

Throughout the first half of the 1990s, the reforms were successful by numerous metrics, sparking growth and reducing inflation in a country previously mired in decades of stunted economic progress. However, not every sector benefited from the neoliberal model. Industrial employment fell from 24 percent of total employment in 1991 to 16 percent in 2000 (Bayón and Saraví 2002), and the overall unemployment rate increased from 6 percent in 1990 to 18 percent in 1996 (Svampa and Pereyra 2003). Labor unions were largely stripped of their power, and the country's largest and most important confederation of unions, the CGT (*Confederación General del Trabajo*), split in 1992 over the decision to continue to support Menem's reinvented Peronist party (Etchemendy 2005). While Menem was popular enough amid a booming economy to reform the constitution and seek reelection in 1995, the seeds of discontent had been planted among the recently unemployed and disenfranchised union members who suffered under the neoliberal economic order.

A new era of contention was inaugurated in 1993 with the *santiagazo* in the northern province of Santiago del Estero. As a result of state decentral-ization efforts by Menem, where Argentine provinces were granted greater fiscal autonomy than ever before and tasked with taking over important public services like healthcare and education, Santiago del Estero soon found itself in a fiscal hole (Carrera and Cotarelo 2001). Angered that they were not receiving their paychecks on time—or in some cases at all—*santiagueño* public employees took to the streets, installing roadblocks, looting stores, and occupying and defacing government buildings throughout the provin-cial capital. To put an end to the most violent *pueblada* in Argentine history, the national government eventually intervened, but not before hundreds were injured and as many as ten were dead, and a slew of important government buildings and even the private homes of prominent public officials had been destroyed (Villalón 2007, Cotarelo 1999).

Unrest spread like wildfire throughout Argentina in the following months and years. Beginning with the southern province of Neuquén in 1996, the *piquetero* movement formed as a response to the 1992 privatization of Argentina's state oil company, YPF (*Yacimientos Petrolíferos Fiscales*), which was the largest source of public employment in the country and served as the economic backbone of oil-producing provinces in the Patagonia region. Following privatization, tens of thousands of state employees accustomed to high-paying, secure employment soon found themselves out of work as the new majority stakeholder in the company, Spanish oil giant Repsol, sought to strip down and make more efficient Argentina's largest and most antiquated state industry. Following the initial roadblocks organized in Cutral-Có, Neuquén, the practice expanded to unemployed workers in other cities and economic sectors, where different groups adopted the *piquetero* moniker in their quest for public assistance amid dire economic circumstances (Garay 2007).

Perhaps most notable about the protests in the 1990s was the extent to which newly forged civic organizations were credited with leading this rising tide of contention (Villalón 2007). In a democracy long dominated by a powerful workers' party (the Peronists), which drew its strength in large part from labor unions, it was striking to observe local neighborhood associations and recently inaugurated confederations of the unemployed mobilizing citizens at such a prodigious rate (Garay 2007). The protests of the 1990s were clearly more than just a response to unfortunate economic circumstances—they also resulted from the construction of dense organizational networks that connected individuals enduring similar economic hardship, and provided the platform by which they could advance their claims. Further, these protests indicated that traditional representational outlets were insufficient for channeling active citizens' demands, and reflected a growing lack of trust in Argentina's formal democratic institutions.

Indeed, beyond merely being adversely affected by the economic reforms undertaken by Menem's reimagined Peronist party, there was a sense among many Argentine citizens that they had been duped by a politician who had said one thing during his presidential campaign but had done virtually the exact opposite once in office (Stokes 2001). Menem ran a classic populist campaign, geared toward winning over union leadership and the working class—the traditional backbone of the PJ. Following his election, he not only embarked on a neoliberal economic campaign that crippled many within his traditional support bloc, but did so in a way that subverted political dialogue and compromise, forcing his agenda through using executive decrees and court-packing, among other democratically questionable tactics (O'Donnell 1993, Carey and Shugart 1998, Helmke 2002). While the initially positive results of Menem's economic strategy kept the backlash in check for a brief period of time, this growing sense of betrayal reared its head when *menemismo* began to produce diminishing returns.

The December 2001 Crisis

Years of building tension amid widespread social unrest came to a head in late 2001 following the October midterm elections, which resulted in the highest rates of absenteeism since Argentina returned to democracy, and an unprecedented number of spoiled or null ballots (in Spanish, dubbed the *"voto bronca"*; Figure 5.1). Menem's second term had come and gone, and Argentina's economic prospects were bleak. Two years into a severe economic recession that had brought on unprecedented unemployment, food shortages, and drastic cuts in social spending, economic minister Domingo Cavallo launched an effort to reduce capital flight by restricting the amount of money Argentines could withdraw from their bank accounts—a measure called the *"corralito"* (Vilas 2006)—with virtually no democratic debate and seemingly following the prescriptions of the International Monetary Fund

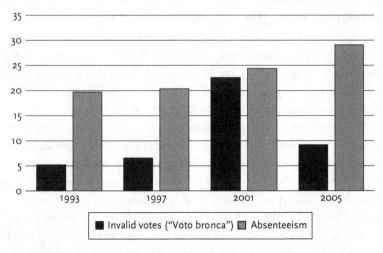

Figure 5.1 Percent absenteeism and "Voto Bronca" in the 2001 Legislative Election
Argentine Ministry of the Interior website.

to a T. Having alienated perhaps the only group of citizens not already protesting in the streets—middle-class Argentines with bank accounts in need of cash but without credit—the government's fate was sealed. In December, citizens of all stripes launched an all-out assault on the incumbent de la Rúa government, setting the stage for perhaps the most contentious moment in Argentine history.

By mid-December 2001, riots had broken out across the country, lootings of supermarkets and neighborhood *kioscos* had become widespread, and massive *cacerolazos*, characterized by the banging of empty pots and pans to symbolize the shortage of basic foodstuffs, were routine (Auyero 2005). De la Rúa declared a state of siege, allowing for the intervention of police and the military to quell the insurrections, which resulted in numerous casualties (Vilas 2006). Nowhere were the protestors bolder and more numerous than in the capital city, where on December 19 and 20 tens of thousands of Argentines staged a *cacerolazo* in the Plaza de Mayo armed with one unifying cry—*"Que se vayan todos!"* (All of them must go!)—a phrase that perfectly captured Argentines' lost faith in the democratic institutions of their country. On December 21, de la Rúa announced his resignation. His successor, Adolfo Rodríguez-Saá, would also resign after barely a week on the job.

More than just a reflection of the dire economic situation, the 2001–2002 protests exposed a growing lack of confidence in formal representative institutions that were deemed corrupt and ineffectual (Levitsky and Murillo 2003). Argentines believed that both of the country's major parties—the Peronists, headed by Menem, and the UCR (*Unión Radical Civil*), represented by de la Rúa's coalition *Alianza* government—had misled voters during their presidential campaigns, and run corrupt administrations that rewarded loyalists and made politically advantageous but economically disastrous policy decisions. The sheer number of null and spoiled votes cast in the October midterms revealed this institutional distrust, as did the sweeping nature of the protestors' rallying cry.

In the weeks leading up to de la Rúa's resignation, political actors had already begun to explore how they might harness the power of these incipient social movements. Auyero's (2007) seminal book on the 2001–2002 riots and lootings in the Buenos Aires capital and *conurbano* area explores this "gray zone" of politics, revealing that Peronist party operatives helped to organize lootings of supermarkets and other protest events as the crisis loomed. Eventually, the former PJ governor of Buenos Aires province, Eduardo Duhalde, would take control of the presidency and help stabilize the Argentine economy. Another Peronist, Néstor Kirchner, succeeded him as president following Menem's withdrawal from the race in the face of certain defeat in the second-round election. Thus, while in many ways the Argentine citizenry accomplished their immediate goal of replacing de la Rúa, they also confirmed the potential usefulness of contentious tactics to a once-powerful political party currently on the fringes of political influence. By 2002, amid heightened citizen engagement and institutional dysfunction, protest had been absorbed in the participatory repertoire in Argentina, deployed almost daily by political elites and citizens alike in pursuit of their goals.

The Kirchner Years—The Consolidation of the Protest State

Much like Menem, Kirchner was a Peronist governor from a peripheral Argentine province—this time the sparsely populated Patagonian province of Santa Cruz—who culminated his meteoric rise in Argentine politics with a *ballotage* victory in April 2003.[1] Having only received about 20 percent of the vote in the first round, Kirchner was tasked with constructing an operational coalition with very little political clout within the traditional Peronist party structure, based largely in the urban core of Buenos Aires, Rosario, and Córdoba.

One of the first places Kirchner looked to build support was among those who were most critical of the government during the crisis years, and particularly the *piquetero* movement, which had emerged as one of the most powerful political groups in the country over the last decade. If Kirchner was going to be able to effectively govern, he needed to prevent the types of destabilizing protests that fomented popular discontent and brought an end to the de la Rúa and Rodríguez-Saá presidencies. So, he reached out to *piquetero* leaders by offering several of them posts in his government, like Jorge Ceballos (*Barrios de Pie*) and Luis D'Elía (*Federación Tierra, Vivienda y Hábitat*). He also renewed the state's commitment to unemployed Argentines in the form of increases in social welfare spending primarily through the *Jefes y Jefas* (Heads of Household) program (Garay 2016). Finally, Kirchner made it a point of emphasis that police officers should not repress protestors, in a conscious effort to avoid making the same mistakes as his predecessors (Levitsky and Murillo 2008).

During Néstor Kirchner's term from 2003 to 2007, the government was able to quell contentious protests for the most part, and secure the election of First Lady and Senator Cristina Fernández de Kirchner to succeed her husband as president. Furthermore, the economy bounced back, as Argentina enjoyed one of the most successful four-year periods of growth in the country's history (Figure 5.2). Fernández de Kirchner won with more

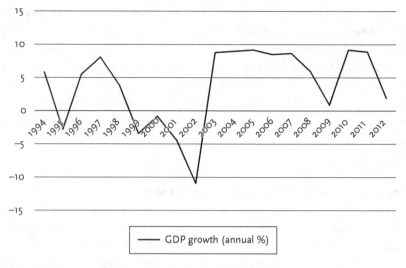

Figure 5.2 GDP Growth in Argentina from 1994–2012
The World Bank: data.worldbank.org/country/argentina

than 45 percent of the popular vote in the first round of the 2007 presidential election—double what her husband received and more than twice as
many votes as her closest competitor—thus precluding the need for a run-
off. However, despite their historic popularity and seeming vice grip on the
Argentine presidency, the Kirchners would find themselves embroiled in
one of Argentina's most contentious moments ever only a few months later.

The first large-scale protests under the two Kirchner governments began
in March 2008. Emboldened by strong economic growth and immense
popularity since Kirchner's 2003 election (see Figure 5.2), Fernández de
Kirchner sought to boost government revenues and decrease domestic
food prices through a controversial export tax that also had the potential to
enervate one of Peronism's most powerful traditional enemies: the agricultural sector (Mangonnet and Murillo 2016). The tax would target soybean
and sunflower exports—two of Argentina's most lucrative commodities on
the international market, due to high commodities prices and demand from
the Asian markets. Almost immediately, Argentine farmers led by rural
labor associations responded with a countrywide "lockout," roadblocks
of major highways, and a massive *cacerolazo* in the Plaza de Mayo, during
which violent clashes between D'Elía's pro-government followers and anti-
government protestors resulted in multiple injuries (Sued 2008).[2] In response, government supporters organized a protest march to counter
that of the farmers in April 2008 that was attended by thousands of
kirchneristas. Finally, when the controversial legislation went up for vote

in the Argentine Senate after passing in the Chamber of Deputies, Vice-President Julio Cobos cast a tie-breaking vote *against* the measure, effectively ending his relationship with the Fernández de Kirchner government.

Since 2008, protest has continued to prosper as a form of political participation in Argentina. An increasingly vocal opposition organized several massive *cacerolazos* in 2012, culminating in a protest event on November 8, 2012 that attracted over 700,000 demonstrators in Buenos Aires alone and hundreds of thousands more in cities across the country (Lindlar 2012). In 2014, a strike by police in Córdoba triggered similar work stoppages nationwide, which eventually resulted in rampant lootings and multiple deaths before provincial governments finally gave in to the protestors' demands. According to Mangonnet and Murillo (2016), whereas rural lockouts were seldom utilized in the prior decade, some 700 similar protests took place in Argentina between 2003 and 2013. Like clockwork, the starts of school years in March of 2015, 2016, and 2017 were delayed by standoffs between teachers' unions and provincial governments, particularly in the chronically underfunded province of Buenos Aires. Fernández de Kirchner's supporters, led by former *piqueteros* and *La Cámpora*, a youth organization founded by her son Máximo, continued to counteract anti-government demonstrations with pro-government ones.

The Argentine Protest State Today

More recently, the mysterious death of an Argentine federal prosecutor, Alberto Nisman, triggered multiple episodes of widespread public demonstrations. As president, Néstor Kirchner tasked Nisman with investigating the 1994 bombing of a Jewish community center in Buenos Aires, the *Asociación Mutual Israelita Argentina* (AMIA). Nearly ten years later, Nisman emerged with allegations that Fernández de Kirchner's government had attempted to make a deal with Iran, whereby Argentine authorities would cover up Iranian involvement in the bombing in exchange for more favorable terms of trade.[3] On the night before the prosecutor was scheduled to present his case in a parliamentary hearing, he was found dead in his apartment with a single gunshot wound to the head.

In response to the tragedy, many Argentines responded by taking to the streets to demand justice for a public servant whose death was highly suspicious, given the serious allegations he had made against the current government. Eventually, a group of Argentina's federal prosecutors organized a massive silent march to demonstrate their support for their fallen colleague, which drew hundreds of thousands to the streets of Buenos

Aires and other cities across the country. As demonstrated by the work of Ernesto Calvo (2016) on social media reactions to Nisman's death, the case revealed the depth of polarization in Argentina after twelve years of Kirchner presidencies, as both sides leapt at the opportunity to accuse the other of wrongdoing. However, it also revealed the alacrity with which any political conflict finds its way to the streets, as political elites called on their followers to join demonstrations, to which citizens responded vociferously.

Another important social movement that has typified the nature of the Argentine protest state is the *Ni Una Menos* ("not one less") movement against femicide and gender violence that arose in 2015. Spurred by a flurry of grisly high-profile murders against young women, activists from women's organizations, political parties, and religious groups organized and staged a massive rally in defense of women's rights in Buenos Aires on June 3, 2015, which drew more than 200,000 attendees (Porter 2015). Activists have continued to convene annually on June 3, and claims have expanded to include rights for the LGBT community, women's reproductive rights, and equal pay. Governments led by Fernández de Kirchner and Mauricio Macri have pledged to respond to the alarming uptick in femicides and domestic violence with educational programs in schools, a national femicide registry, and increased funding for battered women's shelters, but movement leaders have been frustrated by a lack of real progress via formal institutional channels (Bons 2016).

Violence directed at women is a grave problem in Argentina, but it is clearly not unique to that country. According to data from the Small Arms Survey, from 2010–2015 Argentina ranked as one of the least dangerous countries in Latin America for women, and registered less femicides— defined as the killing of a woman because of her sex (Bloom 2008)— per 100,000 women than even the United States. What distinguishes Argentina from other countries in the region, and what made it the first of many where *Ni Una Menos* movements have gained traction, is its level of citizen engagement in politics and the strength of its civil society, nested within a political context where individuals often feel underrepresented via formal institutional vehicles.

Argentina has fully transitioned into a protest state. In Argentina, protest has become so routine that the city government of Buenos Aires actually releases maps of planned roadblocks and demonstrations days before they occur so that commuters can plan accordingly (Figure 5.3). In sum, virtually any political conflict seems to find its way into the streets in Argentina, regardless of the claimant or target of that claim. The following section examines how the makeup of demonstrators lends further empirical support to the theory of the protest state.

Cortes por movilizaciones

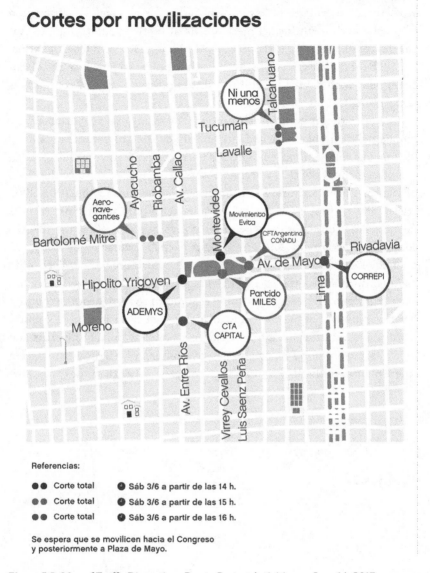

Figure 5.3 Map of Traffic Disruptions Due to Protest Activities on June 14, 2017

QUANTIFYING THE PROTEST STATE IN ARGENTINA

Argentina is a classic example of the protest state. Over the course of time, contentious participation has been absorbed into the "repertoire" of normal, everyday tactics utilized by politically interested and active citizens in the context of a weakly institutionalized democracy (e.g., Levitsky and Murillo 2005). While many social movement scholars have argued over the years that democratization eventually allows for movements' absorption into politics through formal mechanisms of representation, I argue that this process has not occurred as expected in protest states like Argentina, where the combination of a highly organized, engaged populace and disenchantment with formal institutions drives massive levels of contentious social protests.

As argued to this point, where protest is deemed necessary to effectively pursue political objectives and citizens are capable of organizing among likeminded companions, contentious participation can consolidate as an everyday form of political voice. As observed in Figure 5.4, since the dawn of the current era of protest in Argentina leading up to the 2001–2002 crisis, rates of protest have risen steadily, with only slight dips to levels far exceeding those observed before that pivotal crisis. While the spike in contentious activity in 2001 and 2002 is partially explained by a deep economic recession and eventual debt default, which drew the collective ire of Argentines across the sociopolitical spectra, the time period since has been characterized by unprecedented economic prosperity for the country. For this reason, I argue that individuals' lack of faith in formal political institutions, and the success they had in mobilizing during the crisis and precipitating profound changes in the government, paved the way for an era where politics in the streets would be the norm rather than the exception.

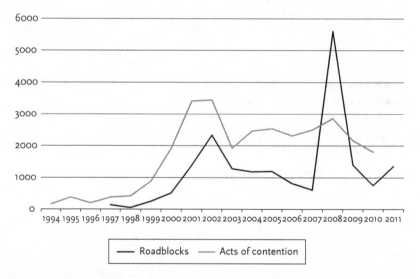

Figure 5.4 The Evolution of Protest in Argentina, 1994–2011
PIMSA 2014, *Nueva Mayoría* 2011

In Argentina, two organizations have taken the initiative to document protest activity since the early 1990s: *Nueva Mayoría* and the *Programa de Investigación sobre el Movimiento de la Sociedad Argentina* (PIMSA). Each measure uses newspaper reports to gather counts of protest events on a monthly basis—in the case of PIMSA, they track dozens of types of contentious acts, whereas the *Nueva Mayoría* measure focuses only on roadblocks.[4] As seen in Figure 5.4, the early to mid-1990s were relatively quiet in terms of protest activity. However, protest rates would surge in the latter part of the decade, with 2001–2002 representing an unprecedented spike in the number of protests that occurred across the country. However, perhaps more noteworthy is the extent to which rates of protest participation have remained high in the aftermath of the crisis, even as the economy has stabilized and, in many ways, prospered. Argentina has had a very healthy recovery following that debacle, growing at some of the most impressive rates in Latin America, which as a region has been thriving since the turn of the century due to high demand for several key commodities (Mangonnet and Murillo 2016). In the case of roadblocks as measured by *Nueva Mayoría*, 2008 (perhaps the peak of Argentina's recent soybean-fueled commodities boom) scores as far and away the most contentious year in recent history. It appears as if a new era of protest was inaugurated around the turn of the millennium, as political actors now seek to utilize protest repertoires to further their goals even in times of relative political and economic stability.

These protest data confirm the extent to which Argentine citizens have increasingly responded in a contentious fashion to a political system that promises democratic representation, yet fails to deliver. As democracy has consolidated in Argentina over the past three decades and individuals have become increasingly politically active, expectations for democracy have risen. The persistence of what citizens view as an overly influential executive branch (i.e., "delegative" democracy according to O'Donnell [1993]), numerous ongoing corruption scandals, and parties that vacillate from one policy stance to the next or disband only to re-form under a different banner, have led many Argentines to sour on formal modes of voicing their claims. In turn, they have looked increasingly to street-based participation as a more aggressive, but frequently effective, alternative method of obtaining representation. This disenchantment is reflected in survey data from the country, in addition to the consolidation of the protest state (Figure 5.4). Figure 5.5 illustrates that Argentina ranks among the bottom in the Americas in system support, a variable constructed by LAPOP to gauge citizen support for key regime institutions like the national legislature, the Supreme Court, and political parties. This places Argentina in a group of similarly contentious cases like Ecuador, Peru, and Brazil, all of

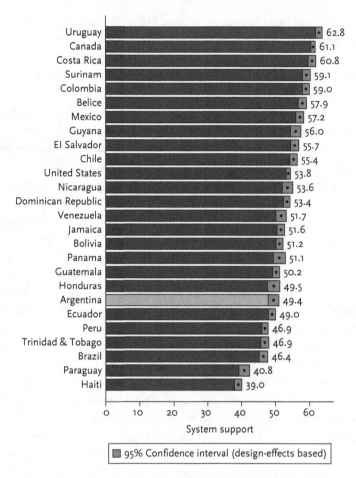

Country	System support
Uruguay	62.8
Canada	61.1
Costa Rica	60.8
Surinam	59.1
Colombia	59.0
Belice	57.9
Mexico	57.2
Guyana	56.0
El Salvador	55.7
Chile	55.4
United States	53.8
Nicaragua	53.6
Dominican Republic	53.4
Venezuela	51.7
Jamaica	51.6
Bolivia	51.2
Panama	51.1
Guatemala	50.2
Honduras	49.5
Argentina	49.4
Ecuador	49.0
Peru	46.9
Trinidad & Tobago	46.9
Brazil	46.4
Paraguay	40.8
Haiti	39.0

System support

■ 95% Confidence interval (design-effects based)

Figure 5.5 System Support in Argentina in Comparative Perspective, 2008–2012
© AmericasBarometer by LAPOP

Support for national institutions is measured by a scale summarizing results of seven B-series questions
(b2 b3 b4 b6 b21 b13 b31) included on the 2008–2012 AmericasBarometer national surveys of Latin
America B2. To what extent do you respect the political institutions of (country)? B3. To what extent do you
think that citizens' basic rights are well protected by the political system of (country)? B4. To what extent
do you feel proud of living under the political system of (country)? B6. To what extent do you think that one
should support the political system of (country)? B13. To what extent do you trust the National Legislature?
B21. To what extent do you trust the political parties? B31. To what extent do you trust the Supreme Court?

which share both low levels of legitimacy in the eyes of their citizens and
surging rates of contentious activity.

On the second key explanatory variable that sheds light on the rise of
the protest state, Argentina also represents a revealing case. Historically,
Argentina is one of the wealthiest Latin American nations and boasts a long
history of high-quality universities, a robust civil society, and the region's
largest middle class. However, key changes in terms of social organization
occurred in the 1990s when Menem began to dismantle labor organizations

and strip Argentines of the mobilizing structures they had utilized to voice their demands in previous decades. The foundation of new neighborhood associations and organized coalitions of the unemployed provided the core organizational framework necessary for Argentine citizens to effectively respond to institutional dysfunction in the late 1990s and early 2000s, and these organizations were in many ways less beholden to traditional hierarchies than labor unions had been in the past (Garay 2007). In the case of the agricultural protests in 2008, disaffected Argentines again tapped into linkages between fellow farmers through labor associations sharing a common interest in maintaining current rates of export taxation (Mangonnet and Murillo 2016). Further, with advances in technology and the rise of social media, Twitter hashtag campaigns like #8N for the anti-government protests on November 8, 2012, and the #NiUnaMenos rallying cry dating back to 2015, have provided an unprecedented opportunity for collective actors to organize almost instantaneously in response to a particular claim (Calvo 2016). In sum, while Argentina is undoubtedly a country characterized by high levels of political engagement historically, at least by regional standards, there is evidence that interest and engagement in politics has reached a zenith just as misgivings about formal institutions have also peaked.

According to data from PIMSA and *Nueva Mayoría*, the number of protests in Argentina surged in the lead-up to the 2001–2002 crisis and has remained high ever since, amid widespread distrust of formal political institutions and surging engagement in politics. In 2008, nearly one in three Argentines claimed to have participated in a protest rally or demonstration in the previous year (LAPOP 2008), and over 5,000 roadblocks were staged nationwide. Without a doubt, protests have become very common, rivaling virtually any other form of political participation in terms of popularity aside from voting (Figure 5.6). But can we classify Argentina as a protest state? In other words, is protest utilized equally across socioeconomic and demographic groups, and do the same variables that predict standard formal modes of political participation also predict which individuals will take part in protests?

In a word, yes. Looking to the AmericasBarometer survey data from Argentina for answers to these questions (LAPOP 2008–2012), we find that in addition to its prevalence as a political activity, several of the classic individual-level predictors of formal political participation—most notably, education and interest in politics (see Verba et al. 1995)—are strongly associated with contentious participation in Argentina (Figure 5.7). Moreover, the degree to which non-contentious forms of community participation and protests are linked, a relationship covered extensively in Chapters 3 and 4, speaks to the "conventional" nature of contentious political participation

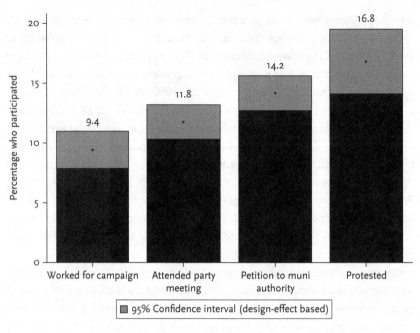

Figure 5.6 Protest Compared to Other Participation in Argentina, 2008–2012
© AmericasBarometer by LAPOP

in Argentina. Perhaps the only standard predictor of conventional participation that is not associated with higher rates of protest is wealth, as no
significant relationship exists between class and protest participation in
Argentina—in fact, protest seems to be equally utilized across the socioeconomic spectrum, net of other explanatory variables (Figure 5.8). However,
while in Argentina socioeconomic class does not appear to be a strong
predictor of participation, evidence from the rest of Latin America has
shown that middle-class individuals are indeed the most likely protestors,
corroborating Verba et al.'s findings from the American context (Moseley
and Layton 2013). Overall, Figure 5.7 demonstrates the degree to which
variables that proxy for political engagement—namely, interest in politics,
years of education, and community participation—serve as the most powerful predictors of protest participation in Argentina.

Just as protest rates appear to be similar across wealth quintiles, protest participation is almost equally prevalent across other key demographic
groups. While 17.1 percent of male respondents surveyed in 2008, 2010,
and 2012 in Argentina responded that they had participated in a protest
during the previous year, 16.5 percent of females responded in the affirmative to the same question—a difference of means indistinguishable from

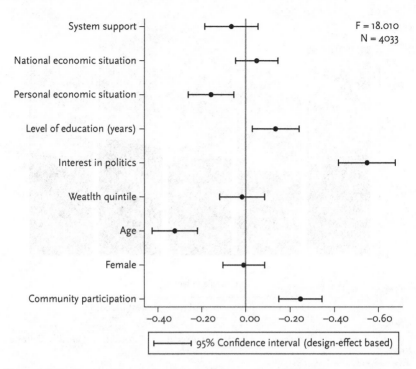

Figure 5.7 Predictors of Protest Participation in Argentina, 2008–2012

© AmericasBarometer, LAPOP, 2008–2012

This figure plots the results of a logistic regression model of protest participation, pooling responses from the 2008, 2010, and 2012 AmericasBarometer national surveys of Argentina. The dots represent coefficients, with those to the right of the centre line being positive and those on the left, negative. Confidence intervals surrounding those point estimates indicate statistical significance at the p<.05 level. Coefficients were normalized here for ease of interpretation. The survey data used for this graph were all nationally representative and stratified by region and urban/rural populations. Design effects associated with the complex nature of the sample, which included clustering, stratification, and weighting, were accounted for in this particular model using the "svy" command on Stata 12. Question wording and model results can be found in the Appendix.

zero. Though protest participation begins to taper off after individuals turn fifty-five years old (probably for obvious reasons related to the sheer physicality of demonstrating in the streets), differences between age brackets below that level are slight (LAPOP 2008–2012). In sum, while protestors appear to make up a younger than average slice of the citizenry, they otherwise constitute a fairly representative cross-section of Argentina's politically active population, deviating little from voters and other habitual participants in politics.

When it comes to individuals who are actually involved in Argentine political parties, the degree to which protest participation has become a routine component of politics is even more evident. Individuals who sympathize with a particular party or have worked for a party—that is, Argentines who are among the most active in *formal* political organizations—are

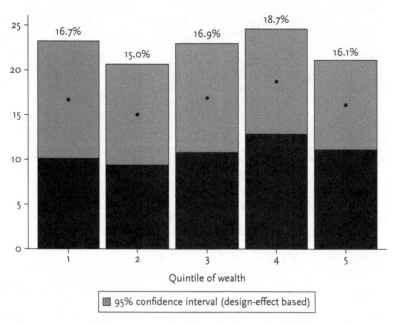

Figure 5.8 Rates of Protest Participation in Argentina According to Wealth Quintile, 2008–2012

© AmericasBarometer by LAPOP

The measure for wealth utilized here draws from a weighted index that measures material possessions based on ownership of certain household goods such as televisions, refrigerators, conventional and cellular telephones, vehicles, washing machines, microwave ovens, indoor plumbing, indoor bathrooms, and computers. See Cordova 2009 for a detailed explanation of this approach.

far more likely to have participated in a protest in the previous twelve months than citizens who maintain no such affiliation. More than one-third of Argentines who report a party affiliation participated in a street march or demonstration during the previous twelve months, and nearly three times as many individuals who worked for a particular campaign reported protesting as those who did not (Figure 5.9). Likewise, as confirmed in Chapter 4, labor association membership is also correlated with higher probabilities of protesting—a relationship well-documented by the literature (Mangonnet and Murillo 2016, Garay 2007). It thus appears that in Argentina, formal political organizations and contentious politics are one and the same, as the most active members of Argentina's most important political organizations are also some of the most likely participants in street protests.

One other indicator of protest's normalization in Argentina is the degree to which clientelistic political parties have adopted "protest-buying" tactics to substitute or supplement traditional vote-buying schemes—a phenomenon covered at some length in Chapter 4. There is a prevailing academic

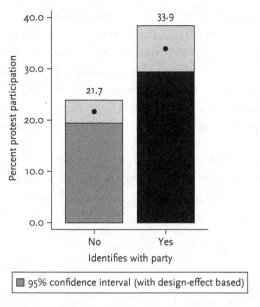

Figure 5.9 Protest Participation by Party Identifiers vs. Non–Party Identifiers, 2008
© AmericasBarometer, LAPOP

consensus (O'Donnell 1993) and ample empirical evidence (Brusco, Nazareno, and Stokes 2004, Calvo and Murillo 2013) to suggest that clientelistic practices are widespread throughout the country. Particularly given that Argentine political parties are not particularly programmatic and lack strong ideological underpinnings, they are deeply reliant on the clientelistic allocation of public resources for electoral support (Calvo and Murillo 2004). This has become increasingly salient since the Peronist party reconfigured its organization from a labor union–based party to clientelistic machines as a way of readapting its partisan structure to the changing trends of economic liberalization (Levitsky 2003). Where protest pays, like in Argentina and other protest states, it makes good sense for clientelistic parties to exchange material gifts for street demonstrations.

CONCLUSION

In this chapter I have attempted to demonstrate that over the past twenty-five years, Argentina has transitioned into a country where protest constitutes a normal form of political voice, utilized by a wide cross-section of Argentine society to address a diverse set of claims. I explain this transition by emphasizing the intersection of weak political institutions and a vibrant civil society, readily mobilized in response to economic and political grievances. I also present data that corroborate this explanation, as the number of roadblocks and acts of contention has remained high in the country since the late 1990s, and protest seems to have normalized to a far greater extent in Argentina than in regimes like Chile and Uruguay.

In the following chapter I shift focus to the subnational level in Argentina, where wide variation exists in terms of the extent to which social protest has taken hold across Argentine provinces. By sorting out how the stark differences observed among subnational units in Argentina influence the quantity and quality of protests that occur within their borders, Chapter 6 seeks to shed further light on the national-level analysis while also deriving new insights regarding the consequences of the uneven nature of democracy in many emerging regimes.

CHAPTER 6

Narrowing the Focus

The Protest State at the Subnational Level in Argentina

Previous chapters have focused on variation in social protest at the national level, first comparing countries utilizing second-level indicators for institutional quality and survey data on protest participation, then further investigating the Argentine case in historical and contemporary perspective. However, this chapter seeks to evaluate the degree to which Argentine provinces differ in terms of democratic quality and citizen engagement, and how that variation might bear on contentious politics within their territories.

Based on an extensive literature on subnational politics in Argentina, I argue that a similar dynamic to what we observe at the national level surfaces, wherein democratic institutions are unresponsive enough in many provinces that contentious participation is deemed necessary by politically active citizens to effect any kind of political change. However, I also expect that certain Argentine provincial systems actually outperform the national regime, achieving a level of competitive multiparty democracy similar to what we find in Latin American countries like Uruguay, Chile, or Costa Rica. On the other hand, Argentine provinces vary a great deal in terms of political engagement, for reasons related both to uneven economic development and stark variation in terms of subnational democracy.

On that note, and deviating slightly from the national-level story, I expect that in certain subnational contexts within Argentina, patrimonial governments dominate political life to the extent that the expectation for democratic representation among citizens has evaporated. Therefore, we might expect low rates of political engagement in these contexts, as individuals are discouraged from forging the organizational networks necessary to mobilize collective action. However, when protest *does* occur in these contexts, I argue it is more likely violent in nature, given the absence of public space for peaceful contention. In other words, while protest activity is generally more prevalent at intermediate levels of democracy, more aggressive collective action should increase at the lowest levels of democratic quality.

In the following pages I first consider how subnational variation in terms of democratic quality might bear on patterns of popular mobilization across Argentine provinces. I draw on extant research to propose an updated, but complementary, theoretical framework for understanding the relationship between subnational democracy and diverse repertoires of contentious politics, vis-à-vis the national-level story. Then, I draw on three specific provincial cases—Buenos Aires, Mendoza, and San Luis—to help illustrate my theoretical perspective. These case studies are based predominantly on fieldwork carried out in each province from March to June 2013 with support from the National Science Foundation (SES-1263807).

SUBNATIONAL DEMOCRACY AND PROTEST IN ARGENTINA

Argentina is undoubtedly a contentious case, as illustrated in the previous chapter. At certain moments the country has seemingly erupted in mass protests nationwide that have had serious consequences for the country's politics, and even resulted in changes in government. Now, it seems that virtually any political conflict is mediated at least in part in the streets. Yet this national-level account of Argentine protests leaves two questions unanswered: Does protest activity vary substantially *within* Argentina? And if so, what explains the uneven nature of protest activity found within the country?

According to data on roadblocks and other acts of contention across Argentina's twenty-three provinces, wide variation exists in terms of the extent to which protest has caught on in Argentine subnational regimes. The most obvious initial conclusion one might draw from Figure 6.1 is that the population of the province is what drives levels of contentious politics, as the top three cases in terms of average annual protest events are the country's three most populous provinces. But it seems as if other factors are at play as well—indeed, several more sparsely populated provinces like Jujuy, Entre Rios, and Neuquén all rank relatively high in terms of annual

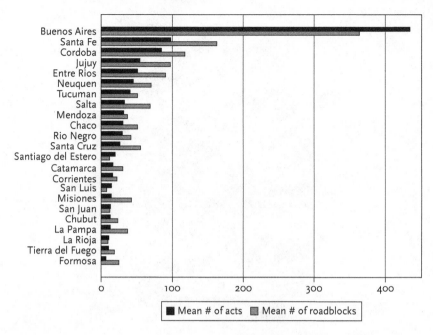

Figure 6.1 Average Annual Acts of Contention and Roadblocks by Province, 1994–2011
Catamarca, Formosa, La Rioja, San Luis, and Santa Cruz have indefinite reelection for the governor, and of that group only Catamarca has experienced a transition in power.

acts of contention, while provinces of a similar size like Formosa and La Rioja register virtually no protests during the period under consideration.

Moving beyond population to other potential explanations of this variation, one might wonder if levels of economic development or even geography might play a role in explaining variation in protest activity. However, at first glance, no obvious relationship surfaces between economic circumstances and variation in protest activity across provinces. Indeed, both poor and rich provinces can be counted among the "most contentious" cases (e.g., Jujuy and Neuquén, respectively), while the same can be said for the group of provinces with lower rates of protest activity (e.g., Formosa and Tierra del Fuego). Clearly the 2001–2002 economic crisis produced a spike in protest activity, but the extremely high number of protests in 2008 occurred during times of relative prosperity at the height of the commodities boom (Mangonnet and Murillo 2016). Further, it seems the spike in protest during 2001 and 2002 did not occur uniformly across provinces. Figure 6.2A and Figure 6.2B illustrates that three provinces—La Rioja, Jujuy, and San Juan—located in western to northwestern Argentina and characterized by relatively small populations and similar levels of development, experienced drastically different rates

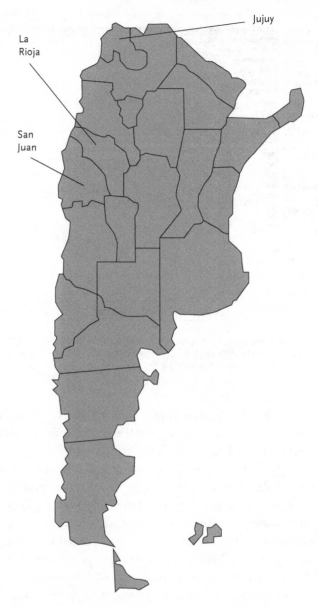

Figure 6.2A Acts of Rebellion in Three Provinces During the 2001–2002 Crisis

of protest participation during Argentina's most dire economic crisis. For all of these reasons, I look to political factors to help explain this striking subnational variation in protest activity.

Since the Third Wave of democracy hit Latin America, scholars have noted that democratization has failed to take hold uniformly within many

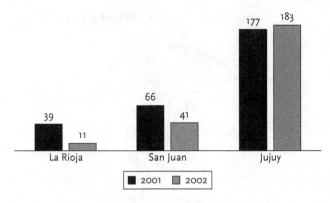

Figure 6.2B 2001–2002 Economic Crisis Acts of contention in La Rioja, San Juan, and Jujuy

of the region's countries—that is, "authoritarian enclaves" remain in regimes that are, at the national level, ostensibly democratic (Fox 1994). In such so-called "brown areas" of institutional and economic development, subnational politics might scarcely resemble modern conceptualizations of democracy, characterized instead by personalistic machines, uncompetitive elections, and political clientelism (O'Donnell 1993). In these subnational regimes, the incumbent government often wins reelection by vast margins, and in the case of several provinces in Argentina they enjoy the perks of indefinite reelection (see Figures 6.3 and 6.4). This subnational "unevenness" has been demonstrated to have important consequences for the political rights of citizens, economic development outcomes, and individuals' attitudes toward the national political regime (e.g., Hiskey 2003, Gibson 2005, Hiskey and Bowler 2005, Hiskey and Moseley n.d.).

A CURVILINEAR RELATIONSHIP BETWEEN INSTITUTIONAL OPENNESS AND PROTEST?

Based on the findings from Chapter 3, one might expect that poor institutional performance in Argentine provinces would have a stimulative effect on protest participation—a perspective that draws on an extensive literature on political opportunities and protest. However, I argue here that this is only partially true. In his seminal 1973 article in the *American Political Science Review*, Eisinger sought to explain why violent uprisings occurred in certain U.S. cities during the American Civil Rights Movement, but not others. While the dominant theoretical school at the time attributed urban

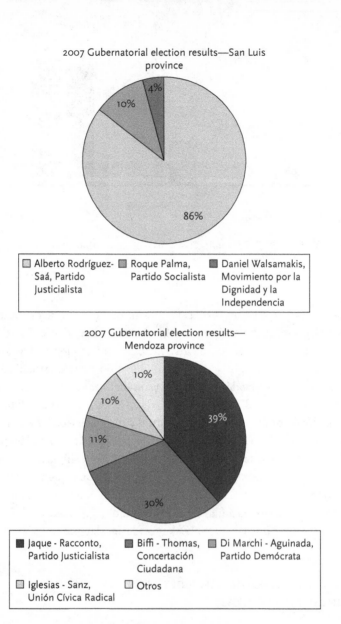

2007 Gubernatorial election results—San Luis province

4%
10%
86%

Alberto Rodríguez-Saá, Partido Justicialista   Roque Palma, Partido Socialista   Daniel Walsamakis, Movimiento por la Dignidad y la Independencia

2007 Gubernatorial election results—Mendoza province

10%
10%
11%
39%
30%

Jaque - Racconto, Partido Justicialista   Biffi - Thomas, Concertación Ciudadana   Di Marchi - Aguinada, Partido Demócrata
Iglesias - Sanz, Unión Cívica Radical   Otros

Figure 6.3 Sample Election Results from San Luis and Mendoza

riots by African Americans to relative deprivation—namely the "perceived discrepancy between value expectations and value capabilities" (Gurr 1970, 37)—Eisinger was interested in how characteristics of local political systems might make citizens more or less likely to adopt contentious tactics. Specifically, his theory was grounded in the degree to which municipal institutions were "open" or "closed" to effective political participation by African Americans. In short, he determined that the relationship between

Province	Number of rotations since 1983
Formosa	0
Jujuy	0
La Pampa	0
La Rioja	0
Neuquén	0
Rio Negro	0
San Luis	0
Santa Cruz	0
Buenos Aires	1
Catamarca	1
Córdoba	1
Misiones	1
Salta	1
Santa Fe	1
Santiago del Estero	1
Tucumán	2
Chaco	3
Chubut	3
Corrientes	3
Entre Rios	3
Mendoza	3
San Juan	3
Tierra del Fuego	3

Figure 6.4 Rotations in the Party of Provincial Governors in Argentina (as of 2012)

political openness and protest participation was a curvilinear one—that is, open systems facilitate effective participation via formal vehicles, thus making protest less consequential, while closed systems prevent widespread protest participation due to the costliness of participating. It is at *intermediate* levels of openness that institutions are not responsive to the extent that they render protest unnecessary, yet are open enough that individuals can draw on existing civil society organizations to mobilize without fear of repression.

While the initial unveiling of this theoretical approach focused on the subnational level, subsequent studies have attempted to apply the political contextual framework to national political institutions. Eventually, a new avenue of empirical research began to crystalize that examined "political opportunities," or "consistent—but not necessarily formal or permanent—dimensions of the political environment that provide incentives for people to undertake collective action by affecting their expectations for success or failure" (Tarrow 1998, 85; see also Tilly 1978). These dimensions can include the nature of political competition, characteristics of party systems and legislative bodies, and rule of law institutions—namely, any political contextual factors that influence social movements' prospects for "(a) mobilizing, (b) advancing particular claims rather than others, (c) cultivating some alliances rather than others, (d) employing particular political strategies and tactics rather than others, and (e) affecting mainstream institutional politics and policy" (Meyer 2004, 126; see also Kitschelt 1986).

Eisinger's conceptualization of American cities in the 1960s according to political openness seems especially pertinent to contemporary politics in a region like Latin America, where subnational regimes are similarly uneven in terms of how effectively they incorporate citizens in the political process (e.g., O'Donnell 1993, Fox 1994, Gervasoni 2010). On the closed end of the democratic openness spectrum, there exists no credible threat to the political machine in power. Opposition parties in these contexts are weakly organized and lack necessary funding, and the dominant political force in the province exerts a great deal of control over local media and civil society. Moreover, political elites in closed systems frequently wield a great deal of control over the judiciary and local law enforcement, and often come from a select group of powerful political families who use their discretionary control over public employment to reward loyalists and punish dissidents (Chavez 2004, Behrend 2011). In many cases, these types of subnational regimes develop in small, peripheral provinces with limited productive activity, thus granting the ruling machine immense influence over the local economy (Gervasoni 2010). Closed regimes might impede consequential formal participation, as the winner in virtually any local election is predetermined, and many voters show up on election day only to ensure they continue to receive clientelistic rewards.

An Adapted Theory of Protest in Uneven Democracies

Given the absence of strong opposition parties and meekness of local media and civil society, citizens in closed regimes encounter difficulties when attempting to mobilize opposition. Further, the ruling machine's access to economic and juridical power makes any potential protestors vulnerable to harsh punishment. Thus, given the costliness of mobilization, I argue that peaceful street marches and demonstrations should occur less frequently within these provincial regimes. However, instances where citizens *do* manage to organize and take to the streets are more likely characterized by aggressive repertoires of contention—such as roadblocks, building occupations, and lootings—given their inability to influence the provincial government through more moderate action. So while closed contexts reduce the number of peaceful demonstrations, they should increase the prevalence of aggressive, oftentimes violent contention.

At high levels of subnational democracy, more than one party competes for political power with realistic hopes of attaining office—in other words, there is "institutionalized uncertainty" (Przeworski 1991). In these more liberal contexts media is free, with different news outlets representing distinct economic and political sectors, some of which are openly critical of the incumbent government. Such provincial regimes also boast independent judiciaries and law enforcement, which treat citizens equitably regardless of their partisan affiliation (Chavez 2004). For these reasons, political engagement is often high. In open provincial regimes, power has changed hands several times without incident, and the indefinite reelection of governors is prohibited. Open regimes should provide citizens with numerous formal outlets for political participation through which they can feel at least somewhat efficacious, given the diversity of electoral options and the general inclusiveness of the provincial regime. Certainly some protest can be expected, as is the case in any democratic regime—especially considering that protestors might take issue with policy decisions and the quality of representation at the national level—but most conflict will be mediated through non-confrontational and, in many cases, formal channels. Moreover, instances of aggressive protests that result in violent stand-offs between the government and demonstrators should be least common in this type of subnational regime.

Finally, regimes at intermediate levels of subnational democracy typify the protest-producing contexts outlined by Eisinger and others, where political structures are not fully accommodating of opposition voices and participation yet are not so closed off that potential movements have no organizational capacity or hope that their actions might make a difference. In other words, nontraditional forms of participation might be deemed necessary to effectively influence policymakers, but are not so costly as to render them unlikely. An example might be a province where one party has always controlled the governorship and legislature, making electoral participation ineffectual in large part. However, elections are increasingly competitive, independent media exists, and repression is rarely utilized to quell anti-government demonstrations. In such a case where a hegemonic provincial party exists but there are still reasons for citizens in the opposition to believe that (1) they are capable of effectively organizing movements via

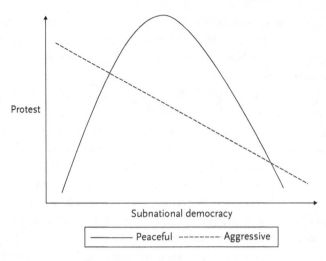

Protest

Subnational democracy

———— Peaceful --------- Aggressive

Figure 6.5 Subnational Democracy and Protest

relatively high levels of citizen engagement and (2) those movements might precipitate a positive response from the government without resorting to aggressive or violent tactics, peaceful protests flourish. However, aggressive contention will be more subdued in these contexts than in more closed settings, as citizens have enough opportunities for meaningful nonviolent mobilization to preclude more drastic options.

In sum, where democratic institutions become less accessible to citizens, and pseudo-authoritarian leaders have a tight grip on local politics, aggressive forms of political protest will become more common. However, the relationship between subnational democracy and protest is more nuanced, as peaceful demonstrations are actually *least* common in closed political contexts, and diminish again in highly democratic settings. Therefore, while the relationship between subnational democracy and aggressive protest is negative, the relationship between subnational democracy and peaceful protests can be characterized as conforming to an inverted "U" shape—that is, Eisinger's curvilinear relationship between openness and protest (Figure 6.5).

Figure 6.6 illustrates how the number of contentious events varies based on provincial regime characteristics. Using Gervasoni's (2010) subnational democracy scores (which will be further discussed in Chapter 7) divided into democracy "terciles," we find the lowest levels of contentiousness among Argentina's *most* and *least* democratic provinces. The highest levels of protest activity are found in mixed contexts, in keeping with the expectations outlined above. However, it must be said that no other variables have been accounted for in this comparison, making these observations

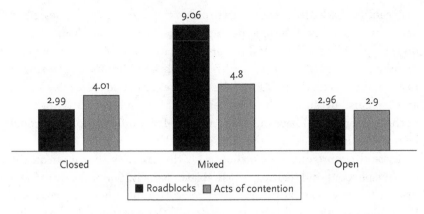

Figure 6.6 Protests across Provincial Political Environments: Average Annual Events per 100,000 Citizens in Argentine Provinces, 1994–2011
Nueva Mayoría 2012, PIMSA 2014

merely suggestive in nature. In the following section I consider three provinces that fall in each category in greater depth, providing more nuanced information as to how subnational political contexts affect individuals' abilities to coordinate and participate in contentious activities.

I must also stress that we are generally dealing with a wider range of democratic regime openness *within* many countries in Latin America than *across* those same countries. For this reason, I argue that protest fades in undemocratic contexts to an extent that we do not observe at the national level. However, the national-level framework presented in previous chapters still applies, in large part. In provinces where democratic institutions fail to fulfill the democratic promise of representation, and levels of citizen engagement in politics are high, I anticipate to find the highest rates of protest activity. Yet in many of the most undemocratic provinces in Argentina and other regimes, political engagement is often suppressed by authoritarian governments that enjoy high levels of economic autonomy (McMann 2006) in the provinces over which they preside. In the following pages I seek to explore both the larger argument regarding the protest state at the provincial level, and the more nuanced subnational adaptation that hypothesizes a decline in peaceful demonstrations in the most undemocratic local contexts.

SUBNATIONAL INSTITUTIONS AND PROTEST: LESSONS FROM THREE PROVINCES

This section draws on three provincial case studies to help illustrate how subnational political environments shape contentious protest repertoires in Argentina. Each case corresponds to one of the three ideal types described above, and a section of the openness spectrum. These case studies are based on (1) my reading of historical research by local academics and provincial media outlets and (2) interviews with protestors, public officials, and other resident experts on the politics of the provinces of Buenos Aires, Mendoza, and San Luis.[1] Because of the delicate nature of the subject matter of some of these interviews, I have omitted any identifying information that could be traced to interviewees in the discussion below.[2]

These three provinces were chosen for the diversity they offer on the key independent and dependent variables—namely, political context and protest activity—but also for their similarities on other key variables. While Buenos Aires is by far the most populous province in Argentina and, for that reason, a different animal in some respects, all three provinces could be characterized as middle income in terms of per capita PBG (*Producto Bruto Geográfico*, or provincial economic productivity) and relatively high in terms of human development (INDEC 2010). While Argentina's northern provinces are very poor and underdeveloped, and its southern energy-producing provinces are located far above the national averages on classic development metrics (e.g., education levels, infant mortality, food scarcity), Argentina's middle corridor of provinces— Buenos Aires, Córdoba, Mendoza, San Luis, and Santa Fé—are all largely agricultural and upper-middle income when compared to other provinces. In sum, while this selection of cases is probably not perfect by Mill's (1843) standards for the "method of difference" approach to comparative analysis, it does provide examples of three provincial environments characterized by similar levels of economic and human development, but vastly different institutional environments and contentious repertoires.

SAN LUIS: THE COMPLEX INTERACTION BETWEEN INSTITUTIONS AND PROTEST IN A CLOSED REGIME

The province of San Luis is located in the *Cuyo* region of Argentina, in the center west (Figure 6.7). San Luis is a sparsely populated province that was underdeveloped historically, lacking the fertile soil of the *Pampas* region or any major urban center. Politically, San Luis has been one of the least competitive and most overtly authoritarian provinces in Argentina since democratization in 1983 at a minimum, but probably well before that. Two brothers from one of the province's most important families, Adolfo and Alberto Rodríguez-Saá, alternated serving as governor of San Luis from 1983 to 2011, during which time each brother also served multiple terms

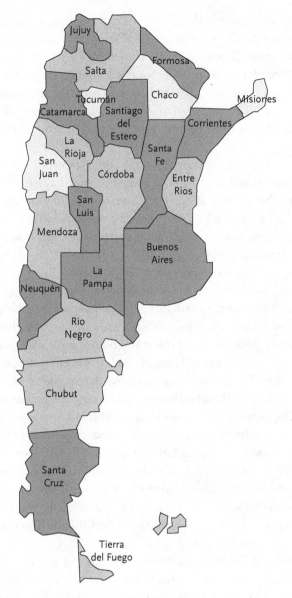

Figure 6.7 A Map of Argentine Provinces

as a national senator. Adolfo actually held the governorship for five consecutive terms, after managing in 1987 to reform the San Luis constitution to include the indefinite reelection of governors.

Beyond simply occupying important elected offices in San Luis politics, the Rodríguez-Saá brothers have also possessed several other distinct advantages that they have used to maintain their political hegemony in the province. Beginning in the 1980s, the two major newspapers (*El Diario de San Luis* and *La Opinión*) and several important television outlets in the province were all eventually purchased by either the Rodríguez-Saá family itself or close friends who occupied important positions in their administrations (Behrend 2011). This has allowed the Rodríguez-Saá brothers to maintain a great deal of control over the content of local media, and the ability to place pro-government propaganda in major media outlets at little cost.

From an economic standpoint, the Rodríguez-Saá brothers have possessed several other sources of influence that have permitted them to dominate the provincial economy and continually obtain reelection. Because of San Luis' small size and relative overrepresentation in the national congress, it, like its fellow smaller provinces, receives a great deal of federal funding under Argentina's co-participation scheme—much more per capita than the most populated provinces. This fact has allowed the Rodríguez-Saá brothers to invest heavily in public housing, welfare programs, and infrastructure (Bianchi 2013). Indeed, a sizeable percentage of the *puntano*[3] population has either been employed by the provincial government[4] or lives in one of the many homes built with public funds, which cost next to nothing and range from humble public housing projects to larger homes for middle-class families.[5] According to local academic Matias Bianchi, from 1983 to 2000 the San Luis government constructed 43,202 public houses[6] that were made available to anyone and ranged from modest, one-bedroom *casitas* to four-bedroom homes found in suburban areas outside of the capital city (Bianchi 2013). One professor at *Universidad Nacional de San Luis* (UNSL) explained to me that the mortgage on his three-bedroom house was about $100 a month—much cheaper than a privately constructed home of similar quality. While he was no fan of the Rodríguez-Saá brothers and openly recognized the illiberal nature of San Luis politics, the offer was too good to refuse.

One prominent Unión Cívica Radical (UCR) leader in San Luis lamented that building the party's base in the province was nearly impossible amidst such high levels of dependence on the government for housing, employment, and sustenance. He listed several cases where his supporters had been fired from their public jobs or denied their monthly cash transfers after Rodríguez-Saá operatives discovered they had attended a UCR rally. In his words, competing against the PJ in San Luis was like playing football on a *cancha inclinada* (uneven playing field). Another *puntana* activist said that the provincial government actually required that individuals participate in a ceremonial handing over of the keys to obtain public housing, which was always attended by one of the Rodríguez-Saá brothers and a small group of journalists who would document the event in the next day's edition of the provincial paper. One of her friends who was also an active member of the province's small political opposition had recently refused to partake in the ceremony, and was shortly notified that her contract was void and she would not receive a house.

Another key facet of the Rodríguez-Saá dominance of San Luis politics has been the Industrial Promotion Law, which went into effect in the 1980s under President Alfonsín. This legislation was originally drafted under the presidency of Juan Perón in 1973 as an effort to compensate the western Argentine provinces that sustained the heaviest casualties during the War for Independence (Catamarca, La Rioja, San Juan, and San Luis). The law essentially created tax-free zones in each of the four provinces, providing strong incentives for companies to relocate at least some phase of production to these four previously lagging provincial economies. This advantage resulted in San Luis' transition to a middle-class province, and built a great deal of political capital for the Rodríguez-Saá brothers for overseeing a period of rapid growth (Bianchi 2013).

According to both *Nueva Mayoría* and PIMSA data, San Luis has maintained one of the lowest rates of protest participation in Argentina since 1993, though their relative standing compared to other provinces becomes somewhat higher when one accounts for population. Interviews with local activists, politicians, and academics reinforced the idea that organizing movements against the Rodríguez-Saá was exceedingly difficult and in some cases dangerous. Generally, opportunities for citizen engagement of any kind are few and far between, given the Rodríguez-Saá brothers' presence in virtually every sphere of social and political life.

One local activist recounted the events of the *multisectorial*—a social movement named for the multiple sectors of *puntano* society that banded together to protest against a highly controversial redistricting effort led by the Rodríguez-Saá brothers in 2004. While the Rodríguez-Saá's local arm of the PJ dominated politics at the provincial level, they were weaker in the capital city, where the UCR continued to win municipal elections on occasion. The brothers viewed this as a threat to their provincial dominance, and concocted a plan that would divide the city government into five different sub-cities, aiming to counteract the mayor elected from the UCR stronghold with four Rodríguez-Saá loyalists—in other words, a San Luis version of American gerrymandering.

For the first time under the reign of the Rodríguez-Saá, a preponderance of *puntano* citizens declared that they had had enough and responded by voicing their grievances in a highly aggressive fashion. Led by opposition parties, anti-Rodríguez-Saá union leaders (mostly associated with the

Central de Trabajadores de la Argentina [CTA]), prominent academics at the UNSL, and religious leaders, a reported 40,000 protestors congregated in front of the *casa de gobierno* to voice their resistance to what they viewed as bald-faced political maneuvering that would have serious consequences for how they would be taxed, what schools their children would attend, and, most importantly, their cultural identities as citizens of San Luis. *Puntanos* were also well aware that towns where the opposition won often found their funding mysteriously disappear, as was the case in the nearby touristic city of Merlo (Rosenberg 2004), and sought to prevent suffering a similar fate in the UCR-controlled section of the capital.

The protests began in March of 2004, and would continue for months. Quickly the events turned violent, as then-governor Alberto Rodríguez-Saá ordered the provincial police to crack down on the protestors with tear gas and batons. Rodríguez-Saá loyalists also took to the streets to carry out a counter-demonstration, and clashed with the anti-government protestors in dramatic fashion (La Gaceta 2004). In retaliation, the demonstrators began peppering the *casa de gobierno* with rocks, vandalizing it and several other public buildings and burning tires in the streets. The most violent confrontation between the police and protestors occurred in May, when fifteen protestors were hospitalized for injuries inflicted by the police, and fifty-five demonstrators were imprisoned (San Martín 2004). As the protestors shifted their focus from the proposed redistricting to myriad other claims regarding the Rodríguez-Saá family's domination of San Luis politics, they began to look to the national government for help, demanding a federal intervention. Eventually, Hebe de Bonafini, founder and leader of the *Madres de la Plaza de Mayo* movement, joined the protestors in San Luis, proclaiming,

> I know the Rodríguez-Saá, and they are corrupt fascists. In Argentina, we can't allow for the existence of hidden dictatorships. San Luis is a hidden dictatorship, and the police repress anyone who works for and demands justice and democracy. (Página12, 2004; author's translation).

Just when it seemed that the multisectorial demonstrations would result in fundamental political change for the province, the national government refused to intervene, the provincial government backed down on their redistricting efforts, and eventually the protests dissipated. As evident in Figure 6.8, which compares San Luis to Buenos Aries and Mendoza, protest rates were low before the events of 2004 and have for the most part remained low since. Yet at the same time, the multisectorial was clearly a much more contentious moment for San Luis than anything experienced

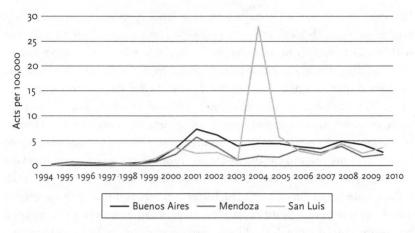

Figure 6.8 Acts of Contention per 100,000 Citizens: Buenos Aries, Mendoza, and San Luis

by the other two provinces. Given the lack of institutional alternatives, protestors seized on a slight opening to mount a massive opposition protest movement, which served as a unique opportunity to voice long-stifled claims in a province where such movements are largely forbidden.

Indeed, on the only occasion when a large-scale protest mobilization occurred in San Luis, it was met swiftly with repression by the provincial government, and while successful in the short term in drawing thousands of citizens to the streets, produced little in the way of long-term political change. Thus, while the 2004 multisectorial attracted the participation of an unprecedented percentage of the San Luis population, it was only a remarkable blip in a province otherwise dominated by the Rodríguez-Saá for the past thirty years. For example, hardly anyone in San Luis protested during the 2001–2002 national economic and political crises, and even during recent years when protests have raged across most of the rest of the country (e.g., 2008), citizens of San Luis have remained conspicuously silent.

One prominent member of the UCR party in San Luis remarked on what he perceived was the dominant strategy utilized by the Rodríguez-Saá to contain social movements: ignoring social protest whenever possible and hoping demonstrators eventually gave up on having their claims addressed:

> in this sense, the strategy followed permanently by the government of San Luis province, which since 1983 has meant the brothers Adolfo and Alberto Rodríguez-Saá, has been to wear down social protest, refusing to implement the types of mechanisms for social conflict resolution that would create dialogue (between protestors and the government). In other words, they resist and resist until eventually the protest loses momentum as time goes by. [7]

However, one thing that became very clear from spending time in San Luis and speaking with local activists and politicians about their experiences with social movements, was that while protests were uncommon due to their relative costliness compared to those in more liberal contexts, the likelihood that violence would ensue if protests *did* get off the ground was high. One veteran activist with whom I spoke led the front lines during the multisectorial and was at one point knocked unconscious by a rock thrown by a member of a pro-Rodríguez-Saá union, and he was eventually thrown in jail. For him, the only available strategy for effecting change in San Luis was this type of direct action, though he admitted it was often hard to rally fellow *puntanos* to his side amid high levels of repression and the potential economic punishments often handed down in an economy so dominated by the provincial state. So, while protests appear to be less common in a closed provincial context like San Luis, the possibility seems high that the protests that do occur will be aggressive in nature.[8]

MENDOZA: DIMINISHED PROTEST IN ARGENTINA'S MOST DEMOCRATIC PROVINCE

Mendoza neighbors San Luis to the west and is also part of the Cuyo region of Argentina, but from a political standpoint the two provinces could not be more different.[9] Since the country's democratization in 1983, Mendoza has played host to strong multiparty competition, an independent and free press, and a diversified economy characterized by nominal public employment and low levels of clientelism. Despite having only one significant urban center—the provincial capital that shares the same name—Mendoza has never been dominated by one family or cadre of political and economic elites, and boasts a political system where the principle of separation of powers is highly observed and valued. It is also home to a diverse collection of citizen organizations, boasting one of the highest concentrations of civil associations per 1,000 citizens in Argentina (MECON 2010).

Unlike at the national level, where Peronism has been the dominant party since its inception with the Radicals running a distant second, Mendoza possesses three significant political parties: the PJ, UCR, and the Democratic Party (PD), a center-right party found only in Mendoza province. The UCR and PJ have alternated in the governorship since 1983, and the PD has maintained a steady presence in the provincial legislature, even winning a plurality of the seats in 1999. All three parties possess strong organizations that carry out community outreach programs throughout the province, build alliances within the provincial and national legislatures (where the PD has aligned itself with the Buenos Aires-based PRO), and maintain fairly consistent and distinguishable ideological platforms.

Among the consequences of multiparty competition in Mendoza has been an independent judiciary and strong rule-of-law institutions, as no dominant political party has been able to parlay their electoral strength into similar authority over judicial/legal institutions (Chavez 2004). Unlike San Luis, Mendoza is also home to several independent provincial newspapers that are owned by different groups and are free to criticize the incumbent government without fear of retribution. For these reasons, Mendoza has routinely been ranked as one of the most democratic provinces in Argentina (e.g., Gervasoni 2010, Giraudy 2010). A former editor of the province's most important newspaper, *Los Andes*, suggested that Mendoza's democratic history could be traced to its "closer proximity to Chile than to Buenos Aires, its strong middle class, and the degree to which those factors produced a strong Radical party that could compete with Peronism,"[10] unlike in many other Argentine provinces.

Another way in which Mendoza differs from provinces like San Luis is its thriving private sector. Mendoza is Argentina's leading producer of wine, which in addition to being widely consumed domestically has over the past decade become one of the country's leading exports (Wines of Argentina 2011).[11] With the growth of the wine industry, Mendoza has also become a popular vacation destination for South American (especially from Brazil), North American, and European wine enthusiasts, who are also attracted to the provinces' many outdoor activities at the foot of the Andes Mountains. So, while in a province like San Luis the government maintains an impressive degree of control over the local economy, which is heavily tied to the provincial state, Mendoza is home to a flourishing private sector that provides ample employment opportunities for citizens of the province.

Mendoza ranks low among Argentine provinces in terms of the number of protests that occur there annually proportional to the size of its population. According to multiple sources, on the rare occasion that Mendoza does erupt in mass protest, those protests are normally directed at the national government and often revolve around issues related to democratic rules of the game. For example, the 1972 *Mendozazo* is still regarded as one of the most important and violent protests to occur under the Argentine military regimes, and it was one of the many mobilizations throughout Argentina that precipitated the brief return of elections in 1973. Since the establishment of the provincial constitution in 1916, Mendoza has been one of only two provinces in Argentina (along with Santa Fé) to continue to ban governors from being reelected, and the only province to prohibit consecutive terms by family members. When governor Francisco Pérez sought a constitutional reform in 2013 to permit one reelection for governors, he was met by widespread protests in the provincial capital. In fact, some of the most significant mobilizations in Mendoza have arisen in response to attempted constitutional reforms—such as when Menem pursued reelection in the mid-1990s and when rumors began to swirl in late 2012 that Cristina Kirchner would seek another term when her mandate ended in 2015. In conclusion, while protests surface on occasion in Mendoza—probably more than in San Luis—they normally look toward Buenos Aires and hardly ever result in long-standing conflict or the widespread use of confrontational tactics like roadblocks and lootings.

BUENOS AIRES: A HOTBED FOR CONTENTION

Representing the middle of the democratic quality spectrum is Buenos Aires, Argentina's largest province in terms of population and economic importance. By some metrics, Buenos Aires is a relatively open subnational democracy—no small cadre of elites has dominated its politics, and it has the country's most varied provincial economy, which has produced a diverse and influential civil society capable of mobilizing large numbers of citizens at a moment's notice. Independent sources of political information abound, as Buenos Aires has a rich collection of newspapers, television channels, and radio stations that fall outside of the provincial government's sphere of influence.

However, Buenos Aires comes up short in terms of democratic quality when compared to a province like Mendoza for several reasons—chiefly, the Peronists' electoral dominance in the province. As of 2013, the only instance where another party had held the governorship of Buenos Aires was during the first four years of democracy following the 1983 transition, and another party held control of the provincial legislature for only four years (the UCR from 1997–2001). In many cases the winning Peronist candidate for governor garnered a margin of victory exceeding 30 percent, offering a strong indication of the power asymmetry that exists in the province between the PJ and its closest rival, the UCR. Moreover, the most populated area of the province—the *conurbano* metropolitan region surrounding the nation's autonomous capital—has been famously dominated by the same clientelistic Peronist mayors and party brokers who maintain monopolies of power over local municipalities and played a critical role in fomenting unrest during the lead-up to the December 2001 crisis (Auyero 2005).

Another reason why Buenos Aires' provincial political institutions fall short of ideal representativeness has little to do with what happens within the province itself. Buenos Aires is the primary victim of Argentina's Co-Participation Law, meaning that *bonaerense* (people from Buenos Aires) citizens receive far less federal funding per capita for education, healthcare, and social programs than Argentines in any other province. For this reason, provincial politicians are often unable to deliver high-quality public services to their constituents—part of the reason why Buenos Aires has higher levels of poverty and unemployment than the national average—and experts on provincial politics have called the governor of Buenos Aires one of the weakest public figures in the country (Di Marco 2013). Recent strikes by police officers and teachers in pursuit of pay raises offer evidence of the extent to which its relatively low levels of federal funding hamstring the provincial government when it attempts to mediate social conflict. In certain situations, the federal government has stepped in to provide a short-term boost in public spending and, given the electoral import of the country's most populous province, claim credit for the generous federal intervention (Moscovich 2013). However, in the eyes of *bonaerenses*, these interventions further highlight the inability of provincial institutions to respond to the demands of the province's citizenry.

In conversations with former politicians and other experts on the politics of Buenos Aires, several interviewees stressed that the province was best understood as having two distinct sections: the *conurbano* and the interior. Traditionally, protests are more common in the *conurbano*, where individuals are more likely to identify as *porteños* (inhabitants of the capital city of Buenos Aires) than as citizens of the province. Indeed, these electoral districts are underrepresented in the provincial legislature in the capital city of La Plata in terms of the number of seats they possess, while the *conurbano* is the most important battleground during presidential elections, meaning citizens of the area often look more to national or municipal elected officials than provincial politicians for solutions to their problems. Given this fact, one provincial pollster said that denizens of the *conurbano* region were often dissatisfied with representation in the provincial legislature, and were sometimes even unaware of basic facts regarding provincial institutions. For them, the politicians in La Plata care far less about what happens in their neighborhood than national political leaders or municipal mayors, who are more visible in the media and spend more time campaigning in the *conurbano* in election years.

Recent social movements in Buenos Aires province offer illustrative examples regarding the role that representational deficits and weak political institutions play in creating an environment ripe for protest. As mentioned above, Peronist mayors and party brokers were pivotal in organizing lootings and riots in the *conurbano* in the lead-up to de la Rúa's resignation in late December 2001 (Auyero 2007). The area's massive population, proximity to the national capital, and Peronist dominance made it an ideal staging area for civil unrest directed at the national government, and much evidence exists to suggest that party brokers continue to draw on clientelistic networks in the *conurbano* to mobilize participation in street demonstrations (e.g., Oliveros 2012, Mangonnet and Moseley 2011.).

During the standoff between the agricultural sector and the Kirchner government in 2008, Buenos Aires province was one of the primary battlegrounds, given the importance of soy and sunflower production in the interior of the province. *Bonaerense* farmers were caught in a difficult situation in terms of their options for overturning the legislation. Citizens of a country with one hegemonic political party at the national level (the PJ), and a province dominated by a powerful branch of that party operating in close concert with the federal government, they were left with few formal options for political representation. Lockouts thus became the key tactic utilized by rural actors, as they attempted to shut down the country's most important productive sector and put the squeeze on their rivals in Buenos Aires (Mangonnet and Murillo 2016). Eventually, their efforts resulted in a surprise success in a Senate vote, which largely resulted from the movement's ability to shift national public opinion in their favor.[12]

Another example would be the seemingly annual conflict between teachers and the governor in Buenos Aires over salaries. In March 2014, Buenos Aires public schools were closed for the initial three weeks of the school year due to ongoing wage negotiations between the *bonaerense* government and teachers' unions led by the Buenos Aires division of the *Confederación de Trabajadores de la Educación de la República de Argentina* (CTERA) and *Sindicato Unificado de Trabajadores de la Educación de Buenos Aires* (SUTEBA). These strikes have become so frequent and, on occasion, dramatic that the leader of SUTEBA, Roberto Baradel, has emerged as a well-known public figure throughout Argentina, grabbing front-page headlines routinely in *La Nación* and *Clarín*. While teachers' strikes are commonplace in Argentina, the contentiousness of the relationship between unions and the *bonaerense* government is heightened by the Buenos Aires governor's fiscal weakness (the province's teachers have some of the lowest salaries in the country) and the lack for Buenos Aires teachers of an effective participatory alternative to striking.

As evident in Figure 6.10, Buenos Aires province has played host to a staggering number of protest events since the early 1990s, and particularly since 2000.[13] Even when one takes into account the size of the province, Buenos Aires ranks as one of the most contentious cases in the country in terms of protests per 100,000 citizens, and registers a significantly higher rate of protest participation than the rest of the country per survey data

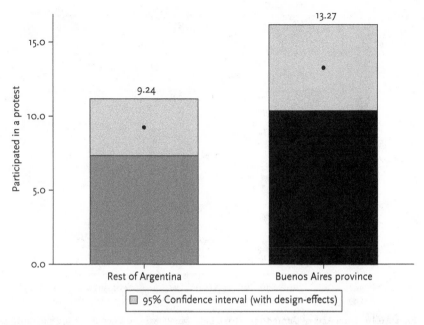

Figure 6.9 Rates of Protest in Buenos Aires versus the Rest of Argentina, 2008–2012
© AmericasBarometer, LAPOP

from 2008, 2010, and 2012 not including the autonomous capital (LAPOP 2008–2012; Figure 6.9). The primary reason for this marked contentious-ness is the combination of a relatively open context characterized by an active civil society and diversified economy, with a political environment marked by single-party dominance and weak provincial governing capacity. In other words, Buenos Aires is a provincial-level protest state.

A former president of the Peronist party in Buenos Aires province claimed that the province's recent history of contentious politics was sim-ilar to the rest of Argentina, if somewhat amplified. For him, *bonaerenses* continued to protest at high rates because it was the most effective way of extracting concessions from the provincial governments, which were in turn loathe to address the root grievances that in part spurred those actions without receiving significant pressure in the form of popular protests:

> There are elevated 'social costs' associated with *planes sociales* (welfare/cash transfer plans in Argentina), which helps explain why we observe such high levels of social protest in Argentina, and particularly in the province of Buenos Aires, which is (in my opinion) the most contentious district in the country. So, if more than eight million Argentines receive social assistance plans from the government, it's mostly because people are permanently carrying out protests

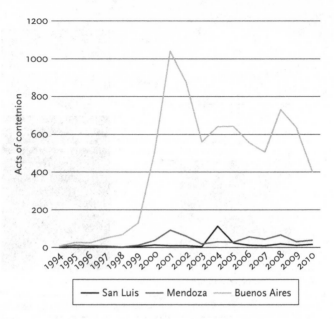

Figure 6.10 Total Acts of Contention in San Luis, Mendoza, and Buenos Aires, 1994–2010

in Argentina (to demand those plans). It's as if protest were a national sport in this country, like football. For this reason, policymakers don't attack the *causes* of this widespread dissatisfaction – poverty, lack of employment opportunities, especially for young people like in Spain and Greece, low salaries, inflation, insecurity, and corruption.[14]

In sum, Buenos Aires is one of the most contentious provinces in Argentina because it combines a highly developed civil society, capable of organizing contention and precipitating policy change, with formal political institutions that are relatively unresponsive to the popular will. However, in spite of its heightened levels of contentious participation, I found less evidence that protests in Buenos Aires frequently resulted in aggressive tactics or violent confrontations between demonstrators and law enforcement, unlike in the case of San Luis. Even in 2001, the lootings in the *conurbano* provoked few cases of police repression, as *bonaerense* officers were often instructed explicitly not to utilize harsh crowd-control tactics even as citizens ransacked local supermarkets (Auyero 2007). Moreover, many of these instances of mass mobilization in Buenos Aires province seem to indicate that peaceful tactics often precipitate meaningful responses from political elites, unlike in the case of San Luis, where the Rodríguez-Saá have virtually no incentive to surrender to moderate forms of contention.

ON CAUSAL MECHANISMS: FEAR OR RESIGNATION?

Key questions emerge from this analysis related to causal mechanisms, notably the distinction between repression and suboptimal representation as the driving force behind observed rates of protest participation across provincial contexts. Here I consider these two perspectives and provide some additional evidence from interviews.

On the one hand, the three cases above might illustrate that what matters in determining the quantity of protests in a given provincial regime is how local governments—and in particular, law enforcement—typically respond to those protests. In Buenos Aires province, despite the staggering number of protest events that have occurred there over the previous fifteen years, instances of repression have been relatively uncommon. Even at the most contentious moment in Argentine history in 2001, local police in the *conurbano* were expressly instructed not to intervene aggressively, even as citizens looted supermarkets (Auyero 2007), and few of the roadblocks mounted in 2008 resulted in violent police interventions. The case of San Luis tells a different story, where the only major mobilization since the early 1990s resulted in police brutality and dozens of arrests. Moreover, numerous interviewees expressed to me how risky it was to oppose the Rodríguez-Saá from an economic standpoint, given their nearly complete control over the local economy and considerable knowledge of the political goings-on within their province of only 300,000 people.

On the other hand, the lack of protests in contexts like San Luis might instead indicate that citizens have simply given up on seeking any response to their claims from the sitting government, given its total disregard for opposition voices and insulation from electoral pressures. In this case, a lack of contentious activity might be better interpreted as *resignation* rather than fear. Eight of Argentina's twenty-three provinces have yet to experience a transition from the party that won the first post-transition gubernatorial election in 1983. One might reasonably wonder why citizens of those provinces should believe that protesting would change anything? Yet in a province like Buenos Aires, protestors can expect some type of response from institutional actors despite the province's recent history of Peronist dominance, given that no individual or ruling family possesses absolute power over the provincial state. Indeed, just as internal competition has been characteristic of the Peronist party at the national level (Levitsky 2003, De Luca et al. 2002), it has also appeared in Buenos Aires province, exemplified by the recent battle for control in the national Chamber of Deputies between former *kirchnerista* Sergio Massa's *Frente Renovador* and the Kirchner-backed Frente para la Victoria. Furthermore, opposition parties (particularly the UCR) have at times upset the Peronist order in Buenos Aires province, particularly in the provincial legislature, and maintain strong ties to the citizenries of interior municipalities like Balcarce and Tandil and in one of the province's two largest cities outside of the *conurbano*, Mar del Plata.

In my fieldwork I found evidence of both perspectives, sometimes in interviews with the same individuals. An opposition deputy in the San Luis provincial legislature theorized about how citizens' lack of efficacy might discourage them from taking to the streets:

> San Luis lacks institutionalized mechanisms for resolving conflicts, compared to the case of 'collective bargaining' systems for salary disputes that exist throughout the rest of the country. So for example, public sector employees in San Luis have no mechanism for salary negotiation like those (that exist for public employees in other provinces). The concentration of power in the hands of the same political force for thirty years has made the people feel discouraged when the time comes to decide if they will mobilize around a cause they consider legitimate and petition the authorities.[15]

On the other hand, he also bemoaned the heavy-handed tactics the Rodríguez-Saá brothers often utilized to suppress any type of mobilization that did occur:

> After the 2001 crisis that devastated the entire country, San Luis province experienced several important social mobilizations that sought a response from public officials to the poverty and economic precariousness generated among a large portion of society . . . Massive social protests uniting multiple sectors marched through the main streets in the capital making their claims. Thousands participated, and the provincial police forces responded with violence. What's worse, many of the beneficiaries of *planes sociales* were called by the governor— in this case, Alberto Rodríguez-Saá—to lead a counter demonstration.[16]

In sum, to disentangle these two competing explanations of lower protest in closed provinces seems highly difficult, given the extent to which they overlap. Even when violent protests emerge in those contexts, it is unclear if they arise in response to repression (see Opp and Roehl 1990) or are a more radical "alternative political technology" (Scartascini and Tommasi 2012) aimed at provoking some kind of positive reaction from a government with little incentive to listen. While I am unaware of any provincial measure of repression in Argentina, there is evidence that points to a general trend toward the criminalization of contentious politics in the era of the Argentine protest state. Of the total number of arrests of protestors that have occurred between 2001 and 2012, more than 50 percent transpired after 2009 (Equipo Nizkor 2012).[17] After the highly visible deaths of dozens of demonstrators during the 2001–2002 crisis, provincial and national public officials attempted to reduce the crackdown on protests, and that is certainly apparent in the Equipo Nizkor data. But more recently, it seems certain repressive tactics might be making a comeback. In San Luis, for example, Juan Larrea, a deputy in the provincial legislature, was roughly detained in January 2015 for defending a group of demonstrators (Diario Registrado 2015). In February 2014, at the order of the provincial governor, twenty individuals were injured and ten detained in Resistencia, the capital of Chaco province in the northeast, while conducting street demonstrations in pursuit of increased social assistance from the provincial government (Schneider 2014).

Even if one could construct a reasonably accurate measure of repression by province, it would seem nearly impossible to discern if incidences of repression were low because the provincial government took a more tolerant view toward protest demonstrations or because citizens were too wary of the government's response to even challenge it in the first place. By focusing on subnational democracy more generally, I thus hope to provide a reasonable test of how institutional characteristics of provinces influence rates of contention within their borders, even if this particular study cannot fully parse out the independent effects of repression versus suboptimal representation—two regime characteristics that undoubtedly overlap, but are not equivalent.

CONCLUSION

Argentina embarked on a striking trend toward being a protest state in the late 1990s, and even following the country's recovery from a catastrophic economic and political crisis in 2001–2002, contentious tactics have remained a hallmark of everyday politics throughout much of the country. Argentina typifies the theory of the protest state, where many individuals have lost faith in traditional representational outlets and turned to protest as their preferred tool for pursuing political influence, drawing on dense organizational networks that have only become more effective in mobilizing protest in the twenty-first century.

While the frequency and intensity of protests, coupled with the extent to which contentious tactics have seemingly normalized over the last decade, make Argentina a critical case in the study of protest behavior, an additional feature of Argentine democracy makes it an ideal laboratory for examining the relationship between institutions and protest. Argentina is home to one of Latin America's most (in)famous federal systems, with vast differences in the quality of democratic institutions found among the country's twenty-three provincial governments (e.g., Chavez 2004, Spiller and Tommasi 2009, Gibson and Suárez-Cao 2010). Moreover, rates of protest activity differ a great deal across provincial contexts as well. As observed in the cases of San Luis, Mendoza, and Buenos Aires, the quality of provincial democratic institutions can bear on a citizenry's ability to organize collective action in nuanced ways.

In San Luis, we observe a province where one elite cadre has tightly controlled local political life since Argentina democratized in 1983, and an environment where contentious actors struggle to gain a foothold given the virtual prohibition on political engagement. However, in the few instances where protest movements have managed to mobilize, they have often resulted in violent clashes between demonstrators and the government. Conversely, the neighboring province of Mendoza probably boasts more effective democratic political institutions than the national regime, characterized by highly competitive elections and strong checks and balances. In Mendoza, both peaceful and aggressive protests are relatively uncommon compared to the majority of Argentine provinces, given the wealth of options for formal representation enjoyed by *mendocinos*. Finally, Buenos Aires province represents the ideal protest-producing context, with a diverse, active civil society and a provincial regime not fully accommodating of opposition voices. While members of the opposition can only rarely hope to challenge the dominant Peronist party in provincial and national elections, they can realistically expect that protest can provoke some kind of response from PJ public officials who are intent on maintaining their party's hegemony over the UCR, or are concerned about a rival offshoot challenging their control of the party. Moreover, prospective protestors in Buenos Aires do not face the barriers to mobilization that exist in state-centric provinces like San Luis, or the strong likelihood of falling victim to repressive police tactics.

While these case studies can best be characterized as suggestive of my theoretical understanding, based on interviews and historical research in only a small sample of three provinces, in the following chapter I provide a more rigorous test of my argument on data from every Argentine province during the period from 1994 to 2011. In so doing, I seek to further demonstrate the powerful, if multifaceted, effects of democratic quality and political engagement on social protest in emerging regimes.

CHAPTER 7

Uneven Democracy and Contentious Politics

An Analysis of Protest Across Argentine Provinces

How does the uneven nature of democracy in developing regimes influence the emergence and sustainability of social protest? While numerous empirical studies have recently sought to explain how national-level political factors help explain the often sharp variation in rates of protest participation observed across countries (e.g., Silva 2009, Dalton et al. 2009, Machado et al. 2011, Bellinger and Arce 2011), only a handful of scholars have endeavored to examine how subnational political context might shape contentious repertoires within countries (Arce and Rice 2009, Boulding 2010, 2014, Arce and Mangonnet 2013). However, as established in Chapter 6, rates of protest participation often vary drastically across state and provincial contexts, particularly in developing countries characterized by significant subnational variation in terms of economic and political development.

Building on the previous chapter's qualitative treatment of this question, this chapter seeks to provide an empirically rigorous, quantitative evaluation of how regime characteristics of Argentine provinces interact with political engagement to impact protest participation within their borders. In so doing, this analysis becomes one of the most thorough empirical examinations of the relationship between subnational regime characteristics and contentious politics to date, and offers an additional test of the theoretical framework that I outlined and tested at the country level in

Chapter 3 of this book. Specifically, I test the argument that subnational democracy has differential effects on distinct protest repertoires. On the one hand, more aggressive protest tactics are likely to emerge as political institutions become more closed off. In other words, subnational democratic quality has a linear, *negative* impact on the occurrence of aggressive, and frequently violent, protests. On the other hand, I argue that more peaceful street demonstrations tend to thrive at intermediate levels of subnational democracy, similar to the argument originally posited by Eisinger (1973) in the American context. In short, pacific street demonstrations thrive where democratic political institutions are not fully accommodating of opposition voices and participation, yet are not so closed off that potential movements have no organizational capacity or hope that such actions might make a difference. To test these arguments, I draw on protest events data from Argentine provinces[1] and individual-level data from the 2008, 2010, and 2012 AmericasBarometer national surveys of Argentina.

In the pages below, I first outline the classic challenges of conceptualizing and measuring subnational democracy in developing regimes, and then introduce my own approach based on Gervasoni's (2010) work on fiscal federalism and subnational democracy in Argentina. This measurement strategy utilizes gubernatorial and provincial legislative elections results to produce subnational democracy scores for each province from 1993 to 2011. Second, I introduce the event-counts data used for this analysis, obtained from two Argentine think tanks—the *Programa de Investigación sobre el Movimiento Social Argentina* (PIMSA) and *Nueva Mayoría*—and discuss the advantages and drawbacks of using these two measures. These data were drawn from newspaper reports on protests in all twenty-three Argentine provinces from 1993–2011, meaning that the analysis requires corresponding independent variables that cover the same sample of provinces over the entire time period under consideration. I also consider another source of data, the 2008–2012 AmericasBarometer national surveys of Argentina, to analyze citizen support for aggressive protest, and participation in peaceful street demonstrations.

Third, I outline my plan for modeling the relationship between provincial regime characteristics and aggressive protest events, which first includes Poisson regression, fixed effects for individual provinces and years, and a number of important control variables. For the survey data on support for aggressive protest, I employ ordinary least squares (OLS) regression and multilevel modeling techniques. To conclude, I utilize the AmericasBarometer data to examine another type of protest repertoire— peaceful street demonstrations—thus bringing to an end a comprehensive analysis of the relationship between subnational regime characteristics and contentious politics in emerging democracies and a test of the theoretical framework put forth in this book.

UNEVEN DEMOCRACY AND SOCIAL PROTEST IN LATIN AMERICA

How might the uneven nature of subnational democracy affect rates of contentious political participation? To this point, most recent work on the political institutional determinants of protest has zeroed in on the national level. While several scholars have found that democratic countries are characterized by higher rates of participation in contentious activities than non-democratic regimes (e.g., Dalton et al. 2009), others have argued that institutional flaws in developing democracies actually tend to amplify rates of protest participation (e.g., Machado et al. 2011). Other studies have found an interactive effect for democracy, wherein the effects of certain grievances or organizational resources are conditional on second-level political factors (e.g., Bellinger and Arce 2011).

Despite important contributions to our understanding of how national regimes shape protest repertoires, these studies do not acknowledge the extent to which democratic quality can vary subnationally, and the considerable spatial variation we observe in terms of the occurrence of protests within a given political system (e.g., Murillo and Ronconi 2004). However, two recent articles have attempted to unravel how certain political factors bear on rates of protest participation at the subnational level in the Latin American context. Arce and Mangonnet (2013) focus on the effects of partisanship and political competition on protest in Argentine provinces, finding that *less* competitive provinces and those where the Peronist party is out of power play host to higher levels of protest (see also Arce 2014). Boulding (2010) examines how NGO activities across Bolivian municipalities are influenced by institutional quality, using electoral competition as a proxy for the strength of democratic institutions. She finds that NGOs are more likely to encourage protest as opposed to more formal modes of participation in less competitive electoral contexts, similar to the findings from Arce and Mangonnet's analysis.

While each of these studies constitutes an important step toward understanding how subnational political factors influence protest, three drawbacks emerge in both. First, neither study offers a thorough conceptualization of how subnational political environments vary and potentially exacerbate or discourage contentious participation. That is, rather than solely focusing on political competition as measured by margin of victory in gubernatorial or municipal elections, one might wonder how subnational regimes differ in terms of alternations in power, term limits, and executive–legislative relations, among other political institutional factors. Second, both studies seek to uncover a *linear* effect for political competition on rates of protest participation, which seems to ignore the possibility that subnational regimes can become so uncompetitive and closed off as to render certain contentious behaviors improbable—a common finding from cross-national studies of contentious politics that include authoritarian countries in the sample (e.g., Tarrow 1998, Dalton et al. 2009). Third, and most importantly, each study treats all kinds of protest as the same, which I argue in Chapter 6 overlooks the possibility that political context exerts differential effects on distinct protest repertoires. Specifically, I argue that while low levels of subnational democracy tend to impede moderate modes of contentious participation, more aggressive repertoires become increasingly likely in such illiberal contexts.

CASE SELECTION: TESTING THE ARGUMENT ON ARGENTINE PROVINCES

Like many of its Latin American neighbors, and as explained in the previous chapter, Argentina is a hodgepodge of subnational regime types. It is home to one of Latin America's most (in)famous federal systems, characterized by vast differences in the quality of democratic institutions found within the country's twenty-three provincial governments (e.g., Spiller and Tommasi 2009, Gibson and Suarez-Cao 2010, Gervasoni 2010, Behrend 2011, Giraudy 2013). In provinces like Mendoza, liberal democracy is the name of the game, exemplified by competitive elections, free media, enforced property rights, and the apolitical dispersion of social programs and public jobs. In other Argentine provinces, like La Rioja or San Luis, powerful bosses (primarily from the long-dominant Peronist party) eliminate their competition through aggressive clientelism, the absence of independent media, and even occasional repression (e.g., Gibson and Calvo 2001, Chavez 2004, Gibson 2012, Gervasoni 2010, Giraudy 2013). In sum, while Argentina has certainly transitioned to liberal democracy at the national level (even if it experiences the occasional hiccup), there is a great deal of evidence supporting the notion that many Argentine provinces have yet to make that transition.

In addition, and as covered extensively in Chapter 6, Argentina offers profound subnational variation in terms of the extent to which protest has taken hold as a vital form of political voice (Murillo and Ronconi 2004). For example, whereas 1,600 roadblocks occurred in Buenos Aires province alone in 2008, other provinces like La Pampa, La Rioja, and San Juan registered less than 200 roadblocks during the entire time period from 1993–2011 (*Nueva Mayoría* 2012). While that result is surely driven to a large extent by the population disparity between Buenos Aires and three more rural provinces, huge gaps also emerge between provinces of a similar size—for example, while Jujuy and San Juan have similarly sized populations, Jujuy averaged nearly five times as many acts of contention annually during the period from 1994–2010 as did San Juan (PIMSA). In sum, due to the considerable variation observed on both the key independent and dependent variables, Argentina offers an exemplary case for testing how uneven democracy influences protest participation across subnational regimes.

MEASURING SUBNATIONAL DEMOCRACY

Unlike at the country level, where democracy scores are published annually by an array of organizations like the World Bank, Polity, and Freedom House, easily accessible and reputable democracy indicators at the subnational level are few and far between. For this reason, students of subnational politics have had to be creative in crafting their own measures of regime characteristics—particularly in developing contexts where good political data are harder to find. Thus, as the literature on subnational politics in the developing world has expanded, so too has a small collection of measurement strategies aiming to quantify just how democratic local regimes really are. In this section, I review extant approaches to conceptualizing and measuring subnational regime types, and eventually argue for what I believe is the best approach for the purposes of this particular analysis.

The first decision any student of subnational democracy must make is that of which conceptualization of democracy is most apt for the question they seek to answer. Generally speaking, subnational regimes found within democratic national contexts are not wholly authoritarian, given that to some extent those subnational units must answer to national political authorities and prevailing democratic rules of the game (Gibson 2005, Gervasoni 2010). However, a great deal of evidence suggests that processes of democratization have occurred unevenly in many developing regimes, and subnational units can fall into some category in between liberal democracy and full-scale dictatorship. While in certain cases, subnational regimes measure up to and even outperform the national regime in terms of democratic norms and procedures, in other cases state and provincial regimes are patrimonial, clientelistic, and exclusionary of minority voices (e.g., Key 1949, Fox 1994, Snyder 2001, Gibson 2005, Gervasoni 2010). These regimes resemble the category of national-level regimes described in the literature on "competitive authoritarian" or "illiberal" democracies, where one personalistic leader or powerful party generally dominates politics, but several key features of democratic rule (e.g., regular elections free of blatant fraud) remain in place (Zakaria 1997, Levitsky and Way 2002). Any conceptualization of subnational democracy must account for these shades of democratic quality, spanning from illiberal but not completely authoritarian (e.g., "closed") to liberal multiparty competition (e.g., "open").

In gauging subnational democracy, some scholars have sought to ascertain the extent to which "institutionalized uncertainty" (Przeworski 1991)—that is, the realistic possibility of change in the ruling party—exists in a particular setting by coding subnational regimes according to whether or not they have undergone a rotation in power from one party to another (see also Alvarez et al. 1996). In a case like Mexico, for example, where true multiparty competition took hold in certain states before the *Partido Revolucionario Institucional* (PRI) finally ceded power at the national level in 2000 while other states have yet to see a non-PRI party win the governorship, a dichotomous rotation measure would seem highly indicative of the extent to which subnational regimes have transitioned to multiparty competition (e.g., Hiskey and Bowler 2005).

In other studies, scholars have argued for a more nuanced conceptualization of local regime types, maintaining that a multidimensional measure that takes into account both *access* to state power (i.e., the presence of inclusive and competitive elections) and the *exercise* of state power (e.g., checks and balances, bureaucratic norms, and judicial independence) is paramount (Gervasoni 2010, Giraudy 2013). While the qualitative differences between these two dimensions of democratic rule seem important, acquiring useful data regarding the exercise of power component can present challenges. For example, while Gervasoni (2010) carried out an innovative expert survey project in Argentina to evaluate subnational democracy on both dimensions from 2003 to 2007, such a laborious endeavor requires a great deal of time and ample research funding, and in the case of Gervasoni's undertaking only yielded democracy scores for one gubernatorial term. Analyzing protest data over a nearly twenty-year period will therefore require a less intensive but more encompassing measure that accurately captures democratic quality across many provinces at various time points, but is realistically attainable with finite resources.

Any measurement strategy adopted should adequately capture the degree to which Argentine provincial regimes offer ample opportunity for individuals to influence policymakers and obtain representation, without having their voices suppressed or ignored by a powerful political leader or party. This measure would thus need to take into consideration countless characteristics of provincial political life that could bear on an individual's ability to obtain effective democratic representation—such as the nature of party competition, checks on executive power, the independence from political influence of the provincial media and judiciary, and the potential consolidation of political and economic power in the hands of a powerful elite, to name a few. But acquiring reasonable measures for all of these variables in each of Argentina's twenty-three provinces over a twenty-year period is difficult, if not impossible, given temporal constraints on available data. The challenge for this analysis is therefore finding high-quality information on provincial political environments that can serve as a proxy for many if not all of the important components of subnational democracy enumerated above, but is also readily available across years and provinces.

CONSTRUCTING THE SUBNATIONAL DEMOCRACY INDEX

The best source for local political information that is accessible across subnational units and time is electoral data (Wibbels 2005, Gervasoni 2010, Giraudy 2013). Indeed, while obtaining information regarding levels of press freedom, civil liberties, and judicial independence might require extensive fieldwork in each local context, which would likely prevent large-N quantitative studies comparing subnational units, utilizing election results to make inferences regarding these factors is much easier and more generalizable. In other words, one might assume that the information provided by provincial election results—such as margin of victory, reelection(s) of a particular party or leader, and inter-branch dynamics—reveals a great deal about the nature of those regimes and can serve as an effective proxy for provinces' overall levels of democratic quality. Put simply, we can reasonably assume that in less democratic provincial contexts, where local leaders utilize clientelistic practices and public funding in their campaigns, own or dominate local media, and control local judges and law enforcement to bias outcomes in their favor, that will be reflected in multiple reelections, uncompetitive contests, and electoral rules that favor the incumbent.

In his 2010 article on fiscal federalism and subnational democracy, Gervasoni uses provincial electoral data to measure two key dimensions of democracy: contestation and constraints on power (see also Dahl 1971). Gervasoni proposes an index based on five particular indicators derived from provincial gubernatorial and legislative elections: *Executive Contestation, Legislative Contestation, Succession Control, Legislature Control,* and *Term Limits. Executive Contestation* gauges how competitive elections for the governorship are by subtracting the percentage of the total vote garnered by the winning candidate from one. *Legislative Contestation* does the same, but with the governor's party in provincial legislative elections.[2] *Succession Control* assesses the degree to which incumbent governors are successful in controlling who follows them in office—this variable is coded as high if the governor himself or a close ally achieves reelection (3), medium if someone from the same party as the governor is elected (2), and low if an opposition party captures the provincial executive office (1). *Legislature Control* measures congruence between the legislature and the governor in terms of legislative seat shares, operationalized as the percentage of lower house seats won by the governor's party in each election. Finally, *Term Limits* codes whether and to what degree limits exist on the length of a governor's reign in power, coded from 0 (reelection is prohibited) to 3 (indefinite reelection). As of 2014, five Argentine provinces allow for indefinite reelection (Formosa, Santa Cruz, San Luis, La Rioja, and Catamarca) and two provinces prohibit reelection for governors altogether (Mendoza and Santa Fé). The rest allow either one or two reelections for governors. Of the five provinces that permit indefinite reelection of governors, four have never experienced a rotation in power since Argentina democratized in 1983, with Catamarca being the only exception.[3]

While Gervasoni's piece provides *Subnational Democracy* scores for every Argentine province aside from Tierra del Fuego from 1983 to 2003, this particular analysis requires that I have democracy scores through 2011, necessitating an extension of Gervasoni's data.[4] To calculate the *Subnational Democracy Index*, I use factor analysis to aggregate the five indicators described above into a single continuous measure, normalized to have a mean of zero and a standard deviation of one.[5] Thus, the most undemocratic provinces will have negative scores, middling provinces will cluster around zero, and more democratic subnational regimes will score positive values.

Below, I present mean subnational democracy scores from each province for the entire time period under consideration, 1993–2011 (Figure 7.1). Unsurprisingly, Formosa, Santa Cruz, La Rioja, and San Luis register the lowest values in terms of *Subnational Democracy*. None of these provinces has yet experienced a transition from PJ rule, and powerful individuals or families have dominated the politics of each province for decades. Another curious note regarding this group of provinces is that four of the past seven Argentine presidents—Menem, Rodríguez-Saá, and the two Kirchners— hail from three of the four *least* democratic provinces in the country: La Rioja, San Luis, and Santa Cruz, respectively.

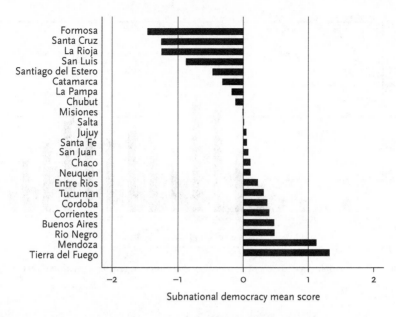

Formosa
Santa Cruz
La Rioja
San Luis
Santiago del Estero
Catamarca
La Pampa
Chubut
Misiones
Salta
Jujuy
Santa Fe
San Juan
Chaco
Neuquen
Entre Rios
Tucuman
Cordoba
Corrientes
Buenos Aires
Rio Negro
Mendoza
Tierra del Fuego

−2   −1   0   1   2

Subnational democracy mean score

Figure 7.1 Subnational Democracy Index, Mean Scores, 1993–2011

DEPENDENT VARIABLES: MEASURING AGGRESSIVE AND PEACEFUL PROTESTS

Aggressive Protest Participation

To test the relationship between subnational democracy and aggressive contention, I first draw on two unique measures of protest at the provincial level, both of which track the number of aggressive protest events that occurred in each province on an annual basis, per 100,000 citizens.[6] Since 1997, the researchers at *Nueva Mayoría* have carried out an ongoing research project on social conflict in Argentina, with a specific emphasis on the common tactic of blocking roads (*"cortes de ruta"*). To track the evolution of this contentious "performance" over time (Tilly and Tarrow 2006), *Nueva Mayoría* investigators have content-analyzed national newspapers[7] and provincial newspapers[8] to record unique instances of roadblocks occurring in each province every year. Since 1997, the number of roadblocks in Argentina has risen steadily, reaching its peak in 2008 thanks in large part to the heated standoff between the government and agricultural sector that resulted in thousands of roadblocks nationwide (Figure 7.2). Roadblocks represent a highly aggressive and confrontational, and oftentimes illegal, component of the participatory repertoire in Argentina (Arce and Mangonnet 2013).

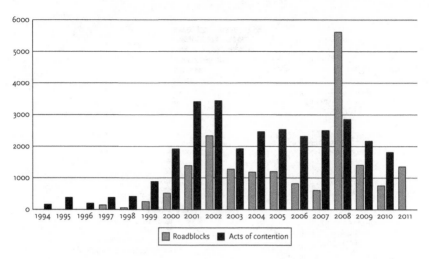

Figure 7.2 Roadblocks and Acts of Contention over Time: Argentine Provinces, 1994–2011

As for the second measure, PIMSA's "acts of contention" ("*hechos de rebelión*") measure captures a wider range of protest activities than just roadblocks. PIMSA's researchers define acts of contention as "actions carried out by representatives of economic, political, or social groups, in order to contest some characteristic or policy of the existing state" (Cotarelo 2009; author's translation). Among other pieces of information regarding each act, PIMSA investigators record the date and location of the event, the identity of the organizers, and the nature of their claim. Unlike *Nueva Mayoría's* more expansive source material, PIMSA uses only national newspaper accounts to code protest events, in this case *Clarín, La Nación, Página 12*, and *Crónica*. It appears that, similarly to roadblocks, the number of acts of contention increased steadily from 1994 to 2001, and while levels of protest fell slightly after the 2001–2002 crisis, they have remained much higher than before that pivotal moment in Argentine history (Figure 7.2). The average number of protest acts by province can be found in Figure 7.3.

There are positives and negatives associated with using each measure. The first drawback of using the PIMSA data is an obvious one—they are based on reports appearing only in national newspapers, all of which are located in Buenos Aires yet are being used to cull information on protest participation across the entire country. Buenos Aires-based papers tend to pay close attention to the goings-on of the capital and *conurbano*, while giving less press coverage to interior provinces. Thus, one might wonder if distance from the capital biases the extent to which protest events are covered in Buenos Aires-based newspapers, and thus if the PIMSA measure accurately

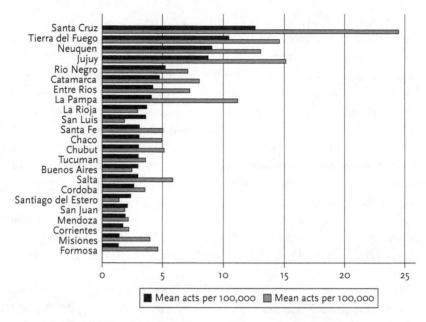

Figure 7.3 Average Protest Acts by Province per 100,000 Citizens, 1994–2011

portrays what is happening outside of the country's largest metropolitan area. Another problem specific to the PIMSA data is that while many of the types of protest registered in this measure are clearly aggressive—roadblocks, lootings, and attacks on public buildings—it is unclear how aggressive other contentious performances included in the data really are. However, I assume that while certain events might not be as combative in nature as others, the presence of more pacific demonstrations in these data would only weaken results to support the hypothesis of a linear negative relationship between subnational democracy and aggressive protest.

Another problem with both measures is that event counts fail to reveal much information regarding protest magnitude, meaning that each coded event is weighted the same regardless of whether five or 500,000 people attended. Indeed, one might envision a scenario where multiple small, relatively inconsequential protests drive up the count in one particular province, while a small number of massive protests in another province are relatively underrepresented in the data. For this reason, many scholars prefer other approaches to measuring protest like surveys, which measure participation at the individual level and thus ensure that each observation is weighted the same (e.g., Dalton et al. 2009).

These data, however, also carry with them several important advantages. First, they cover a time period of nearly twenty years, providing rare temporal breadth in the study of contentious politics at the subnational level. This feature allows us to account for any variation in the prevalence of contentious politics that might occur over time while also increasing the size of the sample, enabling a more robust evaluation of relationships between key variables. Second, these data were collected for each of Argentina's twenty-three provinces, which makes for a sample that includes highly urban areas (the Buenos Aires *conurbano*) and many rural, peripheral provinces (e.g., Santa Cruz or Formosa) that are often forgotten in quantitative analyses based on national-level data. Finally, by utilizing two sources of protest events data, each of which captures a different set(s) of aggressive protest repertoires, I argue that any common findings gleaned from these analyses should be particularly robust. When combined with the analysis of survey data from Argentina, which I will describe in more depth below, the analysis presented here is thus among the most thorough examinations of subnational politics and protest to date.

In addition to using events-count data to measure aggressive protest participation, I also draw on several questions from the 2008–2012 AmericasBarometer national surveys of Argentina regarding support for aggressive forms of contention. While these questions fail to gauge *actual* participation in such activities, any evidence that citizens of less democratic provinces are more supportive of potentially violent anti-state action would lend credence to the notion that aggressive repertoires tend to thrive in the *least* democratic contexts. Specifically, the AmericasBarometer instrument includes questions intended to gauge support for (1) citizens working to overthrow the government, (2) vigilante justice, (3) roadblocks, and (4) occupying property as a form of protest.[9] I utilize all four questions (each of which was measured 1–10 initially, but recoded 0–100 for ease of interpretation) to test if public opinion in Argentina seems to align with the findings from the analysis of protest events across Argentine provinces.[10]

Peaceful Protest Participation

To measure peaceful protest participation, I again look to the AmericasBarometer national surveys of Argentina. As mentioned above, in 2008, 2010, and 2012, the Latin American Public Opinion Project's (LAPOP) AmericasBarometer utilized a national probability sample design of voting-age Argentines, with about 1,500 respondents taking part in face-to-face interviews in Spanish in each round for a total N of 4,408. Each sample has a complex design, featuring stratification and cluster sampling from the Argentine population, and has been stratified by regions within

Argentina (Buenos Aires, Central, Northeastern, Northwestern, Cuyo, and Patagonia) and by urban and rural areas. The sample consists of 286 primary sampling units (municipalities), representing 21 of 23 provinces.[11]

All of these surveys asked Argentines about their protest behavior during the previous year. The dependent variable is thus drawn from a question that inquires if respondents have participated in a protest march or demonstration—inherently peaceful, moderate modes of protest participation—during the previous twelve months. Combining results from all three surveys, about eighteen percent of Argentines reported having participated in a protest during the specified time frame, placing the country third in Latin America behind only Bolivia and Peru in terms of citizens' professed rates of participation (LAPOP 2008–2012).

At first glance, it appears that rates of protest participation by subnational regime category match up fairly well with my theoretical perspective. Here I divide provinces into democracy terciles, corresponding to their annual rank according to the Subnational Democracy Index. Among individuals who live in "mixed" systems, rates of protest participation approach 20 percent and exceed rates of participation in closed and open democratic contexts (Figure 7.4). However, it also appears that more democratic provinces are characterized by significantly higher rates of contentious participation than the least democratic ones, and that mixed and open systems do not differ significantly in terms of participation rates. Thus, contrary to my expectations regarding more aggressive protests, it appears

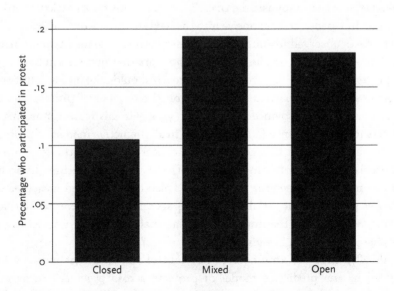

Figure 7.4 Protest Participation by Subnational Democracy Category

that closed provinces play host to the *lowest* rates of peaceful protest participation in the country, though this initial observation clearly requires more rigorous empirical evaluation.

RESULTS

Aggressive Protests across Argentine Provinces

Because I am dealing with count data that span nearly twenty years for all of Argentina's twenty-three provinces, there are several knotty methodological issues that must be sorted out before moving on to the analysis section. Count data are not normally distributed nor can they take on negative values, and the distribution is also discrete rather than continuous. Therefore, these data violate several key assumptions underpinning OLS regression, rendering any findings from a standard OLS approach biased and/or inefficient (King 1988). For these reasons, I utilize Poisson regression, which assumes that the errors follow a Poisson distribution rather than a normal one, and models the natural log of the dependent variable (rather than the variable itself) as a linear function of the independent variables in the model (King 1988, Long 1997).

Another complicating factor for this analysis is the fact that I am using panel data for twenty-three provinces, rather than a dataset consisting of wholly independent, cross-sectional observations.[12] The fact that this dataset includes multiple observations for individual provinces over time means that one cannot assume that the observations for a particular province are independent from one year to the next. In other words, the number of protests observed in Santiago del Estero at time t are inevitably contingent to some degree on the number of protests that occurred in Santiago del Estero at $t - 1$. So, any modeling approach should take into account the unique effects of a particular province on the number of protest events that occur in that province from year to year. For this reason, I use fixed effects for each province (and each year) in all predictive models of protest events in an attempt to account for the concern that something within a particular province is biasing results, or that a snowball effect might occur in provinces from one year to the next. I also include lagged measures of the two protest-count variables, which offers an even more empirically rigorous evaluation of the impact of subnational regime characteristics on protest participation in a given context.

Finally, there are a number of key control variables that must be included in any predictive model of protests across provinces to assure that the inferences made regarding the impact of subnational democracy on contentious participation are valid. First, if one is to isolate the impact of institutional factors, one must also control for relevant economic circumstances that might outweigh political factors in terms of theoretical import. Upticks in unemployment, downturns in economic growth (measured as the percent change in *Producto Bruto Geográfico* [PBG]), and the overall level of development in a province (PBG per capita) are all economic factors that might bear on the prevalence of protest participation in a particular setting.[13]

In the models presented below, I also include control variables for several important political factors. In their 2013 piece on how political competition and partisanship shape protest repertoires, Arce and Mangonnet find that contexts in which the Peronist party is in the opposition often produce higher protest activity, due to the grassroots connections of the PJ and its tremendous mobilization capacity. Thus, a dummy variable for whether or not the PJ holds the governorship will be included in every model. Finally, I have also included an indicator for the number of public employees per 100,000 citizens in each province. This is based on numerous studies that have claimed that high levels of public employment tend to be associated with low quality, patrimonial democracy at the subnational level, and would seemingly diminish contentious activity (see McMann 2006, Gervasoni 2010, Giraudy 2013).

Table 7.1 reports results for Poisson models of annual *Roadblocks* and *Acts of Contention* per 100,000 citizens. Similar to the findings from Arce and Mangonnet (2012) and Boulding (2010), these model results support the hypothesis that aggressive forms of protest become more common in less democratic settings. In all four models, *Subnational Democracy* has a negative effect on the number of protest events that occurred annually in Argentine provinces, and the results for three of those models indicate a significant result at the p<.01 level.[14] From a substantive standpoint, varying levels of *Subnational Democracy* seem to have an important effect on the number of protest events that occur within a given province. For example, holding all other variables in Model 2 at their mean, an increase in the Subnational Democracy Index score from minus two (less democratic) to two (highly democratic) results in about a 50 percent reduction in the predicted number of roadblocks in a given province (Figure 7.5). Likewise, a similar change in democratic quality reduces the number of predicted acts of contention from around six to three annual events (Figure 7.6). In sum, we can say with some degree of confidence that undemocratic provinces will observe roughly twice as many aggressive protests annually as democratic provinces, holding other variables in each model constant.

Table 7.1 PREDICTIVE MODELS OF AGGRESSIVE PROTEST EVENTS ACROSS ARGENTINE PROVINCE (POISSON REGRESSION MODELS)

VARIABLES	Acts of Contention (Annual # of events) Model 1 Coeff. (s.e.)	Roadblocks (Annual # of events) Model 2 Coeff. (s.e.)	Acts of Contention (Annual # of events) Model 3 Coeff. (s.e.)	Roadblocks (Annual # of events) Model 4 Coeff. (s.e.)
PBG per Capita (log)	−0.467** (0.231)	−0.825*** (0.189)	−0.485** (0.235)	−0.368* (0.222)
PBG Change	0.00001 (0.00004)	0.0002*** (0.003)	0.00005 (0.00004)	0.0002*** (0.00006)
Unemployment	0.033*** (0.012)	0.094*** (0.012)	0.034*** (0.013)	0.062*** (0.014)
PJ Governor	−0.197** (0.094)	−0.039 (0.105)	−0.138** (0.097)	0.045 (0.112)
Distance	−0.0004 (0.0003)	0.0003 (0.0003)	−0.0004 (0.0003)	0.0007** (0.0003)
Public Employment	−0.013*** (0.004)	−0.002 (0.004)	−0.010*** (0.004)	−0.009** (0.004)
Subnational Democracy	*−0.166*** (0.046)*	*−0.185*** (0.047)*	*−0.198*** (0.048)*	*−0.077 (0.056)*
Acts of Contention ($t-1$)			0.005 (0.003)	
Roadblocks ($t-1$)				0.012*** (0.002)
Fixed effects for provinces	Yes	Yes	Yes	Yes
Fixed effects for years	Yes	Yes	Yes	Yes
Observations	389	308	367	264

Standard errors in parentheses
*** $p<0.01$, ** $p<0.05$, * $p<0.1$

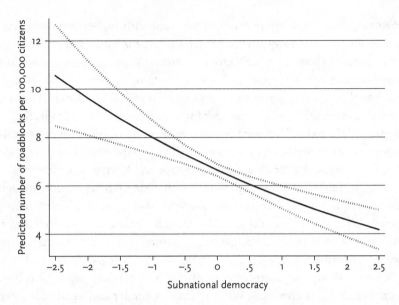

Figure 7.5 Subnational Democracy and Aggressive Protest: Roadblocks

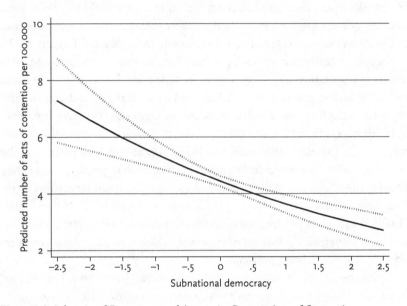

Figure 7.6 Subnational Democracy and Aggressive Protest: Acts of Contention

As for the control variables, as expected, the lagged number of protest events has a positive impact on the number of events observed in the current year in Models 3 and 4, though this effect is only significant in the case of roadblocks. Unemployment has the expected effect on the number of protest events in a particular context, as increases in provincial unemployment rates are generally associated with higher protest counts and seems to wash away any meaningful effect for PBG Change. PBG per capita seems to have a negative effect on protest participation, as wealthier provinces are characterized by lower aggressive protest counts. A high number of public employees also seems to decrease the incidence of protest events, though this effect is stronger for acts of contention. Finally, the indicator "PJ Governor" has a weak negative effect on the number of protests in a particular province in the case of acts of contention, but a stronger effect on roadblocks, lending support to Arce and Mangonnet's findings.

Finally, Table 7.2 presents results from four OLS regression models of support for aggressive protest. As with the provincial event-counts models, a handful of control variables must be included in any individual-level model of protest participation to assure that the relationship between subnational regime characteristics and protest participation is not spurious.[15] First, demographic controls for age, gender, and wealth have been included in each model. While effects for gender and wealth are often inconsequential, age has been found to have a powerful negative impact on the likelihood that one has participated in a protest in the prior year, as older citizens are far less likely than their younger counterparts to take to the streets to make claims on governments (Moseley and Layton 2013).

Second, a collection of sociopolitical factors that are associated with higher probabilities of protesting is included in the models presented below, including interest in politics, level of education, and community engagement. All of these reflect hypotheses from the "resource mobilization" approach to explaining protest, which, as the dominant theoretical paradigm in the contentious politics literature, argues that more civically active, socially connected individuals are more likely protestors, as they possess the necessary skills and access to organizational structures to effectively mobilize contention (e.g., McCarthy and Zald 1977, Meyer 2004). Finally, I include a control for individuals' personal economic situations, system support, and presidential approval, which should capture any overriding grievance driving participation.

As for the key independent variable *Subnational Democracy*, I code provinces according to their scores for the year preceding each survey, given that the AmericasBarometer interviews took place early in the year and the question regarding protest asks specifically about participation over the previous twelve months. Because the coded province in which individuals live is actually a contextual variable—i.e., survey respondents are nested within provinces—the results presented below are from multilevel models, which assess the impact of living in a particular subnational context on one's likelihood of having protested (Gelman and Hill 2006).

Table 7.2 PREDICTIVE MODELS OF SUPPORT FOR AGGRESSIVE PROTEST (ORDINARY LEAST SQUARES REGRESSION MODELS)

VARIABLES	Support for Revolution (0–100) Model 1 Coeff. (s.e.)	Support for Roadblocks (0–100) Model 2 Coeff. (s.e.)	Support for Vigilante Justice (0–100) Model 3 Coeff. (s.e.)	Support for Occupation as Protest (0–100) Model 4 Coeff. (s.e.)
Female	0.130	0.723	-1.827	0.268
	(0.796)	(1.158)	(1.179)	(0.898)
Age	-0.091***	-0.197***	-0.238***	-0.111***
	(0.026)	(0.038)	(0.039)	(0.030)
Quintile of Wealth	-1.190***	-1.824***	-0.966**	-1.981***
	(0.318)	(0.458)	(0.468)	(0.357)
Interest in Politics	0.006	0.078***	-0.057***	0.042***
	(0.013)	(0.019)	(0.020)	(0.015)
Education (level)	0.002	0.051	-0.015	0.034
	(0.030)	(0.043)	(0.045)	(0.034)
Community	-1.498**	-2.324***	-3.653***	-1.750***
	(0.598)	(0.867)	(0.884)	(0.673)
Personal Economic Situation	2.211**	4.374***	0.749	0.862
	(1.118)	(1.614)	(1.640)	(1.263)
Presidential Approval	-0.061***	0.002	-0.088***	-0.013
	(0.018)	(0.026)	(0.026)	(0.020)

(continued)

Table 7.2 CONTINUED

VARIABLES	Support for Revolution (0–100)	Support for Roadblocks (0–100)	Support for Vigilante Justice (0–100)	Support for Occupation as Protest (0–100)
	Model 1	Model 2	Model 3	Model 4
	Coeff.	Coeff.	Coeff.	Coeff.
	(s.e.)	(s.e.)	(s.e.)	(s.e.)
Interpersonal Trust	0.012	-0.001	-0.039*	-0.008
	(0.015)	(0.022)	(0.022)	(0.017)
System Support	-0.045**	0.023	-0.164***	0.009
	(0.018)	(0.026)	(0.026)	(0.020)
Subnational Democracy	*-2.209***	*-0.900*	*-4.271****	*-1.968***
	(0.889)	*(1.152)*	*(1.197)*	*(0.989)*
Constant	34.712***	45.010***	75.717***	36.398***
	(2.838)	(3.834)	(3.933)	(3.154)
Observations	2,284	2,286	2,266	2,280
Number of Provinces	21	21	21	21

Standard errors in parentheses
*** p<0.01, ** p<0.05, * p<0.1

As seen in the results, these models provide strong evidence that individuals residing in less democratic provinces are more prone to supporting more aggressive, potentially violent contentious performances, spanning from roadblocks to vigilante justice. Controlling for a litany of other variables, the quality of the subnational regime within which individuals live has a consistent, powerful negative effect on their support for aggressive behaviors. In other words, the more democratic the province, the less likely individuals are to view such tactics as appropriate or necessary. Taken together, the results from the Poisson models of protest event counts and OLS models of support for aggressive protest make a compelling case that more extreme modes of contention tend to thrive in the *least* democratic subnational contexts.

Peaceful Protest Participation across Argentine Provinces

Having established that a linear, negative relationship exists between subnational democracy and aggressive protest participation, the analysis now moves on to peaceful forms of contention, drawing again on survey data from the AmericasBarometer. To capture the possibility of the hypothesized nonlinear relationship between subnational democracy and protest participation, I code the democracy variable in two ways: (1) the undoctored, continuous index score, and (2) the democracy score squared, which allows for the prospect that values farther from zero (i.e., corresponding to high and low levels of subnational democracy) produce lower rates of peaceful protest participation.

As expected, the Subnational Democracy indicator has no significant linear effect on the likelihood that an individual has participated in a street protest or demonstration in the prior year (Table 7.3). Thus, any attempt to attribute peaceful protests across Argentine provinces to increasing or decreasing levels of subnational democracy appears misplaced, as no direct linear relationship surfaces between the two variables. However, *Subnational Democracy Squared* has a statistically significant, negative impact on an individual's probability of participating in contentious activities. This result indicates that, as predicted, the farther away subnational democracies move from the protest-producing middle region of democratic quality—whether toward liberal democracy or toward outright authoritarianism—the fewer the number of protests we should observe. Figure 7.7 plots the predicted probabilities associated with varying levels of subnational democracy, indicating that at the highest and lowest values, individuals' probabilities of protesting wane.[16] For example, a person living

Table 7.3 PREDICTIVE MODELS OF PEACEFUL PROTEST
PARTICIPATION IN ARGENTINA (LOGISTIC REGRESSION MODELS)

VARIABLES	Protest Participation (1 = Protested) Model 1	Protest Participation (1 = Protested) Model 2
Female	−0.011	−0.009
	(0.127)	(0.127)
Age	−0.017***	−0.016***
	(0.005)	(0.005)
Quintile of Wealth	0.023	0.020
	(0.052)	(0.052)
Interest in Politics	0.016***	0.016***
	(0.002)	(0.002)
Education (level)	0.206**	0.210**
	(0.096)	(0.096)
Community	0.026***	0.026***
	(0.004)	(0.004)
Personal Economic Situation	−0.008**	−0.008**
	(0.004)	(0.004)
Presidential Approval	−0.000	−0.001
	(0.003)	(0.003)
Interpersonal Trust	−0.003	−0.003
	(0.002)	(0.002)
System Support	0.002	0.002
	(0.003)	(0.003)
Subnational Democracy	*−0.098*	*−0.024*
	(0.154)	*(0.154)*
Subnational Democracy Squared		*−0.205**
		(0.115)
Constant	−2.216***	−2.062***
	(0.379)	(0.386)
Observations	3,474	3,474
Number of Provinces	21	21

Standard errors in parentheses
*** p<0.01, ** p<0.05, * p<0.1

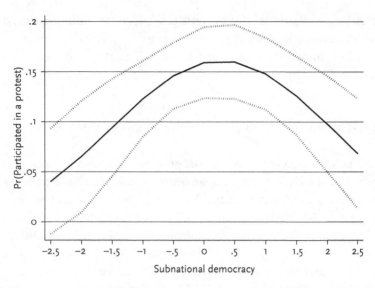

Figure 7.7 Reported Street March Participation by Subnational Democracy Score

in a province at the absolute midpoint in terms of democratic quality (*Subnational Democracy* = 0) is more than three times as likely to participate in a protest compared to a person living in one of the *least* democratic provincial contexts in Argentina (*Subnational Democracy* = -2) and more than twice as likely to protest as someone living in one of the most democratic provinces (*Subnational Democracy* = 2).

While gender and wealth appear unrelated to one's likelihood of protesting, age has a strong negative impact on participation, as expected. Education, community participation, and interest in politics are, as one might anticipate, also strong predictors of having participated in a protest during the previous twelve months. Lastly, having encountered an economic rough patch personally seems to fuel protest participation, which is in keeping with the finding that personal economic circumstances often seem to outweigh sociotropic evaluations when it comes to motivating protest participation.

In sum, while it appears that declining democratic quality fuels aggressive protests in Argentina, this linear relationship fails to emerge when we focus on more peaceful, everyday forms of contention. Indeed, in the least democratic provinces it appears that the types of street demonstrations we commonly associate with the Argentine protest state all but disappear, as individuals are forced to rely on more aggressive tactics to attempt to effect political change. Thus, contrary to assumptions in the existing literature regarding hypothesized linear relationships between institutions and protest, this analysis has uncovered a more nuanced set of relationships between subnational democracy and distinct contentious repertoires. In other words, political institutions affect different types of protest in different ways.

SUBNATIONAL DEMOCRACY AND CITIZEN ENGAGEMENT

To this point, this chapter has focused primarily on subnational democracy rather than the interaction between institutional quality and political engagement, the two factors identified as critical determinants of protest participation in the overarching theory presented in this book. This has been due largely to problems related to data availability in terms of subnational measures of engagement, but also because the interaction between institutions and engagement is fundamentally different at the subnational level, where authoritarian provinces like San Luis almost categorically rule out any sort of widespread political engagement. In this way, subnational democracy measures based on electoral data offer a rough proxy for both concepts, as engagement is inevitably low in illiberal contexts devoid of competition and steeped in patrimonial state-society relations. However, to bring this analysis more in line with the cross-national parlance and results presented in Chapter 3, I take a closer look here at how subnational institutional environments interact with citizen engagement to influence rates of protest participation.

Unlike at the country level, there is no significant result for the interaction between subnational democracy and community participation when including the interaction term in a predictive model of protest participation, though the direction of the effect for the interaction term is consistent with the results in the cross-national chapter. As apparent in Figure 7.8, engaged citizens are clearly more likely to partake of contentious participation than their less engaged counterparts, regardless of institutional context. However, it appears that in Argentina, politically engaged citizens in open and mixed provincial contexts are *equally* likely to participate in protests, which contradicts the country-level finding to some extent, as we would assume that engagement has a stronger impact on participation in mixed (i.e., less democratic) settings. While living in a closed system clearly stifles contentious activity, it appears that differences between high and mixed democratic contexts are minimal in terms of protest participation rates, with the main distinguishing factor being that *un*engaged citizens in mixed contexts are more likely protestors than their counterparts in open provincial democracies. Most notably, Figure 7.8 makes apparent the

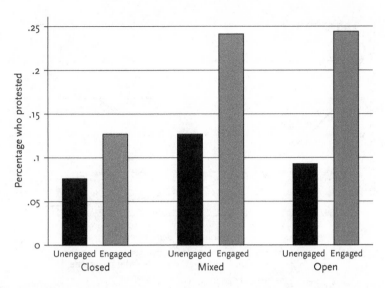

Figure 7.8 The Interaction between Subnational Democracy and Community Engagement
These are absolute percentages, as opposed to predicted probabilities derived from model results. Engaged citizens are those who had participated in at least one community organization during the previous year.

extent to which authoritarian provincial regimes thwart community participation, thus preventing most peaceful protests and pushing individuals toward more aggressive tactics.

While there appear to be slight disparities in how this cross-level relationship plays out within Argentina compared to across Latin American regimes, one must keep in mind that in analyzing the impact of subnational democracy, we are dealing with regimes that are nested within a unique national context. As mentioned in Chapter 3, many individuals in democratic provinces—who are highly engaged in politics—take to the streets to protest against the *national* regime, as has been the case recently in Mendoza. But perhaps most important, Argentine provinces provide a more diverse set of cases in terms of democratic quality, as the least democratic subnational regimes in the country are in many ways more closed off than even the most illiberal national democracies in the region (e.g., Venezuela or Ecuador), which are at least characterized by competitive elections and increasingly vibrant opposition parties.

Another way to investigate the potential interaction between institutional quality and political engagement would be to examine how provincial-level variables influence protest counts across Argentine provinces. In the absence of a direct measure of political engagement, I instead use a provincial-level indicator for per capita income as a proxy which, given the emphasis placed in this book on the role of economic development in

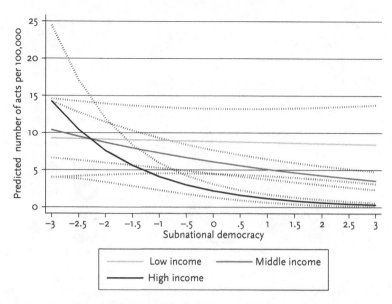

Figure 7.9 The Interaction between Income and Subnational Democracy

facilitating higher rates of political engagement, seems like a reasonable leap. When interacted with subnational democracy in a predictive model of "acts of contention," the interaction term turns out to be statistically significant at p<.001. In Figure 7.9, we observe that the significant negative effect of subnational democracy on incidences of aggressive protest only really holds for middle- and high-income provinces. In other words, low levels of subnational democracy tend to produce particularly high rates of aggressive contention in provinces characterized by at least moderate levels of economic development, which I argue would in turn produce more engaged citizenries. While this proxy is imperfect, considering that development and political engagement do not necessarily go hand in hand, it provides suggestive evidence of a similar dynamic at the subnational level to the cross-national results from Chapter 3.

Another piece of evidence that supports the interactive theory of the protest state emerges in models of support for violent protest. Figure 7.10 illustrates the extent to which subnational democracy and support for aggressive repertoires of participation are more strongly correlated among citizens who are highly engaged in their communities than among inactive individuals. While subnational democracy has virtually no impact on the likelihood that an unengaged individual will be supportive of groups that advocate for the violent overthrow of their government, subnational democracy has a powerful *negative* effect on this type of attitude among

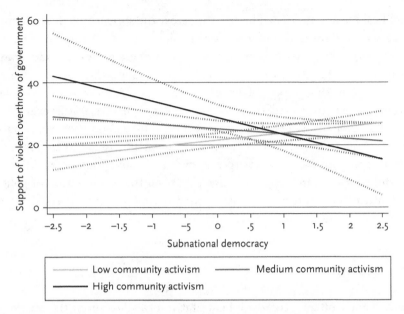

Figure 7.10 Support for Groups Who Want to Overthrow Government

individuals who are least minimally involved in their local communities. Citizens who participate in their communities, and presumably are aware of institutional shortcomings in their home provinces, are far more likely to support revolutionary action in undemocratic settings than in democratic provinces.

For the most part, the results obtained in this chapter corroborate what we observe at the national level, in that flawed subnational democracies play host to more protests than high-quality democracies or illiberal regimes. However, they are by no means a perfect match. At the subnational level in Argentina, the least democratic provinces are far *less* democratic than the least democratic national-level regimes in the region, insofar as local party bosses dominate virtually every facet of economic and political life in their domain. This produces more nuanced outcomes for contentious politics, as aggressive protests thrive in the least democratic settings, while moderate repertoires of contention surge at middling levels of democratic quality. While the severe authoritarian nature of those regimes complicates the interactive relationship between institutional quality and political engagement, we find significant evidence that it plays out in recognizable ways.

The provinces characterized by moderate levels of democratic quality best approximate the national-level protest state. In these contexts, like Buenos Aires province in Argentina, protest plays a critical role in everyday political life and is utilized by citizens across the socioeconomic spectrum as a standard form of political voice. Though protests in these provincial contexts might sometimes become violent, they are most often moderate expressions of a citizenry disenchanted with formal political institutions, intent on making policymakers answer to them in some way, shape, or form. On the other hand, the least democratic provinces serve as examples of what happens in less democratic regimes where opposition is discouraged or repressed, and little political engagement is allowed to flourish. Even if the protest state emerges in part from suboptimal institutional performance, it also results in large part from the liberalization of political institutions and an increasingly permissive environment for citizens to voice their discontent.

CONCLUSION

This chapter offers a thorough quantitative investigation of the relationship between subnational democratic institutions and protest participation in Argentine provinces, utilizing multiple sources of data and modeling strategies. The findings are consistent: rather than unearthing a consistent linear relationship between subnational democracy and protest, it appears that peaceful protests thrive at intermediate levels of democratic quality, while aggressive protests become more likely in less democratic settings. These findings shed light on a heretofore under-examined dynamic in the Latin American context, and call for a recalibration of how we understand why and where protests occur in the developing world more generally. Indeed, rates of mobilization can vary drastically even within the context of a single democratic regime, and uneven processes of subnational democratic development can have important consequences for the participatory repertoires that individuals within those contexts utilize.

As outlined throughout, Argentine provinces offer a more extensive universe of cases in terms of democratic quality than what we find at the national level in Latin America. That is, in certain provinces in Argentina, competition is virtually nonexistent, the current government dominates local media, and the ruling elite's control over access to public jobs and social assistance programs keeps potential political challengers perpetually at bay. Even in Latin America's least democratic country aside from Cuba, Venezuela (Freedom House 2013), recent elections have been characterized by intense competition between incumbent candidates and an increasingly unified opposition, and the government's domination of the economic sphere is nowhere near as complete as it is in provinces like

Formosa, La Rioja, or San Luis. However, the recent violence surrounding citizen protests in Venezuela might reveal that the regime has crossed into uncharted territory—so undemocratic that the opposition demonstrators are adopting increasingly aggressive tactics in their quest to influence the Maduro government.

In conclusion, these findings from Argentina reveal the limitations of the argument that flawed institutions spawn high levels of contentious political behaviors, or that political institutions have the same effects on all protest repertoires. At a certain point, the closing down of opportunities for political expression becomes so complete that individuals abandon moderate forms of protest and resort to more aggressive tactics. In other words, where the democratic promise of representation ceases to exist, so too does the motivation to take to the streets in a peaceful manner in demand of change, and more drastic options take precedent. However, where democratic institutions are only partially flawed—as is the case in numerous developing regimes across the region and in many provinces within Argentina—and political engagement thrives, peaceful street demonstrations become a powerful tool for individuals in pursuit of effective democratic representation. Thus, the protest state emerges not only as a national-level phenomenon but also at the subnational level in uneven democracies throughout the region.

CHAPTER 8

Democracy in the Protest State

The Wave of the Future in Latin America?

In this book I have sought to explain why protests arise so frequently in certain Latin American contexts but not others, and how individual-level and institutional factors interact to explain contentious political participation. The theory I present rests on the idea of the "protest state"—a regime where protest becomes so quotidian, utilized by citizens of all stripes to voice virtually any political claim, that it absorbs into the very fabric of everyday political life. Protest states emerge in regimes characterized by low-quality political institutions and high levels of citizen engagement in politics, a combination that has become increasingly common in Latin America as many of the region's democracies have continued to be plagued by institutional weakness, corruption, and low levels of legitimacy, yet have benefited from an economic boom that produced more engaged citizens than at any point in history.

The empirical results presented in this book demonstrate that characteristics of democratic political institutions help explain the emergence of protest participation in different national and subnational contexts, but that the effects of these institutional factors are not as straightforward as many have argued. Rather, they are best characterized as nonlinear, or conditional on a certain base level of political engagement among a particular citizenry. That is, while underperforming democratic institutions can play a part in triggering contentious modes of political participation, institutions can also be so *un*-democratic that protest movements are prevented from ever getting off the ground. This is particularly evident at the subnational level in uneven democracies like Argentina.

In this concluding chapter, I summarize and offer additional interpretation of the key findings presented to this point. I will also comment on current trends in terms of the Latin American protest state, with a focus on the Brazilian case—a regime that I argue was not a protest state when I began this book project but has recently joined the ranks of Latin America's most contentious democracies. Then, I discuss the implications of my argument at greater length, focusing in particular on whether or not the rise of the protest state is dangerous for democracy in the region, while offering some ideas for extending and improving upon this research. I conclude with some additional remarks on the state of the literature on contentious politics in emerging democracies.

THE RISE OF THE PROTEST STATE IN LATIN AMERICA

Only recently has empirical work begun to examine protest participation across countries, or have comparative studies sought to unravel how characteristics of national political institutions might bear on repertoires of contentious participation within that country's borders.[1] Perhaps more importantly, few scholars have examined how the interaction of country-level political factors with individual-level variables influences patterns of protest participation across *and* within regimes. Contrary to accounts that attribute swelling rates of protest participation to rising political and economic development (Dalton et al. 2009) or institutional weakness (Machado et al. 2011), the analysis presented in this book suggests that institutional quality has no significant linear impact on the likelihood that individuals participate in protests. Instead, results from the predictive models of protest participation analyzed in Chapter 3 uncover a substantial interactive effect for institutional quality and an intervening individual-level variable: political engagement, as measured by community activism, interest in politics, and education. Where engagement is low, institutional quality fails to register a significant impact on the likelihood that an individual will partake of protest. However, as individuals become more involved in their communities, gain access to the organizational resources necessary for mobilization, and acquire information about the political systems they inhabit, institutions begin to exert an important stimulative effect on their probability of protesting. The strongest positive effects for community engagement on protest participation are found in low-quality democratic contexts, where engaged citizens are almost twice as likely to participate in a protest rally or demonstration as their counterparts in high-quality democracies. Thus, for national-level institutions to exert a meaningful effect on protest participation, some minimal level of political engagement within the populace must be present.

This finding is robust to alternative conceptualizations of political engagement, and is especially strong when one examines the stark differences in predicted probabilities of protesting between individuals who have *zero* connections to community organizations and citizens who are at least minimally involved in some local group. Moreover, I find that this interactive relationship manifests itself in different ways beyond merely the cross-level political institutions–engagement nexus. Indeed, I also uncover a significant interactive relationship between system support and community involvement: that is, when individuals lack faith in core political institutions *and* are active in local community associations, they are far likelier to protest than when either factor is absent. Education and interest in politics interact in similar ways with institutional characteristics to what we observe for community engagement, though the findings are not as strong.

In contrast to these confirmatory results for the importance of political institutions in provoking protest among politically engaged citizens, this analysis finds few significant effects for the economic factors that have often been hailed in the literature on contentious politics in Latin America as crucial in explaining instances of mass mobilization (e.g., Walton 1989, Yashar 1998, 2005, Almeida 2007, Silva 2009). Measured at the individual level, wealth itself has little impact on an individual's probability of taking part in a rally or demonstration, nor do individuals' perceptions of the national economic situation. At the country level, measures of inequality, recent economic growth or decline, and human development also fail to lend much explanatory power to answering the question of why individuals participate in protests. While it would seem imprudent to dismiss the notion out of hand that economic conditions matter or that grievances often help ignite protests, these results seem to indicate that protests can occur during times of relative prosperity, and that bad economic times do not always result in throngs of angry demonstrators in the streets.

In Chapter 4 I extend the analysis to test the hypothesis that in protest states, formal political organizations are particularly reliant on mobilizing demonstrators in pursuit of their goals. Whereas in national regimes characterized by strong political institutions, affiliation with a political party is associated with heightened levels of formal participation, linkages to political organizations are often correlated with more contentious modes of political voice in protest states. In tandem with the analysis presented regarding the relationship between clientelism and protest in Argentina and Bolivia, this chapter thus provides strong empirical evidence for the notion that in many developing democracies, the line between institutional politics and grassroots mobilization is increasingly blurred, lending support to a growing body of research on the importance of political elites in driving amplified rates of protest (e.g., Robertson 2007, Beaulieu 2014, Cornell and Grimes 2015, Mangonnet and Murillo 2016).

In sum, these findings call for a recalibration of our understanding of the connection between national political institutions and individual-level protest participation in emerging democracies, and the determinants of contentious political participation more generally. Given the many challenges associated with democratic transition and consolidation (e.g., Linz and Stepan 1996, Schmitter 1994), the number of flawed democracies has exploded in recent years as the third—and now potentially, fourth—"waves" of democratization have spread throughout the world. Moreover, the recent economic progress in many middle-income democracies, which has coincided with stagnated growth in the wealthy countries of Europe and North America, has produced more politically engaged citizens in those regimes than ever before. At the national level, dysfunctional democratic institutions seem to combine with mass-level trends in political engagement to explain why certain individuals are more likely to protest than others.

Where institutions fail to fulfill the democratic promise of representation, politically active citizens often seek alternative means of influencing government policy that are not spelled out on a piece of paper. While the presence of contentious politics itself signals progress in countries where, only a few decades ago, any challenging of the incumbent regime was strictly prohibited, it is also symptomatic of a system that fails to provide high-quality representation and policy responsiveness to its most politically active citizens. Moreover, whereas most prior work has emphasized the mobilizing effects of economic crisis on protest, the argument presented here actually suggests that economic gains might in part *be responsible* for swelling rates of political engagement and thus protest participation.

THE PROTEST STATE AT THE SUBNATIONAL LEVEL

While Chapters 3 and 4 offer compelling evidence that institutional deficiencies at the country level can spur contentious participation by engaged individuals, in Chapters 5, 6, and 7 I narrow my focus to Argentina, a country characterized by flawed national political institutions and high levels of citizen engagement, but also vast subnational variation in terms of protest. Since Argentina's return to democracy, and specifically beginning in the mid-1990s under the Menem government, protests have become increasingly prevalent in the country. Crippled by market reforms that left a record number of Argentines unemployed, and driven by extreme disillusionment with representative institutions, the newly formed *piquetero* movement began to install roadblocks across the country in the late 1990s. In 2001, as the Argentine economic crisis reached its dramatic apex, thousands of citizens descended on the capital city to voice their indignation over the corrupt and unresponsive political actors and institutions they deemed culpable for their current state of despair.

More than just reflective of a deep economic crisis that had serious negative consequences for Argentine citizens' quality of life, the 2001–2002 protests signaled a crisis of representation. Argentine citizens were fed up with a system that seemingly rewarded corrupt and inept leadership, power hungry presidents, and parties that pivoted from one ideological stance to another at the drop of a hat. The rallying cry that resonated with so many Argentinean citizens—"All of them must go!" (*"Que se vayan todos!"*)— perfectly captured the overwhelming lack of faith in formal vehicles for representation that pervaded at the time, and the tactics used by Argentine protestors at this pivotal moment—such as roadblocks and *cacerolazos*— have since consolidated as relatively normal repertoires of political participation. Argentina thus represents the classic example of the protest state.

However, in spite of what this national-level narrative would lead us to believe, protest has taken hold unevenly *within* Argentina. According to data from two leading Argentine think tanks, *Nueva Mayoría* and PIMSA, the country as a whole has indeed become more contentious over the years and protest repertoires have expanded in usefulness and scope, but there are certain provinces where protests are not particularly common. This subnational landscape offers a unique opportunity to explore the question of how subnational variation in democratic quality impinges on varying levels of protest activity *within* a protest state.

In Chapters 6 and 7, I find that characteristics of subnational regime institutions have important consequences for the number, and nature, of protests that occur within a given provincial context. Utilizing the innovative measurement strategy devised by Gervasoni (2010), I calculate (on an annual basis) subnational democracy scores for each of Argentina's twenty-three provinces over the course of nearly twenty years. I find that, net of other factors, the degree of democracy within a province plays an important *but nonlinear* role in the frequency of protests that occur within its borders. Consistent with the more general argument about the quality of representative institutions, but also expanding the scope of the argument to incorporate explicitly undemocratic political systems, I find that aggressive protests tend to surge in the least democratic provinces. Thus, where formal representational outlets are deemed inconsequential, and hegemonic subnational governments exert a great deal of control over local politics, prospective protestors are more likely to adopt more aggressive— and potentially riskier—repertoires of participation. However, I also discover that peaceful protests are less common in both the *most* democratic and *least* democratic contexts. In other words, at intermediate levels of subnational democracy, where representative institutions are most likely to fall short of their democratic promise but are not so illiberal as to preclude any challenging of the incumbent government or force protestors to explore more radical options, moderate protests flourish as a form of political voice.

In provincial political environments like San Luis, opposition movements are ignored, co-opted, or even repressed by an incredibly powerful local machine, making movement organization and mobilization too costly except under extreme circumstances, when highly aggressive tactics are utilized. In provinces like Mendoza, citizens enjoy competitive multiparty democracy and high-quality representation, rendering contentious participation unnecessary for the most part but not obsolete. However, in provinces like Jujuy, Neuquén, and Buenos Aires, where one party often dominates the political realm but not to the extent that they exert total hegemony over political institutions, civil society, and economic opportunities, peaceful protest can thrive as a normal form of political voice.

The results from the subnational analysis of protest across Argentine provinces reveal the limitations of the "bad institutions" argument. While findings from many studies to date on this topic suggest that the worse institutions get, the more likely protest becomes (e.g., Machado et al. 2011, Boulding 2010, 2014, Arce and Mangonnet 2013), it appears that flawed institutions stimulate protest only to a point, after which they become so closed off that many protest movements are incapable of mobilizing at all to articulate their claims. This curvilinear relationship between institutional context and protest harkens back to Eisinger's (1973) work on protest behavior in American cities in the 1960s, but has been conspicuously absent in recent accounts of protest in the developing world.

The findings from the national and subnational analyses in this book largely complement one another, revealing how institutional characteristics interact with individual-level factors to explain contentious political behavior. While I emphasize the role of political engagement more at the national level, it also reveals itself as an important intervening variable in Argentine provinces. However, subnational units in Argentina differ more on certain key variables regarding the quality of democracy than Latin American countries do—that is, the most illiberal Argentine provinces exceed any national regime (other than Cuba) in terms of the extent to which they provide governments with nearly complete control of political life within their borders. In such cases, civil society is often neutered and rarely serves as a mobilizational outlet for disgruntled citizens. Thus, while institutions in such cases as La Rioja, San Luis, and Formosa provide very little responsiveness, they also thwart most opportunities to contest the current government.

By analyzing protest data from Argentine provinces, I expand both the range of this analysis in terms of the openness of political institutions under consideration, but also bring into the fold two measures of what are inherently different, and more aggressive, modes of protest: roadblocks and acts of contention. Subnational political context seems to have different effects on distinct contentious repertoires, making radical modes of protest more common in less democratic contexts while exerting a curvilinear effect on street demonstrations that diminishes individuals' odds of participating in the least democratic subnational contexts. In highlighting how institutional settings can seemingly encourage certain types of contention while rendering others less common, this book has put forth what I argue is a more nuanced account of the complex relationship between democracy and protest than in most recent work on contentious politics in Latin America.

In sum, while political institutions certainly have an impact on the prevalence of contentious politics and the form that it takes within a certain regime, I find that the nature of this impact is less straightforward than previously argued. Institutional weakness does seem to contribute to higher rates of protest participation—however, this effect depends on some minimal level of political engagement among citizens, and can disappear in cases where those institutions become so closed off as to thwart many protest activities. Moreover, not all protest repertoires should be treated equal, as more aggressive tactics thrive in more illiberal contexts, whereas peaceful street demonstrations tend to surge at middling levels of democratic quality.

THE PROTEST STATE IN ARGENTINA AND BEYOND

In this book, I argue that protest can "normalize" where democratic political institutions are weak but citizens' interest and engagement in political life is high. In Latin America, the protest state has emerged due to the consolidation of relatively weak institutions and the emergence of an increasingly activated democratic citizenry, which draws on a budding web of organizational resources to demand more from the region's democracies. To further explore the idea of normalization, I narrow my focus to Argentina—a country characterized by weak institutions but a highly engaged citizenry, which seems to utilize contentious tactics in virtually any political conflict that arises in the country. In Argentina, rates of protest participation have increased since the mid-1990s, and protestors appear to be fairly representative of the general population. Moreover, civil society organizations and political parties often mobilize contentious activities to pursue their goals, and clientelistic support buying seems to have expanded into contentious repertoires of participation, as exemplified by Auyero's (2007) seminal work on the lootings that occurred in the Buenos Aires conurbano in 2001 and 2002.

Evidence from the rest of Latin America is mixed in terms of the degree to which protest has normalized. Only Peru and Bolivia outpace Argentina with respect to participation rates since 2008, and regional analyses generally reveal striking similarities between protestors and citizens who participate in politics through formal vehicles. However, one might also imagine that in certain countries where institutions are of a higher quality, like Chile, Costa Rica, or Uruguay, protestors make up a smaller, less representative subsample of the total population. In Chile, community participation is not associated with protest participation—which offers a striking contrast to what we observe in Argentina and the region at large (LAPOP 2008–2012)—and is instead a much stronger predictor of voting than in Argentina. On the other hand, the analysis in Chapter 4 illustrates that Bolivia is home to a similar "protest-buying" dynamic to that found in Argentina, where the contentious repertoire is so entrenched that political actors actually use clientelistic rewards to mobilize demonstrations on their behalf.

To make a definitive claim about whether or not certain repertoires of participation have consolidated as the years have passed, one would need longitudinal data from within each of those countries, which is beyond the scope of this book. However, in Argentina the data tell a very clear story: thirty years of weak institutions and low-quality democratic representation has birthed a country where contentious participation is the norm, as individuals seek more effective tactics for influencing government. The provinces within Argentina where this is *not* the case are either (1) so authoritarian that normal, everyday protest mobilization is deemed too costly, or (2) high-functioning enough that citizens within that province are content to operate through formal vehicles for democratic representation.

BRAZIL: HARBINGERS OF A PROTEST STATE?

One case that has been conspicuously absent from this book is Brazil, which has rather famously found itself embroiled in mass protests since 2013. The current cycle of Brazilian protest began with demonstrations against the country's staging of the 2014 World Cup during the 2013 Confederations Cup, which was widely viewed as wasteful and corrupt, particularly given substandard public health services, underfunded schools, and the country's crumbling infrastructure (Moseley and Layton 2013). Popular discontent reached its zenith in May 2016 when, only a few years removed from enjoying a prosperous economy and high approval ratings, President Dilma Rousseff was impeached in the Chamber of Deputies and Senate. She has since been removed from office permanently, but mass protests have continued to rage.

What has made recent events in Brazil most remarkable is that it has long been known as one of the least contentious countries in Latin America. As recently as 2012, only about 4 percent of Brazilian citizens reported having participated in a street march or demonstration, placing it in the bottom third of Latin American countries—a position that had remained steady since the AmericasBarometer expanded to Brazil in 2006 (LAPOP 2006–2012). Whereas neighboring countries like Argentina, Bolivia, and Venezuela had experienced multiple explosive episodes of contention in the first decade of the twentieth century, which precipitated changes in government on numerous occasions, Brazil had remained unaffected by such protests since at least the early 1990s. Yet according to the 2014 AmericasBarometer surveys, rates of protest had doubled from 2012 levels, as Brazil climbed from the bottom third to one of Latin America's most contentious countries.

Does the theoretical framework presented above help explain why protest has surged to unprecedented levels over the past three years? In my view, absolutely. In terms of political engagement, Brazil has experienced massive gains in terms of economic and human development since the turn of the century. Whereas in the early 1990s as many as 25 percent of Brazilian citizens lived in extreme poverty, that number fell to 2.2 percent in 2009. In 2011, Brazil's Gini coefficient, a common measure of income inequality, fell to .52—the lowest level in nearly fifty years (World Bank 2013). Along with these improvements, average rates of educational attainment increased by more than two years between 2008 and 2012 (LAPOP 2012). In sum, economy prosperity in Brazil created a more educated and engaged populace, as millions rose from poverty equipped with new tools for organizing themselves and articulating their claims.

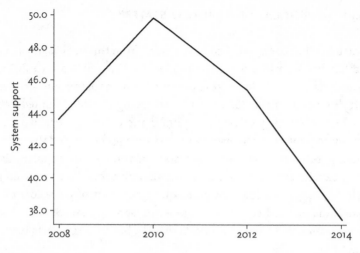

Figure 8.1 System Support in Brazil, 2008–2014
© AmericasBarometer by LAPOP

On the institutional side, Brazil fits the protest state story to a T. In the year preceding the initial protests, Brazilians ranked 22nd of twenty-six countries in the Americas in terms of system support, which gauges trust in core political institutions (LAPOP 2012). Further, more than 65 percent of the Brazilian population believed the political system was corrupt (LAPOP 2012). Perhaps most important, Brazilians reported the third lowest rate of satisfaction with public services (as measured through evaluations of health services, the quality of roads, and public schools), outpacing only Haiti and Trinidad and Tobago among countries in the Americas (LAPOP 2012). In tandem with governance scores from the World Bank, which place Brazil in the middle of the pack in Latin America in terms of institutional quality, there is plentiful evidence to indicate that Brazilian political institutions are plagued by the same types of protest-inducing flaws found in countries like Argentina and Peru.

Yet there is additional, more direct evidence from survey data that the two interacting variables on which the theory of the protest state rests—institutional quality and political engagement—have been trending in a direction that portends higher rates of contention. Figure 8.1 illustrates that since 2010, system support has experienced a steep decline, after peaking during the final term of popular president Lula da Silva (LAPOP 2014). As institutions have increasingly lost their legitimacy in the eyes of Brazilians, so too have citizens become far more active in their communities, as they link up with the types of organizations that can help fuel contentious activity (Figure 8.2).

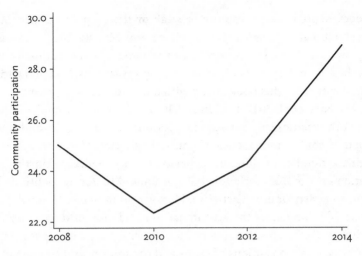

Figure 8.2 Community Participation in Brazil, 2008–2014
© AmericasBarometer by LAPOP

In conclusion, the recent protests in Brazil have been unprecedented in many ways, given the country's recent history as one of Latin America's least contentious regimes. However, according to data from the AmericasBarometer survey, Brazil displayed several harbingers of eventual contention, based on widespread dissatisfaction with public services and core political institutions, and increasingly high levels of education and community engagement, amid decreasing levels of poverty. Thus, despite having little established tradition of contentious activity, the two interacting dynamics that combine to give rise to protest states were present and eventually produced demonstrations that proved massive in terms of both scope and political impact. Now that President Rousseff has been removed from office and the activism of many Brazilian protestors have continued unabated, it seems increasingly evident that protest has been absorbed into everyday political life in the same way it has in countries like Argentina and Bolivia.

TAKEAWAYS

Moving forward, several important implications emerge from this book for future research on political participation and democracy in Latin America and beyond. The first is that uneven institutional development in the region has serious consequences for how democratic citizens engage the political regimes they inhabit. While a significant body of research has documented the persistence of weak or flawed political institutions throughout Latin America (e.g., Levitsky and Murillo 2005, Scartascini and Tommasi 2009), less research has evaluated how institutional quality might bear on patterns of political participation across and within national political contexts. This book, along with a handful of other recent studies (e.g., Machado et al. 2011, Boulding 2010, 2014), offers an empirical evaluation of the relationship between institutional characteristics and the utilization of contentious modes of political behavior. However, one might imagine a number of different behavioral consequences of institutional variation on variables including but not limited to voting, political clientelism, and party or union activism. Plus, variation in institutional quality undoubtedly influences the attitudinal consolidation of democracy (Linz and Stepan 1996), as well as public opinion with regard to support for the political system, perceptions of crime and corruption, and support for extralegal or anti-democratic measures like public lynchings or military coups. Research examining how institutional variation influences mass-level behaviors and attitudes is still somewhat limited in emerging democracies (see Anderson and Singer 2008), especially taking into account the vast differences in institutional quality observed in a region like Latin America, and thus represents a fruitful avenue for deepening our understanding of democratic politics in Latin America.

Another important contribution of this research is that it further underlines the importance of subnational approaches to understanding political phenomena, particularly in the developing world. By conducting a provincial-level analysis of contentious politics in Argentina, a country characterized by stark subnational variation in terms of economic and political development, I marshal additional evidence for my general argument regarding the connection between institutional characteristics and protest participation. The analysis of Argentine provinces presented in this book offers a more expansive universe in terms of the types of protest under consideration, the temporal coverage of the data, and the magnitude of the variation on key institutional characteristics, which results in somewhat distinct findings from the cross-national analysis. Within countries, democracy can take hold at a different pace, and what we think we might know about a given country's politics and development prospects might not apply at all to certain territories within its national boundaries. The differences that I encountered between cities and provinces when living and conducting fieldwork in Argentina made this fact clearer than ever.

On that note, it is important to reiterate how crucial it was for this particular book project that in testing the theory, I was able to draw on different types of data from distinct sources, at multiple levels of analysis. Organizations like LAPOP provide an invaluable resource to students of political behavior, and we are fortunate to have unprecedented access to rich mass-level data that, until recently, only existed for the United States and Europe. However, while to some extent cross-national survey data served as the empirical backbone of this book, this study benefited greatly from the subnational component. By testing my theoretical approach on two distinct sources of event-counts data from Argentina and uncovering results that in many ways corroborated findings from the national level, but also revealed nuanced differences, I believe this project provides a much more convincing test of my argument than would have been possible with only survey data. Moreover, by living in Argentina for a year and conducting interviews in three diverse provinces and the capital city, I gained an on-the-ground understanding of the country's politics that contextualized what I was observing in the data.

From a normative standpoint, the analysis in this book has not revealed any nefarious, anti-democratic characteristics of individuals participating in protests in Latin America—rather, it highlights how active democratic citizens adopt different repertoires of participation depending on the responsiveness of formal political institutions. On the one hand, rising protest activity signals a bellwether moment for Latin American democracy after decades of inconsistent democratic rule. Regardless of protestors' claims, the fact that most citizens across the region can now take to the streets without fear of repression represents a positive step for civil liberties and democratic norms. However, this book argues that protests are often symptomatic of *low-quality* democracy. Protest remains a relatively blunt instrument for obtaining desirable outcomes in terms of representation—that is, even when demonstrations are successful in the short term, they often provoke only piecemeal concessions from governments seeking to avoid public relations nightmares rather than meaningful long-term changes in how public officials respond to the popular will. If policymakers in the region seek to assuage protests, they need to consider serious institutional reforms that more effectively incorporate democratic citizenries hungry for heightened accountability and more responsible governance. While recent innovations like prior consultation in Bolivia, an independent corruption commission in Guatemala, and participatory budgeting in Brazil carry real promise, they also require good faith efforts by governments and citizen groups alike to make them stick. Never before have so many Latin Americans been engaged in democratic politics—it is time that the institutions that represent them reflect that investment.

NEXT STEPS

As much as I would like to say that this book offers the definitive statement on democratic political institutions and protest in Latin America, it leaves numerous questions unanswered that should be addressed in future studies. Setting aside obvious limitations of this book that could only be solved with additional research funding or data that do not currently exist, but might in the future—for example, conducting another national case study to compare with Argentina or obtaining additional national-level survey data for a time-series analysis of protest across countries—here I consider several potential extensions of this project that might advance our understanding of protest in future studies.

One important next step for this project would be to evaluate the *consequences* of the protest state for political representation and democratic politics in Latin America—a topic that this book does little to address. How do governments respond to protests in contexts like Peru, Bolivia, and Argentina, versus countries where contentious participation is less common? How effective are protestors in pursuing their political goals through street-based, extra-institutional activities compared to formal modes of participation? On the one hand, there are numerous examples of protests really *working* in many Latin American contexts, which inevitably explains to some extent why individuals and groups continue to view contentious activities as viable problem-solving strategies. On the other hand, policymakers might suffer from protest fatigue in a "boy who cried wolf" scenario, where contentious actions lose their power through overuse. The protest state might create incentives such that governments respond to protests only enough to quell the masses, without having to provide long-term solutions to real problems. Unlike representation through elections and political parties, protests require no guaranteed feedback between individuals and representatives—if a particular issue fades once it has been resolved in the short term, policymakers are not obligated to follow through on whatever promises they made to ensure that the issue goes away.

It seems to me that there are several potential approaches to studying the effectiveness of protest participation in Latin America. First, one could track specific claims over time and evaluate how those protest-motivating issues were eventually resolved. In so doing, scholars could estimate how frequently protestors are successful in a particular context in accomplishing their goals, and shed light on the conditions under which protests succeed or fail.[2] Second, one might utilize survey data to explore how efficacious and well-represented protestors feel compared to participants in other more formal political activities, while attempting to account for obvious problems related to endogeneity. Finally, students of contentious politics might explore how the policy preferences of protestors correspond to actual policy output, compared to preferences of non-protestors—a strategy that has been used in the American context to examine if voters are better represented than nonvoters (Griffin and Newman 2005).

Debating whether heightened levels of protest are "good" or "bad" for democracy is perhaps an even thornier enterprise. The fact that protestors across Latin America are now able to take to the streets and make claims on governments is undoubtedly an important sign of progress for a region where, only thirty years ago, those same individuals would have been imprisoned or worse. Moreover, widespread protests are indicative of a swelling number of citizens who are engaged in politics and want to have their voices heard, which is a positive sign in an era when scholars in other regions of the world bemoan declining turnout rates and widespread apathy with regard to politics. My experience living and conducting research in Argentina gave me the distinct impression that protestors were often incredibly knowledgeable about the politics of their country and perceived shortcomings of political institutions and actors, and despite their frustration had clear ideas about how they could potentially improve the current situation.

From my research and that of others (e.g., Boulding 2014), it also appears that protestors are not overly extremist or undemocratic in their political views. Figure 8.3 graphs responses to a number of questions in the AmericasBarometer surveys regarding democratic norms and processes, which aim to measure support for democracy as the best form of government, tolerance of unpopular political organizations, and hypothetical support for undemocratic actions like a military coup under conditions of high crime or corruption.[3] By and large, protestors appear very similar to non-protestors in their responses to these questions, and even appear slightly more democratic when it comes to tolerating the participation of groups with whom they disagree. Furthermore, Booth and Seligson (2009) argue and find that protest might actually serve to help appease disgruntled citizens with low levels of support for the political system, making them less likely to undertake more drastic anti-regime activities. Overall, it appears that protestors resemble ordinary citizens with respect to their views toward democracy, and not a threat to consolidating Latin American regimes. However, that does not negate the possibility that protests can be utilized by groups who intend to depose of democratically elected governments on questionable grounds, as was the case in the 2016 impeachment of Brazilian President Dilma Rousseff.

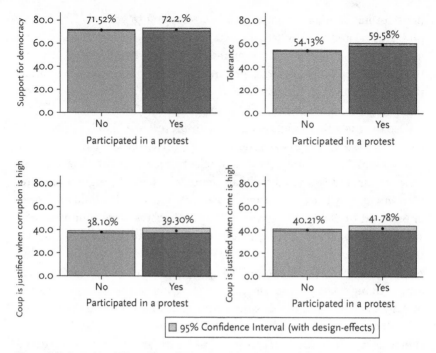

Figure 8.3 Protestors' Views Regarding Democratic Norms and Processes
© AmericasBarometer, LAPOP

At the same time, protests are by definition aggressive, can frequently descend into outright political violence, and often carry with them negative consequences for local and national economies. Regardless of whether it is the protestors or law enforcement officers who are the chief perpetrators, the fact remains that protests are sometimes (if rarely) dangerous in Latin America, raising serious concerns regarding public safety. As mentioned above, protest also remains a relatively blunt instrument for obtaining desirable outcomes in terms of representation—that is, even when demonstrations are successful in the short term, they often provoke only temporary solutions to what are systemic problems, rather than meaningful long-term reforms in how public officials respond to the popular will.

Another potential avenue of research would endeavor to evaluate the representativeness of protestors vis-à-vis partakers of other forms of political participation. Scholars have long expressed concern that voters are not representative of the entire population, particularly in countries without obligatory voting (Lijphart 1997), as voters often consist of a biased cross-section of citizens in terms of class, racial, and ethnic characteristics. Additionally, research from the U.S. context has found that costlier forms of participation like local community and political party activism exacerbate participation biases, as wealthier, whiter, and more educated citizens exert far more influence via civic voluntarism than their poorer, less privileged counterparts (Verba et al. 1995). While in the Argentine case it does seem that protest has normalized across several important demographic variables, there are other ways in which augmented influence for the people who take to the streets might distort policy outcomes in undesirable ways. I briefly expand upon that idea below.

As argued throughout this book, protestors need organization to effectively mobilize. Thus, individuals with access to these crucial organizational resources are likely to exert more influence on policymakers than less connected citizens. In a case like the 2008 agricultural uprising in Argentina, where farmers throughout the country quickly organized to block major highways and cease the delivery of many agricultural products until the government abandoned its proposed export tax increase, a small sliver of the Argentine population was able to achieve a very influential political victory through sheer organizational strength and dexterity. As opposed to elections, where a large percentage of the population has the opportunity to weigh in and provide a more representative depiction of public opinion, protests tend to serve to promote the particularistic interests of an organized few, except in rare instances where massive numbers mobilize to communicate more general claims. In Dahl's terms, this offers a classic case of the *intensity of preferences* winning the day over the majority of preferences (Dahl 1956). While perhaps in some ways deserving of their heightened influence due to their efforts, educated, politically interested, and socially connected citizens might not speak on behalf of their less contentious (and less politically savvy) counterparts, who by abstaining from protests miss out on an important opportunity to influence public policy.

Another omission from this book is that I largely neglect variation in protest "type" as an important distinction at the national level. Not all repertoires are created equal—peaceful street demonstrations are different from roadblocks, which are in turn distinct from organized lootings of grocery stores. As we find in the case of Argentina, it is possible that institutional characteristics encourage certain types of contention but not others. Future work might further divide repertoires by type, analyzing whether or not institutional deficiencies exert the same type of influence on peaceful demonstrations as they do on more confrontational, violent tactics in different Latin American regimes. My expectation is that the national level would play out much in the same way as the provincial level in Argentina— while protests might be less common in more illiberal contexts, the protests that arise in those settings have a higher probability of becoming violent, as was the case of the "*multisectorial*" in San Luis in 2004–2005. This expectation would be relevant to the case of Venezuela, for example, which seems to be creeping closer to the type of closed institutions explored in the subnational chapters of this book.

Another omission from this manuscript concerns my underemphasizing of the role of social media in mobilizing protests in twenty-first century Latin America. While I include social media usage in several of the models reported in Chapter 3, one could really dedicate an entire book to the increasing ease with which (particularly young) people can organize compared to even a decade ago. Just as protest repertoires differ a great deal in terms of cause, type, and consequence, so do organizational resources. The rise of the Internet in Latin America, a region with some of the highest usage rates in the world according to recent studies (The Economist 2013), certainly plays some part in explaining expanded citizen engagement in politics and organizational capacity and thus, protest participation.

Finally, perhaps the gravest missing piece from this book is my inattention to how systematic differences in law enforcement responses to protestors might shape protest repertoires. Indeed, the characteristics of protestors themselves and the typical response by police to contentious behaviors would seem highly consequential in explaining patterns of contention in a particular context. For example, in a country with weak institutions like Argentina, protest appears to be relatively normal across demographic and socioeconomic groups. Because public manifestations are so common, and protestors are composed of such a large, diverse cross-section of the total population, demonstrations are most often peaceful and non-confrontational (with obvious exceptions like the 2001–2002 riots). However, in a country like Chile, where protest is far less common and utilized by a less representative subsection of the population (usually younger and more leftist), we have found on occasion that tactics are more aggressive and are often met by police with tear gas and nightsticks (e.g., the student protests of 2011 and 2012). I leave these dynamics relatively unexplored in this book, but future studies would do well to take the next step and explore these intriguing puzzles.

CLOSING THOUGHTS

This manuscript has contributed to our understanding of why people protest at different rates across Latin America, and how characteristics of national and provincial political institutions interact with individual-level factors to explain why individual citizens adopt contentious tactics in their quest to make democracy work for them. It has also shed light on a particularly contentious case in Argentina, a country where protest continues to shape democratic politics on an everyday basis, and how uneven democratization at the subnational level can influence patterns of political participation within a single country. In so doing, this book connects the two dominant strains of comparative research—institutions and behavior—to offer a comprehensive examination of one of the most important sociopolitical phenomena in Latin America today.

Moving beyond twenty-first-century Latin America, the findings from this book might also help understand how gains in social development and political engagement, coupled with low-quality formal political institutions, could lie at the root of mass protests in other regions and time periods. Indeed, an increase in civic engagement and the use of social media to share political information clearly played an important role in Arab Spring countries, where citizens began to demand institutional reforms that made leaders more accountable to the citizenry. In Europe, citizens in countries like Greece and Spain—both of which possess myriad educated and engaged citizens—have not only been devastated by a severe economic recession, but frustrated by their inability to have their voices heard by policymakers amid EU-prescribed austerity measures. Even in the United States, the reemergence of racial oppression as a central motivating grievance, as embodied by the Black Lives Matter movement and the uptick in activism by groups spanning from women to academics in the wake of Donald Trump's election, highlight the usefulness of the theoretical framework presented here. Thus, this book casts light on a broader set of phenomena and informs scholars as they attempt to understand the causes and consequences of future episodes of protest across the world.

Despite this book's contributions, it also serves to highlight how much work is left to be done on the topic of contentious politics in the twenty-first century. Democracy is changing, as increasingly engaged citizens across the world grow impatient with the unresponsive nature of formal institutions and thus utilize an expanding array of organizational tools to mobilize contentious repertoires of participation in making their voices heard. Only by expanding upon this book to include other cases and repertoires of contention, and further delving into the consequences of the protest state, will we begin to fully grasp how contentious behaviors are revolutionizing democratic politics in Latin America and beyond.

APPENDIX

Table A1 WORLD BANK GOVERNANCE INDICATOR SCORES, 2007–2011 (CHAPTER 3)

	Voice and Accountability	Government Effectiveness	Rule of Law	Institutions Index
Chile	1.03	1.19	1.28	**1.17**
Uruguay	1.07	0.56	0.65	**0.76**
Costa Rica	0.97	0.29	0.44	**0.57**
Panama	0.56	0.13	−0.14	**0.18**
Trinidad and Tobago	0.52	0.31	−0.52	**0.10**
Jamaica	0.51	0.23	−0.45	**0.10**
Brazil	0.5	−0.03	−0.21	**0.09**
Belize	0.65	−0.44	−0.33	**−0.04**
Suriname	0.37	−0.08	−0.48	**−0.06**
Guyana	0.08	−0.09	−0.22	**−0.08**
Mexico	0.1	0.22	−0.61	**−0.10**
Argentina	0.35	−0.18	−0.61	**−0.15**
Colombia	−0.18	0.06	−0.38	**−0.17**
El Salvador	0.07	−0.11	−0.74	**−0.26**
Peru	0.04	−0.35	−0.69	**−0.33**
Dominican Republic	0.08	−0.577	−0.69	**−0.40**
Bolivia	−0.03	−0.51	−1	**−0.51**
Honduras	−0.44	−0.6	−0.92	**−0.65**
Paraguay	−0.15	−0.86	−0.95	**−0.65**
Guatemala	−0.29	−0.64	−1.1	**−0.68**
Ecuador	−0.26	−0.74	−1.14	**−0.71**
Nicaragua	−0.43	−0.92	−0.79	**−0.71**
Venezuela	−0.84	−1	−1.58	**−1.14**
Haiti	−0.68	−1.49	−1.37	**−1.18**

Table A2 QUESTION WORDING AND DESCRIPTIVE STATISTICS (CHAPTER 3)

Variable	Question Wording or Explanation	N	Mean	Standard Deviation	Min	Max
	Dependent Variable					
Protest	"In the last 12 months, have you participated in a demonstration or protest march?" Yes (1); No (0).	105,600	.103	.304	0	1
	Independent Variables					
Community Engagement	"Now, changing the subject. In the last 12 months have you tried to help to solve a problem in your community or in your neighborhood? Please, tell me if you did it at least once a week, once or twice a month, once or twice a year, or never in the last 12 months." This was repeated for religious organization, parents' association, community improvement organization, an association of professionals, or a political party. 4-point scale; higher values = more participation. Answers to these questions were then converted into an index.	116,526	19.628	16.661	0	100
External Efficacy	"Those who govern this country are interested in what people like you think. How much do you agree or disagree with this statement?" 100-point scale; higher values = more efficacy.	111,596	39.365	32.099	0	100

		N	Mean	SD	Min	Max
System Support Index	"I am going to ask you a series of questions. I am going to ask that you use the numbers provided in the ladder to answer. 1. To what extent do you think the courts in (country) guarantee a fair trial? 2. To what extent do you respect the political institutions of (country)? 3. To what extent do you think that citizens' basic rights are well protected by the political system of (country)? 4. To what extent do you feel proud of living under the political system of (country)? 5. To what extent do you think that one should support the political system of (country)?" 7-point scale; higher values = more positive evaluation of institutions. Answers to these questions were then converted into an index.	113,147	52.234	22.548	0	100
Personal Economic Situation	"How would you describe your overall economic situation? Would you say that it is very good, good, neither good nor bad, bad, or very bad?" 100-point scale; higher values = good.	115949	49.441	20.987	0	100
National Economic Situation	"How would you describe the country's economic situation? Would you say that it is very good, good, neither good nor bad, bad, or very bad?" 100-point scale; higher values = good.	115,512	42.121	23.367	0	100
Satisfaction with Public Services	"And thinking about this city/area where you live, are you very satisfied, satisfied, dissatisfied, or very dissatisfied with the condition of the streets, roads, and highways?" Repeated for public health services and schools. 100-point scale; higher values = more satisfied.	34,685	50.194	19.471	0	100

(continued)

Table A2 CONTINUED

Variable	Question Wording or Explanation	N	Mean	Standard Deviation	Min	Max
Interest in Politics	How much interest do you have in politics: a lot, some, little or none? 100-point scale; higher values = more interest.	115,418	35.277	.772	0	100
Shared Information Via Social Network	And in the last twelve months, have you read or shared political information through any social network website such as Twitter or Facebook or Orkut? Coded as 1 if "yes", 0 if "no."	38,126	.111	.327	0	1
Perception of Corruption	Taking into account your own experience or what you have heard, corruption among public officials is very common, common, uncommon, or very uncommon? 100-point scale; higher values = higher perception of corruption.	109,775	72.385	28.472	0	100
Age	Respondents' age in years.	116,042	39.193	15.803	16	99
Wealth Quintile	A weighted index that measures wealth based on the possession of certain household goods such as televisions, refrigerators, conventional and cellular telephones, vehicles, washing machines, microwave ovens, indoor plumbing, indoor bathrooms, and computers.	116,275	2.933	1.422	1	5
Education	Level of formal education. 4-point scale; 0 = None, 1 = Primary, 2 = Secondary, 3 = Superior	116,656	1.817	0.772	0	3
Female	1 if female, 0 if male.	116,655	0.501	0.500	0	1

Table A3 DESCRIPTIONS OF WORLD BANK GOVERNANCE INDICATORS (CHAPTER 3)

Voice and Accountability: "Reflects perceptions of the extent to which a country's citizens are able to participate in selecting their government, as well as freedom of expression, freedom of association, and a free media."

Government Effectiveness: "Reflects perceptions of the quality of public services, the quality of the civil service and the degree of its independence from political pressures, the quality of policy formulation and implementation, and the credibility of the government's commitment to such policies."

Rule of Law: "Reflects perceptions of the extent to which agents have confidence in and abide by the rules of society, and in particular the quality of contract enforcement, property rights, the police, and the courts, as well as the likelihood of crime and violence."

Table A4 COMMUNITY ENGAGEMENT AND PROTEST: INSTRUMENTAL VARIABLES REGRESSION (CHAPTER 3)

VARIABLES	Model 1 IVReg (2SLS)
	Second stage (DV: Protest)
Community Participation	.0007***
	(.0001)
Female	−.024***
	(.002)
Age	−.0004***
	(.00006)
Interest in Politics	.001***
	(.00003)
Education	.027***
	(.001)
Wealth	−.0002
	(.0007)
Internal Efficacy	−.00007**
	(.00003)
Constant	.030***
	(.005)

(continued)

Table A4 CONTINUED

VARIABLES	Model 1 IVReg (2SLS)
First stage **(DV: Community Participation)**	
Church Attendance	.200***
	(.001)
Female	.423***
	(.003)
Age	.013***
	(.003)
Interest in Politics	.072***
	(.002)
Education	−.027
	(.072)
Wealth	.015
	(.037)
Internal Efficacy	018***
	(.002)
Constant	5.374***
	(.001)
Cragg-Donald Wald F-statistic	19557.97
Number of Observations	96,546

Standard errors in parentheses
*** p<0.01, ** p<0.05, * p<0.1
Two-tailed tests:
Church attendance was chosen as the instrument—a variable that strongly correlates with community participation but is unassociated with protest participation. Indeed, the Cragg-Donald Wald F-statistic indicates that this is a *very* strong instrument. The assumption I then make in the analysis above is that church attendance does not influence protest participation through any pathway other than community engagement. The results for community engagement remain strong, and comparable to those presented in the body of the chapter.

Table A5 QUESTION WORDING AND DESCRIPTIVE STATISTICS (CHAPTER 6)

Variable	Question Wording or Explanation	N	Mean	Standard Deviation	Min	Max
	Dependent Variable					
Protest	"In the last 12 months, have you participated in a demonstration or protest march?" Yes (1); No (0).	4,313	0.168	0.374	0	1
	Independent Variables					
Community Engagement	"Now, changing the subject. In the last 12 months have you tried to help to solve a problem in your community or in your neighborhood? Please, tell me if you did it at least once a week, once or twice a month, once or twice a year, or never in the last 12 months." This was repeated for religious organization, parents' association, community improvement organization, an association of professionals, or a political party. 4-point scale; higher values = more participation. Answers to these questions were then converted into an index.	4,406	11.105	13.722	0	100
System Support Index	"I am going to ask you a series of questions. I am going to ask that you use the numbers provided in the ladder to answer. 1. To what extent do you think the courts in (country) guarantee a fair trial? 2. To what extent do you respect the political institutions of (country)? 3. To what extent do you think that citizens' basic rights are well protected by the political system of (country)? 4. To what extent do you feel proud of living under the political system of (country)? 5. To what extent do you think that one should support the political system of (country)?" 7-point scale; higher values = more positive evaluation of institutions. Answers to these questions were then converted into an index.	4,277	49.541	24.190	0	100

(continued)

Table A5 CONTINUED

Variable	Question Wording or Explanation	N	Mean	Standard Deviation	Min	Max
Personal Economic Situation	"How would you describe your overall economic situation? Would you say that it is very good, good, neither good nor bad, bad, or very bad?" 100-point scale; higher values = good.	4,365	53.923	20.223	0	100
Interest in Politics	How much interest do you have in politics: a lot, some, little, or none? 100-point scale; higher values = more interest.	4,338	40.672	31.878	0	100
Age	Respondents' age in years.	4,383	38.069	15.610	17	99
Wealth Quintile	A weighted index that measures wealth based on the possession of certain household goods such as televisions, refrigerators, conventional and cellular telephones, vehicles, washing machines, microwave ovens, indoor plumbing, indoor bathrooms, and computers.	4,408	2.907	1.390	1	5
Interpersonal Trust	And speaking of the people from around here, would you say that people in this community are very trustworthy, somewhat trustworthy, not very trustworthy, or untrustworthy...? 100 point scale; higher values = more trustworthy.	4,308	59.278	27.348	0	100
Presidential Approval	Speaking in general of the current administration, how would you rate the job performance of President [NAME]? 100 point scale; higher values = more favorable.	4,182	59.278	27.348	0	100
Education	Level of formal education. 4-point scale; 0 = None, 1 = Primary, 2 = Secondary, 3 = Superior	4,398	1.994	0.746	0	3
Urban	1 if urban, 0 if rural	4,408	.510	1.109	1	2
Female	1 if female, 0 if male.	4,408	0.510	0.500	0	1

Table A6 PREDICTIVE MODELS OF AGGRESSIVE PROTEST EVENTS ACROSS ARGENTINE PROVINCE (**POISSON REGRESSION MODELS INCLUDING SOY AND OIL DUMMIES**)

VARIABLES	Acts of Rebellion (Annual # of events) Model 1 Coeff. (s.e.)	Roadblocks (Annual # of events) Model 2 Coeff. (s.e.)	Acts of Rebellion (Annual # of events) Model 3 Coeff. (s.e.)	Roadblocks (Annual # of events) Model 4 Coeff. (s.e.)
PBG per Capita (log)	−0.467**	−0.825***	−0.485**	−0.368*
	(0.231)	(0.189)	(0.235)	(0.222)
PBG Change	0.00001	0.0002***	0.00005	0.0002***
	(0.00004)	(0.00005)	(0.00004)	(0.00006)
Unemployment	0.033***	0.094***	0.034***	0.062***
	(0.012)	(0.012)	(0.013)	(0.014)
PJ Governor	−0.197**	−0.039	−0.138**	0.045
	(0.094)	(0.105)	(0.097)	(0.112)
Distance	0.002	0.003***	−0.0004	0.0007**
	(0.0004)	(0.0003)	(0.0003)	(0.0003)
Public Employment	−0.013***	−0.002	−0.010***	−0.009**
	(0.004)	(0.004)	(0.004)	(0.004)
Oil	1.344***	1.841***	1.216***	1.132***
	(0.257)	(0.220)	(0.267)	(0.257)
Soy	2.846***	2.441***	2.785***	1.132
	(0.698)	(0.004)	(0.715)	(0.700)

(continued)

Table A6 CONTINUED

VARIABLES	Acts of Rebellion (Annual # of events) Model 1 Coeff. (s.e.)	Roadblocks (Annual # of events) Model 2 Coeff. (s.e.)	Acts of Rebellion (Annual # of events) Model 3 Coeff. (s.e.)	Roadblocks (Annual # of events) Model 4 Coeff. (s.e.)
Subnational Democracy	**-0.166***	**-0.185***	**-0.198***	**-0.077**
	(0.046)	**(0.047)**	**(0.048)**	**(0.056)**
Acts of Rebellion ($t-1$)			0.012	
			(0.002)	
Roadblocks ($t-1$)				0.012***
				(0.002)
Fixed effects for provinces	Yes	Yes	Yes	Yes
Fixed effects for years	Yes	Yes	Yes	Yes
Observations	389	308	367	264

Standard errors in parentheses
*** p<0.01, ** p<0.05, * p<0.1

In response to the criticism that the results for the Subnational Democracy variable might be driven by the 2008 protests in soy-producing provinces, or the fact that many of Argentina's most important social movements can be traced to the *piquetero* protests in oil-producing provinces during the 1990s, I include indicators for Argentina's five leading soy and oil producers according to data from the Ministry of the Economy website. As predicted, both variables have significant positive effects on the number of protest events that occurred in a particular province per 100,000 citizens, but do not change the results for subnational democracy.

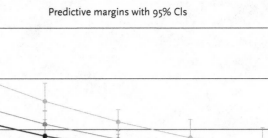

Figure A1 Predicted Probabilities: Institutional Context and Education (Chapter 3)

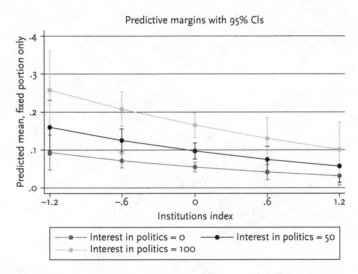

Figure A2 Predicted Probabilities: Institutional Context and Interest in Politics (Chapter 3)

NOTES

CHAPTER 2

1. While there have certainly been exceptions to these statements over the past thirty years—the *Sandinistas* in Nicaragua, *Sendero Luminoso* in Peru, and FARC in Colombia spring to mind—it seems that democracy has consolidated in Latin America to the extent that the debate has largely shifted from examining its durability to an increased focus on its quality throughout the region (e.g., Smith 2005, Levitsky and Murillo 2005, Levine and Molina 2011). Even when democratic norms and processes appear to be under assault (e.g., Chávez's Venezuela), leaders often appeal to democratic ideals to sell constitutional reforms and infringements on political rights (Rodríguez-Vargas 2013). Moreover, the most notable militarized political conflicts have begun to fade in recent years, with the demise of the *Sendero Luminoso* and weakening of FARC.
2. With the notable exception of Machado et al. 2011 and Boulding 2014, which are discussed below.
3. Recent events in Venezuela might indicate a shift toward increased government repression of social movements and street demonstrations; however, the empirical analysis conducted in this book extends only to 2012, when state repression of protestors was a less common occurrence in the country. At the subnational level, powerful local politicians have utilized repression at certain times in countries like Argentina and Mexico, and I will explore this phenomenon in Chapter 6.
4. *A la* current U.S. politics, where we certainly are seeing more protests as well.
5. This assertion echoes Tilly's (1978) and Tarrow's (1998) work on repertoire change—namely that it occurs slowly, over long periods of time.
6. See Chapter 5 for a more complete qualification of these statements.
7. Again, Venezuela seems like a case where this might no longer ring true. I return to Venezuela in Chapter 3 and discuss what the continuing trend toward authoritarianism under Nicolás Maduro might portend for protests there moving forward.
8. Also see Scartascini and Tommasi (2012) for a more thorough examination of institutionalized versus non-institutionalized policymaking.

CHAPTER 3

1. The findings presented in this chapter were originally published in the *Journal of Politics in Latin America* in 2015 (7[3]: 3–48).
2. Despite this trend in the protest literature, some recent work has delved into the potential causal influence of specific types of grievances in spurring protest involvement (Finkel and Muller 1998). Land and income inequality (Muller and

Seligson 1987, Sen 2002, Jenkins et al. 2003), neoliberal reforms and associated austerity measures (Walton and Ragin 1990, Arce 2008, Roberts 2008, Silva 2009, Bellinger and Arce 2011), and political repression or exclusion in authoritarian regimes (Loveman 1998, Bunce 2003) have all been attributed causal weight in spurring mass mobilizations. Moreover, journalistic accounts of virtually any episode of mass mobilization—from Occupy Wall Street to the Arab Spring to recent protests in Brazil—tend to focus on the grievances being voiced by demonstrators as a primary causal factor, rather than the longer-term economic and political trends that might facilitate instances of mass mobilization.

3. In particular, the resource mobilization school received a boon from studies on the U.S. Civil Rights Movement published in the 1960s and 1970s. While in many ways, blacks in the United States encountered the same grievances they had faced during the decades leading up to this time period, access to organizational resources changed drastically in the direct lead-up to the Civil Rights movement. Indeed, it seemed that increased urbanization, the growth of historically black universities, and an expanding black middle class led to the removal of traditional paternalistic social relations between (particularly Southern) whites and blacks, and paved the way for a thriving national movement (McAdam 1982, Jenkins 1983).

4. Democratic quality can be defined as the extent to which regimes adhere to democratic norms like "freedom, the rule of law, vertical accountability, responsiveness, and equality" (Diamond and Morlino 2004, 21).

5. Their dependent variable measures participation in four types of protest activities over an indefinite time period, across a mix of democratic and authoritarian regimes. Unfortunately, failing to specify a time period for participation casts serious doubt on those results (which will be further discussed below in the discussion of measurement), and the most common form of protest participation reported was petition signing, an activity that falls outside of most conceptualizations of contentious politics. Similarly, relying only on a rule of law indicator to measure political development leaves out of the analysis several potentially important institutional factors that might moderate rates of protest participation.

6. See Appendix for specific question wording for all variables included in the analysis.

7. Summary statistics for each variable are included in the appendix.

8. The most recent version of the World Values Survey questionnaire available online (2005) states that "during the last five years" has since been added to this question. However, all previous surveys—which have been used in the studies cited above, including the key study by Dalton and co-authors (2009)—ask if respondents have ever participated in any of the enumerated activities without limiting responses to a certain time period.

9. For country values on each of these of these indicators, please see the table in the Appendix.

10. As a reference point, the score for the United States during this time period was 1.39.

11. These logistic regression models account for the complex nature of the survey data, which include stratification and clustering. Both models were also run including fixed effects for countries and years, with Uruguay and 2012 as the baseline, but, given that this did not affect results, those coefficients are not reported in Table 3.2. All countries are weighted to an equal N.

12. Predicted probabilities are calculated using Stata 12's "margins" command while holding other variables in the model at their mean. Graphs were made using the "marginsplot" command, which graphs the results from "margins."

13. In any attempt to propose and test a causal argument using cross-sectional data, endogeneity is justifiably a concern. In this case, the most plausible alternative explanation would be that protest actually increases community engagement, in that demonstrations might link formerly unassociated protestors to established civic organizations. Replacing a potentially problematic variable with an instrument unrelated to the outcome variable can help solve this problem (Sovey and Green 2011). A two-stage least squares model instrumenting for protest with ideology (an instrument deemed "not weak") coupled with a Hausman test somewhat assuages concerns that the causal arrow flows from community engagement to protest and not the other way around, as I was unable to reject the null hypothesis of exogeneity. However, in the Appendix I include results from an instrumental variables regression model that instruments for community engagement. While the predicted effect of community engagement on protest is somewhat attenuated, it remains one of the strongest predictors in the model.

14. This alternative coding of the engagement variable controls for the possibility that a small number of hyper-engaged citizens—such as individuals who are active in three or more community organizations—are driving results.

15. While Chile recently transitioned from a compulsory to a voluntary voting system whereas Argentina maintains mandatory voting requirements, that reform did not occur in Chile until after the data used for these analyses were collected.

CHAPTER 4

1. For decades, the conventional wisdom viewed clientelism as antithetical to contentious politics—a demobilizing endeavor by machine parties aimed to suppress protest activity and atomize collective actors (e.g., Caciagli and Belloni 1981; Diani and McAdam 2003). According to this perspective, clientelism is a hierarchical arrangement between patron and client; a subordinating linkage that precludes the horizontal and cooperative ties necessary for engaging various forms of contentious politics (Diani and McAdam 2003). Because clientelism encompasses a set of diffuse, particularistic bonds built on economic deprivation and social exclusion, it was thus theorized to depress protest involvement and depoliticize civil society.

2. These provinces are as follows: Buenos Aires, Catamarca, Chaco, Córdoba, Chubut, Corrientes, Entre Ríos, Formosa, Jujuy, La Rioja, Mendoza, Misiones, Neuquén, Río Negro, Salta, San Juan, San Luis, Santa Fe, Santiago del Estero, Tierra del Fuego and Tucumán. This wide territorial diversity is an important comparative advantage when contrasting this survey with the one conducted by Brusco, Nazareno, and Stokes (2004), which has only covered three provinces (Buenos Aires, Córdoba, and Misiones).

3. These departments are as follows: La Paz, Santa Cruz, Cochabamba, Oruro, Chuquisaca, Potos, Pando, Tarija, Beni.

4. In line with PIMSA (*Programa de Investigación del Movimiento de la Sociedad Argentina*) yearly reports, a well-known Buenos Aires-based research center for the study of contentious events and social movements, there have been 9,937

rallies for the 2002–2009 period, representing the 49 percent of the total of protests and being the most-used protest performance in the country.

5. In Argentina, roadblocks have become a "normal" mode of protest since the 2001–2002 crises, rising from year to year. According to CENM (*Centro de Estudios Nueva Mayoría*), while there were 4,676 blockades in 1997–2002, that amount swiftly increased to 10,601 in the 2003–2008 years. Hand-in-hand with roadblocks, Argentine unemployed federations have also grown: while the unemployed federations numbered only 6 in 1999, in 2003 there were 34 of them in the whole country (Garay 2007, 312).

CHAPTER 5

1. Kirchner actually defeated Menem to become president, after the latter dropped out before the run-off election in the face of certain defeat.
2. Most accounts point to D'Elía's band of supporters as the aggressors, even suggesting that police nearby were aware of the violence but had been instructed not to intervene.
3. Nisman's allegation against the president has yet to be proved, and serious doubts exist over its validity after his case was made public in January 2015.
4. Chapter 7 provides a detailed description of how researchers at each organization track protest events using news reports, and the relative advantages and disadvantages of each measure.

CHAPTER 6

1. Thirty-seven total sit-down interviews were carried out in Buenos Aires capital, Buenos Aires province, Mendoza, and San Luis in Spring 2013. Subjects were initially drawn from a list of experts utilized in Gervasoni's (2010) elite surveys project, and then additional interviews were obtained through these contacts. I also carried out dozens of informal interviews in Buenos Aires with protestors throughout late 2012 and early 2013—notably, at the three massive *cacerolazos* that occurred on September 13, 2012, November 8, 2012, and April 18, 2013.
2. This was conditional for approval by the Vanderbilt University Institutional Review Board: IRB# 101398.
3. The nickname *"puntano"* comes from the capital city's location at the foot of the Punta de los Venados mountain range.
4. See McMann 2006 for her excellent research on the relationship between levels of public employment and the quality of democracy.
5. In 2004, forty-seven out of every 1,000 *puntanos* were public employees, outpacing the national average by ten (MECON 2004).
6. Keep in mind that in 2000, the population of San Luis province was 365,168 (INDEC 2001).
7. Author's translation.
8. This seems reminiscent of the *santiagazo* in the province of Santiago del Estero discussed above—another illiberal province where the federal government eventually intervened to remove the governing Juárez family from power in 2004 for alleged corruption and involvement in several mysterious murders and disappearances in the province (Gibson 2012). While we also observe diminished rates of protest participation in Santiago del Estero, the few instances where contention has emerged have resulted in violent confrontation between demonstrators and the government.

9. In numerous conversations, *mendocinos* proudly pointed to the democratic history of their province, and in some cases mocked neighboring San Luis by quoting an old slogan the province had at one point used to promote tourism: "*San Luis, es otro pais!*" One *mendocina* activist even shared with me that the only province in the country where her organization had yet to gain a foothold was San Luis, due to a combination of factors related to the provincial government, according to her.

10. Author's translation.

11. See the "Wines of Argentina" website for updated information on changes in the amount of wine exported annually: (www.winesofargentina.org/es/estadistica/exportacion).

12. The Senate vote to overturn the export tax was one of the most dramatic in Argentine history, with Vice President Julio Cobos forced to cast a tie-breaking vote that would either sever his ties with the Kirchner government or undermine his long-standing alliance with the agricultural sector (Cobos was a member of the UCR in Mendoza before joining the Kirchner ticket for the 2007 election). Cobos voted to abolish the tax, thus ending his short-lived partnership with the Kirchners and FPV. He would eventually return to the UCR in 2009 after being expelled in 2007, once again highlighting the fluidity of party platforms and attachments in Argentina.

13. These figures do not include the autonomous national capital, which is not technically part of Buenos Aires province.

14. Author's translation; emphasis added.

15. Author's translation.

16. Author's translation.

17. See the *Equipo Nizkor* website for the full report, which includes detailed information about arrests and deaths in Argentina since 2001, and which sectors of society have been disproportionately targeted for repression by public authorities: "Informe sobre Criminalización de Protesta en Argentina": http://www.derechos.org/nizkor/arg/doc/protesta.html.

CHAPTER 7

1. These data were obtained while conducting fieldwork in Argentina during the 2012–2013 academic year with the support of a dissertation grant from the National Science Foundation (SES-1263807).

2. In provinces with bicameral legislatures, the measure is calculated for the lower house.

3. All electoral data used for the creation of the Subnational Democracy Index were gathered from Andy Tow's comprehensive website on subnational politics in Argentina, where he has compiled data on elections at the provincial and municipal level since the country's 1983 transition to democracy: www.andytow.com. I would like to thank Dr. Tow for his continued efforts in providing this invaluable resource to students of subnational politics in Argentina.

4. I thank Dr. Gervasoni for graciously providing detailed code for creating the Subnational Democracy Index, in addition to his data for the period from 1983 to 2003 to check against values on my own measures.

5. Factor analysis of the five measures results in a clear one-factor solution (the eigenvalue for the first factor was 2.39, while the second was .38).

6. The measure I choose for the dependent variable accounts for the massive population differences between Argentine provinces, ranging from Tierra del Fuego (~125,000 citizens) to Buenos Aires (~15,600,000).

7. *La Nación, El Clarín, Página/12, La Prensa, Crónica, La Razón, Diario Popular, El Cronista, Ambito Financiero, The Buenos Aires Herald*.

8. *El Ancasti* (Catamarca), *El Chubut* (Chubut), *La Voz del Interior* (Córdoba), *Corrientes Noticias* (Corrientes), *El Diario* (Entre Ríos), *La Mañana* (Formosa), *Pregón* (Jujuy), *La Arena* y *El Diario de la Pampa* (La Pampa), *El Independiente* (La Rioja), *Los Andes* (Mendoza), *El Territorio* (Misiones), *La Mañana del Sur* (Neuquén), *El Tribuno* (Salta), *El Zonda* (San Juan), *El Diario de la República* (San Luis), *La Opinión Austral* (Santa Cruz), *La Capital* (Santa Fe), *El Liberal* (Santiago del Estero), *El Sureño* y *el Tiempo Fueguino* (Tierra del Fuego), *La Gaceta* (Tucumán).

9. See Appendix for specific question wording.

10. For the reasons enumerated above, I exclude the capital city from this analysis as well.

11. Samples were self-weighting, and estimates will represent the desired target population. The total number of respondents surveyed in urban areas was 3,927 and in rural areas, 481.

12. I have chosen to omit the autonomous capital of Buenos Aires for all of these analyses, due to its unique status as the home of Argentina's national government, and thus the gathering place for many protestors who seek not to make claims on the local city government, but the national government itself. For this reason, protests in the capital would seem qualitatively different from those found in other provinces, where local protests are primarily directed at local authorities.

13. *Producto Bruto Interno* is calculated by Argentina's national statistical agency, *Instituto Nacional de Estadística y Censos* (INDEC), and represents a measure of gross domestic product by province. INDEC data were also used for measures of population, unemployment, and public employment.

14. It appears that including lagged roadblocks prevents a significant finding in Model 4, though in the case of acts of contention (Model 3), including a lagged variable actually strengthens the results.

15. Question wording for all variables can be found in the Appendix.

16. This finding holds when I create a variable that represents the absolute value of provinces' democracy scores—in other words, increasing a province's distance from zero in terms of subnational democracy decreases the probability of protesting among individuals.

CHAPTER 8

1. Examples would be articles by Dalton et al. 2009 and Machado et al. 2011, and Boulding's 2014 book.

2. To my knowledge, the only studies to this point that have addressed the policy consequences of protest have been Tenorio's (2014) piece on social policy responses to mass protests and Franklin's (2009) article on how Latin American governments respond differently to distinct repertoires of contention. However, there are more examples of this type of research on contentious politics in the United States (e.g., Gillion 2013).

3. The support for democracy measure comes from the following question, which was asked in every country from 2008 to 2012: ING4. Changing the subject

again, democracy may have problems, but it is better than any other form of government. To what extent do you agree or disagree with this statement?" responses were given in a 1–7 agree/disagree scale and transformed to a 0–100 scale. Higher values indicate higher support for democracy. Tolerance is measured by an index based on the following questions: D1. There are people who always speak badly of _____'s form of government, not only the current administration, but the kind of government. How strongly do you approve or disapprove of these peoples' right to vote? D2. How strongly do you approve or disapprove that these people can conduct peaceful demonstrations in order to express their points of view? D3. How strongly do you approve or disapprove that these people can run for public office? D4. How strongly do you approve or disapprove that these people appear on television to give speeches? Individuals respond to each question on a 1–10 scale; the questions are combined into a composite scale that is coded to run from 0 to 100, where 0 indicates the lowest level of tolerance and 100 indicates the highest. The questions regarding shutting down Congress or coups during times of corruption ask respondents to respond yes or no depending on whether or not they would support such actions. The percentages represent the number who responded in the affirmative across the region.

REFERENCES

Albó, Xavier. 2006. "El Alto, la Vorágine de una Ciudad Única." *Journal of Latin American Anthropology* 11(2): 329–350.

Almeida, Paul D. 2007. "Defensive Mobilization: Popular Movements against Economic Adjustment Policies in Latin America." *Latin American Perspectives* 34(3): 123–139.

Almond, Gabriel A. 1988. "The Return to the State." *American Political Science Review* 82(3): 853–874.

Alvarez, Mike, José Antonio Cheibub, Francisco Limongi, and Adam Przeworski. 1996. "Classifying Political Regimes." *Studies in Comparative International Development* 31(2): 3–36.

Anderson, Christopher, and Silvia Mendes. 2006. "Learning to Lose: Election Outcomes, Democratic Experience and Political Protest Potential." *British Journal of Political Science* 36(1): 91–111.

Anderson, Christopher J., and Matthew M. Singer. 2008. "The Sensitive Left and the Impervious Right: Multilevel Models and the Politics of Inequality, Ideology, and Legitimacy in Europe." *Comparative Political Studies* 41(4–5): 564–599.

Anria, Santiago. 2013. "Social Movements, Party Organization, and Populism: Insights from the Bolivian MAS." *Latin American Politics and Society* 55(3): 19–46.

Arce, Moisés. 2008. "The Repoliticization of Collective Action after Neoliberalism in Peru." *Latin American Politics and Society* 50(3): 37–62.

Arce, Moisés. 2014. *Resource Extraction and Protest in Peru*. Pittsburgh, PA: University of Pittsburgh Press.

Arce, Moisés, and Paul T. Bellinger Jr. 2007. "Low-Intensity Democracy Revisited: The Effects of Economic Liberalization on Political Activity in Latin America." *World Politics* 60(1): 97–121.

Arce, Moisés, and Jorge Mangonnet. 2013. "Competitiveness, Partisanship, and Subnational Protest in Argentina." *Comparative Political Studies* 46(8): 895–919.

Arce, Moisés, and Roberta Rice. 2009. "Societal Protest in Post-Stabilization Bolivia." *Latin American Research Review* 44(1): 88–101.

Assies, Willem. 2003. "David versus Goliath in Cochabamba: Water Rights, Neoliberalism, and the Revival of Social Protest in Bolivia." *Latin American Perspectives* 30(3): 14–36.

Auyero, Javier. 2000. "The Logic of Clientelism in Argentina: An Ethnographic Account." *Latin American Research Review* 35(3): 55–81.

Auyero, Javier. 2005. "Protest and Politics in Contemporary Argentina," in *Argentine Democracy: The Politics of Institutional Weakness*, eds. Steven Levitsky and Maria Victoria Murillo. University Park, PA: Penn State University Press, 250–268.

Auyero, Javier. 2006. "Protest in Contemporary Argentina: A Contentious Repertoire in the Making," in *Out of the Shadows*, eds. Patricia Fernández-Kelly and Jon Shefner. University Park, PA: Penn State University Press, 165–190.

Auyero, Javier. 2007. *Routine Politics and Violence in Argentina: The Gray Zone of State Power*. New York, NY: Cambridge University Press.

Auyero, Javier, Pablo Lapegna, and Fernanda Poma. 2009. "Patronage Politics and Contentious Collective Action: A Recursive Relationship." *Latin American Politics and Society* 51(3): 1–31.

Bateson, Regina. 2012. "Crime Victimization and Political Participation." *American Political Science Review* 106(3): 570–587.

Bayón, Cristina, and Gonzalo Saraví. 2002. "Vulnerabilidad Social en la Argentina de los Años Noventa: Impactos de la Crisis en el Gran Buenos Aires," in *Trabajo y Ciudadanía: Los Cambiantes Rostros de la Integración y la Exclusión Social en Cuatro Áreas Metropolitanas de América Latina*, eds. Rubén Kaztman y Guillermo Wormald, Montevideo, UY: Editorial Cebra, 61–132.

Beaulieu, Emily. 2014. *Electoral Protest and Democracy in the Developing World*. New York, NY: Cambridge University Press.

Becker, Marc. 2011. "Correa, Indigenous Movements, and the Writing of a New Constitution in Ecuador." *Latin American Perspectives* 38(1): 47–62.

Behrend, Jacqueline. 2011. "The Unevenness of Democracy at the Subnational Level: Provincial Closed Games in Argentina." *Latin American Research Review* 46(1): 150–176.

Bellinger, Paul, and Moises Arce. 2011. "Protest and Democracy in Latin America's Market Era." *Comparative Political Studies* 64(3): 688–704.

Bianchi, Matias. 2013. "The Political Economy of Sub-National Democracy: Fiscal Rentierism and Geography in Argentina." Doctoral Dissertation. Institut d'Études Politiques de Paris.

Bloom, Shelah S. 2008. *Violence against Women and Girls: A Compendium of Monitoring and Evaluation Indicators*. US AID.

Bons, Sarah. 2016. "Why Women in Argentina Called for a National Day of Mourning." *Americas Quarterly*, October 19. Retrieved from http://www.americasquarterly.org/content/why-women-argentina-have-called-day-mourning.

Booth, John A., and Mitchell A. Seligson. 2009. *The Legitimacy Puzzle in Latin America: Political Support and Democracy in Eight Nations*. New York, NY: Cambridge University Press.

Boulding, Carew. 2010. "NGOs and Political Participation in Weak Democracies: Subnational Evidence on Protest and Voter Turnout from Bolivia." *Journal of Politics* 72(2): 456–468.

Boulding, Carew. 2014. *NGOs, Political Protest, and Civil Society*. New York, NY: Cambridge University Press.

Boylan, Delia. 2002. *Defusing Democracy: Central Bank Autonomy and the Transition from Authoritarian Rule*. Ann Arbor, MI: University of Michigan Press.

Bratton, Michael, Robert B. Mattes, and Emmanuel Gyimah-Boadi. 2005. *Public Opinion, Democracy, and Market Reform in Africa*. New York, NY: Cambridge University Press.

Brockett, Charles. 1991. "The Structure of Political Opportunities and Peasant Mobilization in Central America." *Comparative Politics* 23(3): 253–274.

Bruhn, Miriam. 2008. *License to Sell: The Effect of Business Registration Reform on Entrepreneurial Activity in Mexico*. Washington, DC: World Bank Publications.

Brusco, Valeria, Marcelo Nazareno, and Susan Stokes. 2004. "Vote Buying in Argentina." *Latin American Research Review* 39(2): 66–88.

Bunce, Valerie. 2003. "Rethinking Recent Democratization: Lessons from the Postcommunist Experience." *World Politics* 55(2): 167–192.

Caciagli, Mario, and Frank P. Belloni. 1981. "The 'New' Clientelism in Southern Italy: The Christian Democratic Party in Catania," in *Political Clientelism, Patronage, and Development,* eds. S. Shmuel Noah Eisenstadt, and Renâe Lemarchand. Beverly Hills, CA: Sage Publications, 35–55.

Calvo, Ernesto. 2016. *Anatomía Política de Twitter en Argentina*. Buenos Aires, AR: Capital Intelectual.

Calvo, Ernesto, and Maria Victoria Murillo. 2004. "Who Delivers? Partisan Clients in the Argentine Electoral Market." *American Journal of Political Science* 48(4): 742–757.

Calvo, Ernesto, and Maria Victoria Murillo. 2013. "When Parties Meet Voters Assessing Political Linkages Through Partisan Networks and Distributive Expectations in Argentina and Chile." *Comparative Political Studies* 46(7): 851–882.

Carey, John M., and Matthew Soberg Shugart, eds. 1998. *Executive Decree Authority*. New York, NY: Cambridge University Press.

Carlin, Ryan E., and Mason Moseley. 2014. "Good Democrats, Bad Targets: Democratic Values and Clientelistic Vote Buying." *Journal of Politics* 77(1): 14–26.

Carrera, Nicolás Iñigo, and María Celia Cotarelo. 2001. "Las Huelgas Generales, Argentina 1983-2001: Un Ejercicio de Periodización." *PIMSA Documentos y Comunicaciones*, 33.

Ceobanu, Alin M., Charles H. Wood, and Ludmila Ribeiro. 2010. "Crime Victimization and Public Support for Democracy: Evidence from Latin America." *International Journal of Public Opinion Research* 23(1): 56–78.

Chavez, Rebecca. 2004. "The Evolution of Judicial Autonomy in Argentina: Establishing the Rule of Law in an Ultrapresidential System." *Journal of Latin American Studies* 36(03): 451–478.

Collier, David, and Steven Levitsky. 1997. "Democracy with Adjectives: Conceptual Innovation in Comparative Research." *World Politics* 49(3): 430–451.

Collier, Ruth B., and Samuel Handlin, eds. 2009. *Reorganizing Popular Politics: Participation and the New Interest Regime in Latin America*. University Park, PA: Penn State University Press.

Collier, Ruth B., and James Mahoney. 1997. "Adding Collective Actors to Collective Outcomes: Labor and Recent Democratization in South America and Southern Europe." *Comparative Politics* 29(3): 285–303.

Cordova, Abby. 2009. "Methodological Note: Measuring Relative Wealth Using Household Asset Indicators." *The AmericasBarometer Insight Series* No. 6. Retrieved from http://www.vanderbilt.edu/lapop/insights/I0806en.pdf.

Cornell, Agnes, and Marcia Grimes. 2015. "Institutions as Incentives for Civic Action: Bureaucratic Structures, Civil Society, and Disruptive Protests." *Journal of Politics* 77(3): 664–678.

Cotarelo, María Celia. 1999. "N°19. El Motin de Santiago del Estero. Argentina, Diciembre de 1993." PIMSA 3: 83–119.

Cotarelo, María Celia. 2009. "Conflicto Social en Argentina entre 2002 y 2008." *Actas XII Jornadas Interescuelas Departamentos de Historia, Bariloche, Universidad Nacional de Comahue, 28*. San Carlos de Bariloche.

Dahl, Robert A. 1956. *A Preface to Democracy Theory*. New Haven, CT: Yale University Press.

Dahl, Robert A. 1971. *Polyarchy: Participation and Opposition*. New Haven, CT: Yale University Press.

Dalton, Russell J., and Alix van Sickle. 2005. "The Resource, Structural, and Cultural Bases of Protest." Working Paper. University of California, Irvine, CA.

Dalton, Russell J., Alix van Sickle, and Steven Weldon. 2009. "The Individual-Institutional Nexus of Protest." *British Journal of Political Science* 40(1): 51–73.

De Luca, Miguel, Mark. P. Jones, and María Inés Tula. 2002. "Back Rooms or Ballot Boxes? Candidate Nomination in Argentina." *Comparative Political Studies* 35(4): 413–436.

Diamond, Larry. 2002. "Thinking About Hybrid Regimes." *Journal of Democracy* 13(2): 21–35.

Diamond, Larry. 2015. "Facing Up to the Democratic Recession." *Journal of Democracy* 26(1): 141–155.

Diamond, Larry Jay, and Leonardo Morlino. 2004. "An Overview." *Journal of Democracy* 15(4): 20–31.

Diani, Mario, and Doug McAdam, eds. 2003. *Social Movements and Networks: Relational Approaches to Collective Action: Relational Approaches to Collective Action*. New York, NY: Oxford University Press.

Diario Registrado. 2015. "San Luis: Detuvieron a Legislador por Defender a Manifestantes." January 3. Retrieved from http://www.diarioregistrado.com/politica/san-luis--detuvieron-a-legislador-por-defender-a-manifestantes_a563169ed42bd9ca81b194f28.

Di Marco, Laura. 2013. "Cuentas Fuertes, Lealtades Débiles: El Secreto del Poder de los Intendentes." *La Nación*, November 3. Retrieved from http://www.lanacion.com.ar/1634629-cuentas-fuertes-lealtades-debiles-el-secreto-del-poder-de-los-intendentes.

Dunning, John. 2014. *Economic Analysis and Multinational Enterprise*. New York, NY: Routledge.

Eckstein, Susan. 2001. "Power and Popular Protest in Latin America," in *Power and Popular Protest: Latin American Social Movements*, eds. Susan Eckstein and Garretón Merino. Berkeley and Los Angeles, CA: University of California Press.

Economic Commission for Latin America and the Caribbean (ECLAC) and Organization for Economic Cooperation and Development (OECD). 2013. "Latin American Economic Outlook 2013: SME Policies for Structural Change." Retrieved from http://www.eclac.org/publicaciones/xml/5/48385/LEO2013_ing.pdf.

The Economist. 2013. "Follow the Leader: Social Networking Latin America." August 10. Retrieved from http://www.economist.com/news/americas/21583263-how-presidents-tweet-follow-leader.

Eisinger, Peter. 1973. "The Conditions of Protest in American Cities." *American Political Science Review* 67(1): 11–28.

Equipo Nizkor. 2012. "Informe Sobre Criminalización de la Protesta en Argentina." March 1. Retrieved from http://www.derechos.org/nizkor/arg/doc/protesta.html.

Escobar, Cristina. 1994. "Clientelism and Social Protest: Peasant Politics in Northern Colombia," in *Democracy, Clientelism and Civil Society*, eds. Roniger, Luis, and Ayşe Güneş-Ayata. London, UK: Lynne Rienner Publishers, 65–85.

Etchemendy, Sebastián. 2005. "Old Actors in New Markets," in *Argentine Democracy: The Politics of Institutional Weakness*, eds. Steven Levitsky and Maria Victoria Murillo. University Park, PA: Penn State University Press, 62–87.

Etchemendy, Sebastián, and Ruth Collier. 2007. "Down but Not Out: Union Resurgence and Segmented Neocorporatism in Argentina (2003–2007)." *Politics & Society* 35(3): 363–401.

Eulau, Heinz, and Paul D. Karps. 1977. "The Puzzle of Representation: Specifying Components of Responsiveness." *Legislative Studies Quarterly* 2(3): 233–254.

Falleti, Tulia G. 2010. *Decentralization and Subnational Politics in Latin America*. New York, NY: Cambridge University Press.

Finkel, Steven E., and Edward N. Muller. 1998. "Rational Choice and the Dynamics of Collective Political Action: Evaluating Alternative Models with Panel Data." *American Political Science Review* 92(1): 37–49.

Fox, Jonathan. 1994. "Latin America's Emerging Local Politics." *Journal of Democracy* 5(2): 105–116.

Franklin, James C. 2009. "Contentious Challenges and Government Responses in Latin America." *Political Research Quarterly* 62(4): 700–714.

Freedom House. 2013. "Freedom in the World 2013: Democratic Breakthroughs in the Balance." Retrieved from https://freedomhouse.org/report/freedom-world/freedom-world-2013.

Freedom House. 2015. "Freedom in the World: The Annual Survey of Political Rights and Civil Liberties." Washington, DC: Freedom House.

Garay, Candelaria. 2007. "Social Policy and Collective Action: Unemployed Workers, Community Associations, and Protest in Argentina." *Politics & Society* 35(2): 301–328.

Garay, Candelaria. 2016. *Social Policy Expansion in Latin America*. New York, NY: Cambridge University Press.

Geddes, Barbara. 1990. "How the Cases You Choose Affect the Answers You Get: Selection Bias in Comparative Politics." *Political Analysis* 2(1): 131–150.

Gelman, Andrew, and Jennifer Hill. 2006. *Data Analysis Using Regression an Multilevel/Hierarchical Models*. New York, NY: Cambridge University Press.

Gervasoni, Carlos. 2010. "Measuring Variance in Subnational Regimes: Results from an Expert-Based Operationalization of Democracy in the Argentine Provinces." *Journal of Politics in Latin America* 2(2): 13–52.

Gervasoni, Carlos. 2010. "A Rentier Theory of Subnational Regimes: Fiscal Federalism, Democracy, and Authoritarianism in the Argentine Provinces." *World Politics* 62(02): 302–340.

Gibson, Edward L. 2005. "Boundary Control: Subnational Authoritarianism in Democratic Countries." *World Politics* 58(1): 101–132.

Gibson, Edward L. 2012. *Boundary Control: Subnational Authoritarianism in Federal Democracies*. New York: Cambridge University Press.

Gibson, Edward, and Ernesto Calvo. 2001. "Federalismo y Sobrerrepresentación: La Dimensión Territorial de la Reforma Económica en la Argentina," in *El Federalismo Electoral Argentino: Sobrerrepresentación, Reforma Política y Gobierno Dividido en la Argentina*, eds. Ernesto Calvo and Juan Manuel Abal Medina. Buenos Aires, AR: INAP - Eudeba, 179–204.

Gibson, Edward L., and Julieta Suárez-Cao. 2010. "Federalized Party Systems and Subnational Party Competition: Theory and an Empirical Application to Argentina." *Comparative Politics* 43(1): 21–39.

Gillion, Daniel Q. 2013. *The Political Power of Protest: Minority Activism and Shifts in Public Policy*. New York, NY: Cambridge University Press.

Giraudy, Agustina. 2010. "The Politics of Subnational Undemocratic Regime Reproduction in Argentina and Mexico." *Journal of Politics in Latin America* 2(2): 53–84.

Giraudy, Agustina. 2013. "Varieties of Subnational Undemocratic Regimes: Evidence from Argentina and Mexico." *Studies in Comparative International Development* 48(1): 51–80.

Gonzalez-Ocantos, Ezequiel, Chad Kiewiet De Jonge, Carlos Meléndez, Javier Osorio, and David W. Nickerson. 2012. "Vote Buying and Social Desirability Bias: Experimental Evidence from Nicaragua." *American Journal of Political Science* 56(1): 202–217.

Griffin, John D., and Brian Newman. 2005. "Are Voters Better Represented?" *Journal of Politics* 67(4): 1206–1227.

Gurr, Ted Robert. 1970. *Why Men Rebel*. Princeton, NJ: Princeton University Press.

Gusfield, Joseph. 1968. "The Study of Social Movements," in *International Encyclopedia of the Social Sciences, Volume 14*, ed. David Sills. New York, NY: Macmillan, 445–452.

Helmke, Gretchen. 2002. "The Logic of Strategic Defection: Judicial Decision-Making in Argentina under Dictatorship and Democracy." *American Political Science Review* 96(2): 291–330.

Hipsher, Patricia. 1996. "Democratization and the Decline of Urban Social Movements in Chile and Spain." *Comparative Politics* 28(3): 273–297.

Hiskey, Jonathan. 2003. "Demand-Based Development and Local Electoral Environments in Mexico." *Comparative Politics* 36(1): 41–59.

Hiskey, Jonathan T., and Shaun Bowler. 2005. "Local Context and Democratization in Mexico." *American Journal of Political Science* 49(1): 57–71.

Hiskey, Jonathan T., and Mason W. Moseley. (n.d.) "Severed Linkages: Democratic Accountabilty in Uneven Regimes." Working Paper. Vanderbilt University, Nashville, TN.

Huntington, Samuel P. 1968. *Political Order in Changing Societies*. New Haven, CT: Yale University Press.

Huntington, Samuel P. 1991. *The Third Wave: Democratization in the Late Twentieth Century*. Norman, OK: University of Oklahoma Press.

Inglehart, Ronald. 1990. *Culture Shift in Advanced Industrial Society*. Princeton NJ: Princeton University Press.

Instituto Nacional de Estadística y Censos (INDEC). 2001. "Censo 2001." Retrieved from http://www.indec.gob.ar/micro_sitios/webcenso/.

Instituto Nacional de Estadística y Censos (INDEC). 2010. "Censo 2010." Retrieved from www.indec.gov.ar/nivel4_default.asp?id_tema_1=2&id_tema_2=41&id_tema_3=135.

International Monetary Fund (IMF). 2012. "Growth in Latin America Moderating but Resilient." Retrieved from http://www.imf.org/external/pubs/ft/survey/so/2012/car101212c.htm.

Jackman, Robert W. 1985. "Cross-National Statistical Research and the Study of Comparative Politics." *American Journal of Political Science* 29(1): 161–182.

Javeline, Debra. 2003. "The Role of Blame in Collective Action: Evidence from Russia." *American Political Science Review* 97(1): 107–121.

Jenkins, J. Craig. 1983. "Resource Mobilization Theory and the Study of Social Movements." *Annual Review of Sociology* 9(1): 527–553.

Jenkins, J. Craig, David Jacobs, and Jon Agnone. 2003. "Political Opportunities and African-American Protest, 1948-1997." *American Journal of Sociology* 101(2): 277–303.

Jung, Courtney. 2003. "The Politics of Indigenous Identity: Neoliberalism, Cultural Rights, and the Mexican Zapatistas." *Social Research* 70(2): 433–461.

Kam, Cindy D., and Robert J. Franzese. 2006. *Modeling and Interpreting Interactive Hypotheses in Regression Analysis*. Ann Arbor, MI: University of Michigan Press.

Kaufmann, Daniel, Aart Kraay, and Massimo Mastruzzi. 2007. "The Worldwide Governance Indicators Project: Answering the Critics." World Bank Policy Research Working Paper #4149.

Key Jr., V. O. 1949. *Southern Politics*. New York, NY: Alfred A. Knopf.

King, Gary. 1988. "Statistical Models for Political Science Event Counts: Bias in Conventional Procedures and Evidence for the Exponential Poisson Regression Model." *American Journal of Political Science* 32(3): 838–863.

King, Gary, Robert Keohane, and Sidney Verba. 1994. *Designing Social Inquiry*. Princeton NJ: Princeton University Press.

Kitschelt, Herbert. 1986. "Political Opportunity Structures and Political Protest: Anti-Nuclear Movements in Four Democracies." *British Journal of Political Science* 16(1): 57–85.

Krauss, Clifford. 2001. "Reeling From Riots, Argentina Declares a State of Siege." December 31. *The New York Times*. Retrieved from http://www.nytimes.com/2001/12/20/world/reeling-from-riots-argentina-declares-a-state-of-siege.html.

Kurtz, Marcus J. 2004. "The Dilemmas of Democracy in the Open Economy: Lessons from Latin America." *World Politics* 56(2): 262–302.

La Gaceta. 2004. "Aumentarían los Sueldos: Choque de Manifestantes en San Luis." May 7. http://www.lagaceta.com.ar/nota/amp/74958/choque-manifestantes-san-luis.html.

Lapalombara, Joseph. 1968. "Macrotheories and Microapplications in Comparative Politics." *Comparative Politics* 1(1): 52–78.

Latin American Public Opinion Project. 2004. "AmericasBarometer 2004." Retrieved from http://www.vanderbilt.edu/lapop/ab2004.php.

Latin American Public Opinion Project. 2006. "AmericasBarometer 2006." Retrieved from http://www.vanderbilt.edu/lapop/ab2006.php.

Latin American Public Opinion Project. 2008. "AmericasBarometer 2008." Retrieved from http://www.vanderbilt.edu/lapop/ab2008.php.

Latin American Public Opinion Project. 2010. "AmericasBarometer 2010." Retrieved from http://www.vanderbilt.edu/lapop/ab2010.php.

Latin American Public Opinion Project. 2012. "AmericasBarometer 2012." Retrieved from http://www.vanderbilt.edu/lapop/ab2012.php.

Latin American Public Opinion Project. 2014. "AmericasBarometer 2014." Retrieved from http://www.vanderbilt.edu/lapop/ab2014.php.

Lawson, Chappell, and Kenneth F. Greene. 2014. "Making Clientelism Work: How Norms of Reciprocity Increase Voter Compliance." *Comparative Politics* 47(1): 61–85.

Lazar, Sian. 2004. "Personalist Politics, Clientelism and Citizenship: Local Elections in El Alto, Bolivia." *Bulletin of Latin American Research* 23(2): 228–243.

Lazar, Sian. 2007. *El Alto, Rebel City: Self and Citizenship in Andean Bolivia*. Durham, NC: Duke University Press.

Levine, Daniel H., and José E. Molina. 2011. *The Quality of Democracy in Latin America*. Boulder, CO: Lynne Rienner.

Levitsky, Steven. 2003. "From Labor Politics to Machine Politics: the Transformation of Party–Union Linkages in Argentine Peronism, 1983-1999." *Latin American Research Review* 38(3): 3–36.

Levitsky, Steven, and Lucan Way. 2002. "The Rise of Competitive Authoritarianism." *Journal of Democracy* 13(2): 51–65.

Levitsky, Steven, and Maria Victoria Murillo. 2003. "Argentina Weathers the Storm." *Journal of Democracy* 14(4): 152–166.

Levitsky, Steven, and Maria Victoria Murillo. 2005. *Argentine Democracy: The Politics of Institutional Weakness*. University Park, PA: Penn State University Press.

Levitsky, Steven, and Maria Victoria Murillo. 2008. "Argentina: From Kirchner to Kirchner." *Journal of Democracy* 19(2): 16–30.

Levitsky, Steven, and Maria Victoria Murillo.2009. "Variation in Institutional Strength." *Annual Review of Political Science* 12: 115–133.

Lichbach, Mark. 1987. "Deterrence or Escalation? The Puzzle of Aggregate Studies of Repression and Dissent." *Journal of Conflict Resolution* 31(2): 266–297.

Lieberson, Stanley. 1991. "Small Ns and Big Conclusions: An Examination of the Reasoning in Comparative Studies Based on a Small Number of Cases." *Social Forces* 70(2): 307–320.

Lijphart, Arend. 1971. "Comparative Politics and the Comparative Method." *American Political Science Review* 65(3): 682–693.

Lijphart, Arend. 1997. "Unequal Participation: Democracy's Unresolved Dilemma. Presidential Address, American Political Science Association, 1996." *American Political Science Review* 91(1): 1–14.

Lindlar, Charlie. 2012. "Argentina Protests: Up to 700,000 March in Frustration at President Cristina Kirchner." *HuffPost United Kingdom,* November 11. Retrieved from http://www.huffingtonpost.co.uk/2012/11/10/argentina-protests-thousands-pictures_n_2109363.html.

Linz, Juan J., and Amando de Miguel. 1966. "Within-Nation Differences and Comparisons: The Eight Spains," in *Comparing Nations: The Use of Quantitative Data in Cross-National Research*, eds. Richard Merritt and Stein Rokkan. New Haven, CT: Yale University Press.

Linz, Juan J., and Alfred Stepan. 1996. *Problems of Democratic Transition and Consolidation: Southern Europe, South America, and Post-Communist Europe*. Baltimore, MD: Johns Hopkins University Press.

Long, J. Scott. 1997. *Regression Models for Categorical and Limited Dependent Variables*. Thousand Oaks, CA: Sage Publications.

Loveman, Mara. 1998. "High-Risk Collective Action: Defending Human Rights in Chile, Uruguay, and Argentina." *American Journal of Sociology* 104(2): 477–525.

Machado, Fabiana, Carlos Scartascini, and Mariano Tommasi. 2011. "Political Institutions and Street Protests in Latin America." *Journal of Conflict Resolution* 55(3): 340–365.

Mahoney, James. 2007. "Qualitative Methodology and Comparative Politics." *Comparative Political Studies* 40(2): 122–144.

Mainwaring, Scott, and Timothy Scully. 2010. *Democratic Governance in Latin America*. Redwood City, CA: Stanford University Press.

Mangonnet, Jorge, and Mason W. Moseley. 2011. "Contentious Clients: Disentangling the Relationship between Clientelism and Social Protest." Presented at the Annual Meeting of the American Political Science Association, Seattle, WA.

Mangonnet, Jorge, and Victoria Murillo. 2016. "Protests of Abundance: Commodity Rents and Rural Lockouts in Argentina." Presented at the Annual Conference of the American Political Science Association, Philadelphia, September.

McAdam, Doug. 1982. *Political Process and the Development of Black Insurgency 1930-1970.* Chicago, IL: University of Chicago Press.

McAdam, Douglas, Sidney Tarrow, and Charles Tilly. 2001. *Dynamics of Contention.* New York, NY: Cambridge University Press.

McAdam, Douglas, Sidney Tarrow, and Charles Tilly. 2009. "Contentious Politics and Social Movements," in *Ideas, Interests, and Institutions: Advancing Theory in Comparative Politics,* eds. Mark Lichbach and Alan Zuckerman. 2nd ed. New York, NY: Cambridge University Press, 260–290.

McCarthy, John, and Mayer Zald. 1973. *The Trend of Social Movements in America: Professionalization and Resource Mobilization.* Morristown, NJ: General Learning Press.

McCarthy, John, and Mayer N. Zald. 1977. "Resource Mobilization and Social Movements: A Partial Theory." *American Journal of Sociology* 82(6): 1212–1241.

McMann, Kelly. 2006. *Economic Autonomy and Democracy: Hybrid Regimes in Russia and Kyrgyzstan.* New York, NY: Cambridge University Press.

Meyer, David S. 2004. "Protest and Political Opportunities." *Annual Review of Political Science* 30: 125–145.

Ministerio de Hacienda y Finanzas Públicas (MECON). 2004. "Economic and Financial Data for Argentina." Retrieved from http://www.mecon.gov.ar/progeco/dsbb.htm.

Ministerio de Hacienda y Finanzas Públicas (MECON). 2010. "Presupuesto Resumen." Retrieved from http://www.mecon.gov.ar/onp/html/presupresumen/resum10.pdf.

Mill, John Stuart. 1843. *A System of Logic.*

Moore, Will. 1998. "Repression and Dissent: Substitution, Context, and Timing." *American Journal of Political Science* 42(3): 851–873.

Moreno, Daniel, and Mason Moseley. 2011. "Who Protests in Latin America? Individual-Level Determinants of Protest in the Region's Developing Democracies." Working Paper. Vanderbilt University, Nashville, TN.

Moscovich, Lorena. 2013. "Gobernadores Versus Organizaciones: Apoyos Federales, Política Provincial y Potesta." *Revista SAAP (ISSN 1666-7883)* 7(1): 131–159.

Moseley, Mason, and Matthew Layton. 2013. "Prosperity and Protest in Brazil: The Wave of the Future in Latin America?" AmericasBarometer Insights Series No. 92, Latin American Public Opinion Project, Vanderbilt University, USAID.

Muller, Edward N. 1979. *Aggressive Political Participation.* Princeton, NJ: Princeton University Press.

Muller, Edward N., and Mitchell Seligson. 1987. "Insurgency and Inequality." *American Political Science Review* 81(2): 425–451.

Murillo, Maria Victoria. 1997. "La Adaptación del Sindicalismo Argentino a las Reformas de Mercado en la Primera Presidencia de Menem." *Desarrollo Económico* 37(147): 419–446.

Murillo, Maria Victoria. 2001. *Labor Unions, Partisan Coalitions, and Market Reforms in Latin America.* New York, NY: Cambridge University Press.

La Nación. 2012. "Para la Federal, Fueron Solo 70,000 Personas." November 10. Retrieved from http://www.lanacion.com.ar/1525179-para-la-federal-fueron-solo-70000-personas.

Nichter, Simeon. 2008. "Vote Buying or Turnout Buying? Machine Politics and the Secret Ballot." *American Political Science Review* 102(1): 19–31.

Niemi, Richard G., Stephen C. Craig, and Franco Mattei. 1991. "Measuring Internal Political Efficacy in the 1988 National Election Study." *American Political Science Review* 85(4): 1407–1413.

Norris, Pippa. 2002. *Democratic Phoenix: Reinventing Political Activism.* New York, NY: Cambridge University Press.

Norris, Pippa, Stefaan Walgrave, and Peter Van Aelst. 2005. "Who Demonstrates? Antistate Rebels, Conventional Participants, or Everyone?" *Comparative Politics* 37(2): 189–204.

North, Douglas. 1990. *Institutions, Institutional Change and Economic Performance.* New York, NY: Cambridge University Press.

Nueva Mayoría. 2009. "Con 5608 Cortes de Ruta y Vías Públicas, el 2008 Registró la Mayor Cantidad de Cortes Desde 1997." January 28. Retrieved from http://www.nuevamayoria.com/index.php?option=com_content&task=view&id=1192&Itemid=30.

Nueva Mayoría. 2012. "Evolución Sociopolítica." Retrieved from http://www.nuevamayoria.com/index.php?option=com_content&task=category&sectionid=5&id=29&Itemid=30.

Ocampo, José Antonio. 2008. "The End of the Latin American Boom." Working Paper. Rice University, Houston, TX.

O'Donnell, Guillermo. 1993. "Delegative Democracy?" Kellogg Institute Working Paper #192.

Oliveros, Virginia. 2012. "Public Employees as Political Workers: Evidence from an Original Survey in Argentina." Manuscript. Columbia University.

Oliveros, Virginia. 2014. "Making it Personal: Clientelism, Favors, and the Personalization of Public Administration in Argentina." *Comparative Politics* 48(3): 373–391.

Olson, Mancur. 1965. *The Logic of Collective Action.* Cambridge, MA: Harvard University Press.

Opp, Karl-Dieter, and Roehl, Wolfgang. 1990. "Repression, Micromobilization, and Political Protest." *Social Forces* 69(2): 521–547.

Página 12. 2004. "Otra Multitud en San Luis." May 14. Retrieved from http://www.pagina12.com.ar/diario/elpais/1-35317-2004-05-14.html.

Penfold-Becerra, Michael. 2007. "Clientelism and Social Funds: Evidence from Chavez's Misiones." *Latin American Politics & Society* 49(4): 63–84.

Porter, Tom. 2015. "Argentina: 200,000 Rally against Femicide and Domestic Violence in Buenos Aires." *International Business Times,* June 4. Retrieved from http://www.ibtimes.co.uk/argentina-200000-rally-against-femicide-domestic-violence-buenos-aires-1504391.

Programa de Investigación Sobre el Movimiento de la Sociedad Argentina (PIMSA). 2014. Retrieved from http://www.pimsa.secyt.gov.ar/.

Puddington, Arch. "Freedom in the World 2012: The Arab Uprisings and their Global Repercussions." *Freedom in the World* (2012): 1–40.

Przeworski, Adam. 1991. *Democracy and the Market: Political and economic reforms in Eastern Europe and Latin America.* New York, NY: Cambridge University Press.

Przeworski, Adam. 2010. *Democracy and the Limits of Self-Government.* New York, NY: Cambridge University Press.

Roberts, Kenneth M. 1996. "Economic Crisis and the Demise of the Legal Left in Peru." *Comparative Politics* 29(1): 69–92.

Roberts, Kenneth M. 1997. "Beyond Romanticism: Social Movements and the Study of Political Change in Latin America." *Latin American Research Review* 32(2): 137–151.

Roberts, Kenneth M. 2008. "The Mobilization of Opposition to Economic Liberalization." *Annual Review of Political Science* 11: 327–349.

Robertson, Graeme B. 2007. "Strikes and Labor Organization in Hybrid Regimes." *American Political Science Review* 101(4): 781–798.

Rodríguez-Vargas, Mariana. 2013. "The Sustainability of Populism in Times of Crisis: Explaining the Chávez Phenomenon." Doctoral Dissertation. Vanderbilt University, Nashville, TN.

Rokkan, Stein. 1970. "The Growth and Structuring of Mass Politics in Western Europe: Reflections of Possible Models of Explanation." *Scandinavian Political Studies* 5(A5): 65–83.

Rosenberg, Jaime. 2004. "Rodríguez Saá Borró de los Mapas a Merlo, Bastión de la Oposición." March 31. *La Nación*. Retrieved from http://www.lanacion.com.ar/587910-rodriguez-saa-borro-de-los-mapas-a-merlo-bastion-de-la-oposicion.

San Martín, Claudia. 2004. "La Represión Policial Dejó 15 Hospitalizados." May 2. *La Nación*. Retrieved from http://www.lanacion.com.ar/597473-la-represion-policial-dejo-15-hospitalizados.

Sartori, Giovanni. 1970. "Concept Misformation in Comparative Politics." *American Political Science Review* 64(4): 1033–1053.

Savolainen, Jukka. 1994. "The Rationality of Drawing Big Conclusions Based on Small Samples: In Defense of Mill's Methods." *Social Forces* 72(4): 1217–1224.

Scartascini, Carlos, and Mariano Tommasi. 2009. "The Making of Policy: Institutionalized or Not?" Inter-American Development Bank: Working Paper 4644.

Scartascini, Carlos, and Mariano Tommasi. 2012. "The Making of Policy: Institutionalized or Not?" *American Journal of Political Science* 56(4): 787–801.

Schmitter, Philippe C. 1994. "Dangers and Dilemmas of Democracy." *Journal of Democracy* 5(2): 57–74.

Schneider, Sergio. 2014. "Dura Represión en Chaco a una Protesta Social: Hay 20 Heridos y 10 Detenidos." *Clarín*, February 2. Retrieved from http://www.clarin.com/politica/Dura-represion-Chaco-protesta-detenidos_0_1083491658.html.

Schumpeter, Joseph. 1976. *Capitalism, Socialism, and Democracy*. New York, NY: Routledge.

Schussman, Alan, and Sarah Soule. 2005. "Process and Protest: Accounting for Individual Protest Participation." *Social Forces* 84(2): 1083–1108.

Sen, Amartya. 2002. "Globalization, Inequality and Global Protest." *Development* 45(2): 11–16.

Silva, Eduardo. 2009. *Challenging Neoliberalism in Latin America*. New York, NY: Cambridge University Press.

Smith, Peter H. 2005. *Democracy in Latin America: Political Change in Comparative Perspective*. New York, NY: Oxford University Press.

Snyder, Richard. 2001. "Scaling Down: Subnational Approaches to Comparative Politics." *Studies in Comparative International Development* 36(1): 93–110.

Sovey, Allison, and Donald Green. 2011. "Instrumental Variables Estimation in Political Science: A Reader's Guide." *American Journal of Political Science* 55(1): 188–200.

Spiller, Pablo, and Mariano Tommasi. 2007. *The Institutional Foundations of Public Policy in Argentina*. New York, NY: Cambridge University Press.

Stimson, James. 1999. *Public Opinion in America: Moods, Cycles, and Swings*. Boulder, CO: Westview Press.

Stokes, Susan. 2001. *Mandates and Democracy: Neoliberalism by Surprise in Latin America*. New York, NY: Cambridge University Press.

Stokes, Susan. 2005. "Perverse Accountability: A Formal Model of Machine Politics with Evidence from Argentina." *American Political Science Review* 99(3): 315–325.

Stokes, Susan, Thad Dunning, Marcelo Nazareno, and Valeria Brusco. 2013. *Brokers, Voters, and Clientelism: The Puzzle of Distributive Politics*. New York, NY: Cambridge University Press.

Sued, Gabriel. 2008. "Cacería para Ganar la Plaza Fueron Golpeados Manifestantes que Apoyaban el Reclamo del Campo." *La Nación,* March 26. Retrieved from http://www.lanacion.com.ar/998778-caceria-para-ganar-la-plaza.

Svampa, Maristella, and Sebastián Pereyra. 2003. *Entre la Ruta y el Barrio: La Experiencia de las Organizaciones Piqueteras*. Buenos Aires, AR: Editorial Biblos.

Szwarcberg, Mariela. 2012. "Uncertainty, Political Clientelism, and Voter Turnout in Latin America: Why Parties Conduct Rallies in Argentina." *Comparative Politics* 45(1): 88–106.

Szwarcberg, Mariela. 2013. "The Microfoundations of Political Clientelism: Lessons from the Argentine Case." *Latin American Research Review* 48(2): 32–54.

Szwarcberg, Mariela. 2015. *Mobilizing Poor Voters: Machine Politics, Clientelism, and Social Networks in Argentina*. New York, NY: Cambridge University Press.

Tarrow, Sidney. 1998. *Power in Movement: Social Movements and Contentious Politics*. New York, NY: Cambridge University Press.

Tenorio, Barbara Z. 2014. "Social Spending Responses to Organized Labor and Mass Protests in Latin America, 1970-2007." *Comparative Political Studies* 47(14): 1945–1972.

Teune, Henry, and Adam Przeworski. 1970. *The Logic of Comparative Social Inquiry*. New York, NY: Wiley-Interscience.

Tilly, Charles. 1978. *From Mobilization to Revolution*. Reading, MA: Addison-Wesley.

Tilly, Charles. 2006. *Regimes and Repertoires*. Chicago, IL: University of Chicago Press.

Tilly, Charles, and Sidney Tarrow. 2006. *Contentious Politics*. Boulder, CO: Paradigm Publishers.

Traynor, Ian, and Constanze Letsch. 2013. "Turkey Divided More Than Ever by Erdoğan's Gezi Park Crackdown." *The Guardian,* June 20. Retrieved from https://www.theguardian.com/world/2013/jun/20/turkey-divided-erdogan-protests-crackdown.

Trejo, Guillermo. 2014. "The Ballot and the Street: an Electoral Theory of Social Protest in Autocracies." *Perspectives on Politics* 12(2): 332–352.

Tufekci, Zeynep, and Christopher Wilson. 2012. "Social Media and the Decision to Participate in Political Protest: Observations from Tahrir Square." *Journal of Communication* 62(2): 363–379.

Ujhelyi, Gergely, and Ernesto Calvo. 2010. "Political Screening: Theory and Evidence from the Argentine Public Sector." Working Paper. University of Houston, Houston, TX.

Valenzuela, Sebastián, Arturo Arriagada, and Andrés Scherman. 2012. "The Social Media Basis of Youth Protest Behavior: The Case of Chile." *Journal of Communication* 62(2): 299–314.

Van Cott, Donna Lee. 2000. *The Friendly Liquidation of the Past: The Politics of Diversity in Latin America*. Pittsburgh, PA: University of Pittsburgh Press.

Van Laer, Jeroen. 2010. "Activists Online and Offline: The Internet as an Information Channel for Protest Demonstrations." *Mobilization: An International Quarterly* 15(3): 347–366.

Verba, Sidney, Kay Lehman Scholzman, and Henry E. Brady. 1995. *Voice and Equality: Civic Voluntarism in American Politics.* Cambridge, MA: Harvard University Press.

Vilas, Carlos. M. 2006. "Neoliberal Meltdown and Social Protest: Argentina 2001–2002." *Critical Sociology* 32(1): 163–186.

Villalón, Roberta. 2007. "Neoliberalism, Corruption, and Legacies of Contention Argentina's Social Movements, 1993-2006." *Latin American Perspectives* 34(2): 139–156.

Walton, John. 1989. "Debt, Protest, and the State in Latin America," in *Power and Popular Protest: Latin American Social Movements,* ed. Susan Eckstein. Berkely and Los Angeles, CA: University of California Press, 299–328.

Walton, John, and Charles Ragin. 1990. "Global and National Sources of Political Protest: Third World Responses to the Debt Crisis." *American Sociological Review* 55(6): 876–890.

Weitz-Shapiro, Rebecca. 2014. *Curbing Clientelism in Argentina: Politics, Poverty, and Social Policy.* New York, NY: Cambridge University Press.

Weitz-Shapiro, Rebecca, and Matthew S. Winters. 2017. "Can Citizens Discern? Information Credibility, Political Sophistication, and the Punishment of Corruption in Brazil." *Journal of Politics* 79(1): 60–74.

Weyland, Kurt. 2013. "Latin America's Authoritarian Drift: The Threat from the Populist Left." *Journal of Democracy* 24(3): 18–32.

Wibbels, Erik. 2005. "Decentralized Governance, Constitution Formation, and Redistribution." *Constitutional Political Economy* 16(2): 161–188.

Williamson, Vanessa, Theda Skocpol, and John Coggin. 2011. "The Tea Party and the Remaking of Republican Conservatism." *Perspectives on Politics* 9(1): 25–43.

Wiñazki, Nicolás. 2012. "Fue Multitudinaria la Protesta contra el Gobierno." *Clarín,* November 9. Retrieved from https://www.clarin.com/politica/multitudinaria-protesta-Gobierno_0_Byr8CpjPXg.html.

Wines of Argentina. 2011. "Estadísticas de Exportación." Retrieved from http://www.winesofargentina.org/es/estadistica/exportacion.

World Bank. 2013. "Fair and Efficient Growth; the Biggest Challenge for Latin America." March 15. Retrieved from http://www.worldbank.org/en/news/feature/2013/03/15/crecimiento-america-latina.

Yashar, Deborah J. 1998. "Contesting Citizenship: Indigenous Movements and Democracy in Latin America." *Comparative Politics* 31(1): 23–42.

Yashar, Deborah J. 1999. "Democracy, Indigenous Movements, and the Postliberal Challenge in Latin America." *World Politics* 52(1): 76–104.

Yashar, Deborah J. 2005. *Contesting Citizenship in Latin America: The Rise of Indigenous Movements and the Postliberal Challenge.* New York, NY: Cambridge University Press.

Zaller, John. 1992. *The Nature and Origins of Mass Opinion.* New York, NY: Cambridge University Press.

Zakaria, Fareed. 1997. "The Rise of Illiberal Democracy." *Foreign Affairs* 76(6): 22–43.

INDEX

Note: Numbers followed with an italics *f* or *t* indicate figures or tables, respectively.

Dominican Republic, corruption in, 30
Duhalde, Eduardo, 106
Dunning, John, 80

economic factors, as element in protest
    participation, 181
economic shocks, large-scale, 23
Ecuador
    democratic backsliding in, 48
    indigenous protest groups in, 18
    police riots in, 6
    political parties in, 29
    protest participation in, 49
    protests in, 4
education, protest participation and, 55,
    56, 58, 59t, 68, 171, 180, 181
#8N, 2
Eisinger, Peter, 125–30, 150, 184
elections, 25
    data from, local political information
        and, 155–56
    losses in, protest potential and, 53
    protests and , 77
elites
    in closed systems, 128
    electoral protests and, 77
    grassroots activism and, 77–78
    labor unions and, 77
    losing control over protestors, 98
    mobilizing protest participation, 12,
        37–38, 75–76
    operation of, in protest states, 81–86
    political parties as vehicles for, 78–79
    in protest states, 76–79, 99
    street-based activism and, 79
    voices of, in low-quality
        democracies, 76
El Salvador
    protest participation in, 54
    protests in, 7, 53
emerging democracies
    protest activity increasing in, 18
    protests in, variations between, 8
    socioeconomic gains in, 8–9
enforcement, in democratic institutions,
    50–51
endogeneity, 96
Erdogan, Recep Tayyip, 2
Escobar, Cristina, 80

Executive Contestation, measurement
    of, 155
executive dominance, mass protest
    participation and, 30t

farmers, contentious politics by, 79
Fernández de Kirchner, Cristina, 1–2,
    102, 107–8, 140, 156, 215n12
Fernández de Kirchner government, 12,
    109–10
flawed institutions, closing off
    protest, 184
Formosa province (Argentina), 156
Frente para la Victora (Argentina), 145
Frente Renovador (Argentina), 145

Garay, Candelaria, 32–33, 47–48
GDP growth, as predictor of protest
    participation, 61
gender violence, 110
Gervasoni, Carlos, 13, 130, 150,
    154–55, 183
governance, measurement of, 56
Government Effectiveness measure
    (WGI), 56
governments, as components of
    contentious politics, 17
grassroots activism, elites and, 77–78
Greece, 73
    protests in, 23
    repression in, 28
grievances, 28
    collective action resulting from,
        22–24, 48–49
    constancy of, 34
    responses to, 34–35
    shifts in, 23
    vehicles for addressing, 25
Grimes, Marcia, 27, 49, 53, 78
Guatemala, protest movements in, 53
Gurr, Ted Robert, 22–23

Haiti
    institutional quality of, 57
    protest participation in, 54
Honduras, government's legitimacy in, 51
human development, as predictor of
    protest participation, 61
Huntington, Samuel P., 31

protest participation in, 49, 54, 186
social movements in, 18
weak political institution in, 10
PIMSA. See *Programa de Investigación sobre el Movimiento de la Sociedad Argentina*
Piñera, Sebastian, 6
piquetero movement (Argentina), 101, 104, 107, 183
PJ. *See* Peronist party
political behavior, conflict and, 21
political context, protest movements emerging in, 24
political engagement, 180–81
  alternative conceptions of, 181
  increase in, 8–9
  measurement of, 32
  protest movements and, 31–33
  suppression of, 131
political entrepreneurs, role of, 76–77
political expression, limitations on, 36–37
political institutions, citizen engagement and, 35–36
political interest, protest participation and, 56, 58, 59*t*, 68, 171, 172
political liberalization, process of, 52
political mobilization, clientelism and, 80, 81
political opportunities, examination of, 127–28
political opportunities approach, 24, 52
political organization, as element in protest participation, 181–82
political participation
  clientelism and, 76
  modes of, contexts for, 22
  repertoires of, 78
  and unevenness of subnational democracies, 151
political parties, 25, 26, 37, 76
  as protagonists, 77
  protest participation and, 82–83, 118
  role of, 52
  socioelectoral strategy of, 77
  as vehicles for elites, 78–79
political regimes, influencing contentious actions, 24
political systems, openness of, 126–27
Poma, Fernanda, 80

power, constraints on, measurement of, 155–56
PRI. See *Partido Revolucionario Institucional*
professional associations, protests and, 27
Programa de Investigación sobre el Movimiento de la Sociedad Argentina (PIMSA), 113, 115, 158–59
protest buying, 100, 118–19, 186
protestors
  characteristics of, 23, 60, 69, 80, 81
  elites losing control over, 98
  representativeness of, 38, 194–95
protest participation
  decreases in, variables associated with, 58–59
  NGOs and, 52–53
  party membership and, 86–92
  predictors of, 49, 58–60, 116, 117*f*
  variables affecting, on subregional levels, 163–72
protests, 46
  aggressive, 13, 37, 130–31
  clientelism and, 97–98, 100
  confrontational vs. non-confrontational, 18
  data analysis of, 154–55
  decision-making calculus of, 35*f*
  definition of, 39
  democratic openness and, 52
  deprivation leading to, 23
  determinants of, 11
  elites' involvement in, 12
  individual-level motivations for, 22
  institutional quality and, 29–31, 52–53
  institutional sources of, 30*t*
  law enforcement response to, 196
  legal decisions and, 52
  likelihood of, factors affecting, 3
  local governments' response to, 145
  low-quality democracy and, 20, 191
  macro-level stimuli for, 22
  measurement of, 39–40
  neoliberalism and, 4–5
  normalization of, 33, 36, 38, 75, 102, 185–86
  organization of, 195
  organizational networks underlying, 10
  organizational structures and, 26

protests (*cont.*)
  peaceful, 13, 160–62
  perpetuating the protest state, 99
  predictors of, 55
  research on, in Latin America, 3–4
  subnational democratic effects on
    repertoires of, 149
  substituting for conventional
    participation, 23
  success of, 192–94
  as threat to democracy, 22
  violent, 129
  See also mass-level political
    engagement
protest state, 16, 36
  Argentina as, 71, 109–19, 122, 147–48
  clientelism in, 37, 80–86
  conditions for, 9, 46
  consequences of, 192–93
  elites in, 38, 75–79, 81–86, 99
  emergence of, 28–29, 185–86
  enriched by elite-protest
    relationship, 99
  political parties in, and political
    participation, 79
  protest as everyday component in, 29
  protestors' representativeness in, 38
public employment
  levels of, and subnational
    democracy, 163
  protest participation and, 165–66
puntano society (Argentina), 135–36

qualitative approach, advantages of,
    41–42
quantitative approach, advantages of, 41

relative deprivation, 27
religious groups, 26
repoliticization school, 5
representation, 28
  expectation of, 25, 72
  as stimuli for protests, 22, 24–25
  suboptimal, 46
repression, 28, 36–37, 131, 137
  effect of, on protest technologies, 22,
    25–26
  political participation limited under, 26
Repsol (Spain), 104
resignation, regarding protesting, 145, 146

resource mobilization approach, 27, 49,
    58, 77, 80, 166, 212n3
roadblocks, 4, 40, 49, 78, 85, 96, 104,
    110, 112*f*, 113, 123*f*, 152–53, 157–58
Robertson, Graeme B., 77
Rodríguez-Saá, Adolfo, 106, 132–37, 144,
    145, 146, 156
Rodríguez-Saá, Alberto, 132–37, 144,
    145, 146
Rodríguez-Saá family (Argentina), 42
Rodríguez-Saá presidency, 107
Rousseff, Dilma, 3, 7, 187, 189, 193
Rule of Law measure (WGI), 56

Sánchez de Lozada, Gonzalo, 85
San Luis province (Argentina), 42, 132–38,
    144*f*, 145–48, 152, 153, 156
Santa Cruz province (Argentina), 156
santiagazo (Argentina), 103
Santiago del Estero (Argentina), 103–4
Scartascini, Carlos, 20
Seligson, Mitchell, 51, 193
*Sindicato Unificado de Trabajadores de la
    Educación de Buenos Aires*, 142
social media
  effects of, 73
  organizing and, 56, 115, 196
social movements
  formation of, 27
  resources for, 49
  sustainability of, 49
social policy, expansion of, and citizen
    engagement, 48
social protest
  clientelism and, 79–81
  normalizing of, 16
Spain, 23, 73
stability, of democratic institutions,
    50–51
street demonstrations, 5
  peacefulness of, 150
  as symptom of low-quality
    institutions, 20
subnational democracy, 129
  aggressive contention and, 157, 159–60
  effects of, on protest repertoires, 149
  measurement of, 13, 130, 150, 153–56
  protest participation by category of,
    161–62
  protests in, 34, 129–31